# MEASURE OF THE MAN

*John Ciardi*

# MEASURE OF THE MAN

edited by Vince Clemente

The University of Arkansas Press
Fayetteville    1987 —————

Copyright © 1987 by The Board of Trustees
The University of Arkansas Press, Fayetteville, Arkansas 72701
All rights reserved
Manufactured in the United States of America

Designer: Chiquita Babb
Typeface: Linotron 202 Bodoni Book
Typesetter: G&S Typesetters, Inc.
Printer: Thomson-Shore, Inc.
Binder: John H. Dekker & Sons, Inc.

The paper used in this publication meets the minimum requirements of the American National Standard for Permanence of Paper for Printed Library Materials Z39.48-1984. ∞

LIBRARY OF CONGRESS CATALOGING-IN-PUBLICATION DATA

John Ciardi: measure of the man.

   Bibliography: p.
   Includes index.
   1. Ciardi, John, 1916–      . 2. Poets, American—
20th century—Biography.   I. Clemente, Vince.
PS3505.I27Z74      1987      811'.52 [B]      86-19139
ISBN 0–938626-79-5
ISBN 0–938626-80-9 (pbk.)

for Judith Ciardi


*I marry you from time and a great door*
*is shut and stays shut against wind, sea, stone,*
*sunburst, and heavenfall.*

# *Acknowledgments*

Lewis Turco's "Sasquatch" is from *A Cage of Creatures*. Copyright 1978 by Lewis Turco. Karl Shapiro's "John Ciardi: Heart Like a Halfback" is *Section #92, The Bourgeois Poet*. Copyright 1964 by Karl Shapiro. "The Stranger in the Pumpkin," lines from "The Man Who Sang the Sillies," lines from "As I Was Picking a Bobble-Bud," and lines from "There Was a Hunter from Littletown" are from *The Man Who Sang the Sillies*. Copyright 1961 by John Ciardi. "Last Word about Bears" and lines from "Sometimes I Feel This Way" are from *You Read to Me, I'll Read to You*. Copyright 1962 by John Ciardi. Lines from "The Lesson for Tonight" are from *The Monster Den or Look What Happened at My House—and to It*. Copyright 1966 by John Ciardi. "An Inscription to Richard Eberhart" is from *39 Poems*. Copyright 1959 by Rutgers, The State University. Lines from "There Once Was an Owl" are from *The Reason for the Pelican*. Copyright 1959 by John Ciardi. "A Note on John Ciardi at Michigan" by Roy W. Cowden is from *Tuftonian*, Vol. IV, No. 3, Fall 1944, and printed with permission of Tufts University Archives. "John Ciardi, Tufts Poet" by John Holmes is from *Tuftonian*, Vol. XII, No. 1, Fall 1955, and printed with permission of Tufts University Archives. "'A Man Is What He Does with His Attention': An Interview with John Ciardi" by Vince Clemente is from *Poesis: A Journal of Criticism*, Bryn Mawr College, Vol. VII, No. 2. "Saturday, March 6" and "Machine" are from *For Instance*. Copyright 1979 by John Ciardi. John Frederick Nims' "John Ciardi: The Many Lives of Poetry" was first delivered as the Cockefair Chair Lecture, University of Missouri-Kansas City, on March 19, 1986. "About Being Born, and Surviving It" by John Ciardi is excerpted from *Contemporary Authors Autobiography Series*, Volume 2, edited by Adele Sarkissian. Copyright 1985 by Gale Research Company; reprinted by permission of the publisher. John Stone's "Treinte-Sei for John Ciardi" appeared in *The American Scholar*. Miller Williams' "John Ciardi—'Nothing Is Really Hard but to Be Real'" is excerpted from *The Achievement of John Ciardi*. Copyright 1969 by Scott, Foresman. "True or False" is from *The Birds of Pompeii*. Copyright 1985 by John

Ciardi. "The Last Photograph of John Ciardi" by Samuel Hazo, © 1987 by Samuel Hazo. Used by permission.

With special thanks to my wife, Ann Clemente, for her nurturing spirit. Also to the libraries and staff at Suffolk County Community College, and to the administration for a sabbatical during which time this book came together in its final form.

V.C.

# *Contents*

*"It Is for the Waking Man to Tell His Dreams"*
John Ciardi                                                    1

*About Being Born, and Surviving It*
John Ciardi                                                    3

*John Ciardi: The Many Gifts*
Vince Clemente                                               20

*John Ciardi's Early Lives*
X. J. Kennedy                                                24

*Thanks, John, for Being*
Richard Eberhart                                             32

*Ciardi the Taler*
Lewis Turco                                                  34

*John Holmes and Roy W. Cowden: Teachers of a Teacher*
Vince Clemente                                               40

*John Ciardi, Tufts Poet*
John Holmes                                                  42

*A Note on John Ciardi at Michigan*
Roy W. Cowden                                                49

*English C, 1947*
Donald Hall                                                  52

*Letter to an Old Friend*
Dan Jaffe                                                    55

*From Dissertation to Friendship: The Joy of Knowing John Ciardi*
Jeff Lovill                                                        61

The Mid-Century *Fifteen, a Memoir*
Philip Booth                                                      68

*Ciardi's Dante*
W. S. Di Piero                                                    71

*Form and Style in Ciardi's Dante*
Charles Guenther                                                  74

*John Ciardi and* Treat It Gentle
Richard Elman                                                     79

*Writing* Treat It Gentle: *A Letter to Vince Clemente*
John Ciardi                                                       82

*A Blade*
William Heyen                                                     84

*John Ciardi: Heart Like a Halfback*
Karl Shapiro                                                      86

*John Ciardi and "Jabberwocky" in the Indiana Cornfields*
Norbert Krapf                                                     87

*John Ciardi: The Many Lives of Poetry*
John Frederick Nims                                               91

*Ciardi at* The Saturday Review
Norman Cousins                                                   114

*John Ciardi: National Treasure*
Lucien Stryk                                                     117

*Seeing Ciardi Plain*
Stanley Burnshaw                                                 119

*For John Ciardi: In Praise of Humor*
William White                                                   123

*Looking for John Ciardi at Bread Loaf*
John Williams                                                   126

x

*John Ciardi and the "Witch of Fungi"*
Maxine Kumin                                        131

*Dionysian Memories*
Diane Wakoski                                       133

*Ciardi Remembered*
Judson Jerome                                       135

*John Ciardi: His Wit and Witness*
John Stone                                          141

*A Trenta-sei for John Ciardi (1916–1986)*
John Stone                                          148

*Light Years Near: Ciardi's Poems for Children*
Joann P. Krieg                                      150

*Energy and Gusto: A Note on John Ciardi*
William Jay Smith                                   153

*A Note on "Ciardi's Dialogue with Children"*
Vince Clemente                                      155

*Ciardi's Dialogue with Children*
Terri Arrigon                                       157

*John Ciardi—"Nothing Is Really Hard but to Be Real"*
Miller Williams                                     162

*Some Clerihews for John*
Richard Wilbur                                      178

*John Ciardi, Science Fiction Writer*
Elly Welt                                           180

*John Ciardi and the White Line under the Snow*
Isaac Asimov                                        185

Una Festa con John Ciardi: *Random Thoughts*
John Tagliabue                                      188

*Ciardi's Winter Words: Some Oblique Notes on a Southern Education*
Edward Krickel                                      192

*The Good Influence of John Ciardi*
  George Garrett                                          199

*The Last Photograph of John Ciardi*
  Samuel Hazo                                             211

*"A Man Is What He Does with His Attention":*
*A Conversation with John Ciardi*
  Vince Clemente                                          213

*Notes on Contributors*                                   229

*Selected Bibliography*                                   233

*Index*                                                   239

MEASURE OF THE MAN

It is for the Waking Man to Tell His Dreams

somnum
narrare vigilantis est
-- Seneca

In the stupors before sleep
I used to hear in my head
poems at which God might weep
each line an angel's bread.

They dried awake, their myth
like the gold plates, God bright,
Maroni brought to Smith
and then took back each night.

I wired my bed and taped
those canticles. Come day,
I heard: "The cat escaped
when Jesus ran away

with Mary's lamb, no doubt."
.. And then a snore
until the tape ran out.
The dog scratched at the door

hearing its master's voice.
It is a dog's mistake
to watch and rejoice
because the fool's awake.

John Ciardi

# It Is for the Waking Man to Tell His Dreams
## John Ciardi

somnum
narrare vigilantis est
— Seneca

In the stupor before sleep
I used to hear in my head
poems at which God might weep,
each line an angel's bread.

They died awake, their myth
like the gold plates, God-bright,
Moroni brought to Smith
and then took back each night.

I wired my bed and taped
those canticles. Come day,
I heard: "The cat escaped
when Jesus ran away,

with Mary's lamb, no doubt."
—And then a snore
until the tape ran out.
The dog scratched at the door

hearing its master's voice.
It is a dog's mistake
to wagtail and rejoice
because the fool's awake.

*Photo Credit: Michael Mardikes*

# *About Being Born, and Surviving It*

## John Ciardi
## 1916–1986

An autobiographical note may be little more than the act of choosing memories, but do we choose them, or do they come looking for us? I have never been sure to what extent my life has been something I did, and to what extent it has been something done to me, the conscious decisions—as often as not wrong (but in my case, I think, blessed by egregious luck)—being only on the surface of unreckoned, or dimly reckoned, forces that decide. I approach seventy with a sense that I am a lucky survivor of forces usually beyond my control. I have wrestled with those forces, often painfully, as I have wrestled with poetry and with language, always joyously, but seldom with any sense that I was in decisive control. One important reason for poetry is that the poem sometimes makes possible a momentary illusion of being in control. I doubt that it is ever more than illusion, but what else are we born for? I take what comes and do what I can with it, failing as we must, but almost winning for a while. . . .

I was born June 24, 1916, at 25 Sheafe Street in Boston's North End, which was then as now, though more so then, Little Italy. Sheafe Street is a single block of five-story walk-up tenements, most of the floors divided into a front and rear flat. The street runs from Salem Street a bit below the Old North Church, past a narrow lane called Margaret Street that runs downhill on one side, to be capped at the other end by Snowhill Street, beyond which stands a large garage complex made famous around 1950 as the scene of the great Brinks robbery. Beyond the garage the Atlantic Avenue El used to run from South Station to North Station until it was torn down and the steel was sold to Japan to be returned to us in various denominations in World War II. Beyond the El, by a back reach of Boston Harbor, there used to be some large molasses tanks, roughly like gas tanks as I was told, that blew up in a freak accident that damaged the El, knocked down some houses that fronted the scene from across the street, and filled their cellar holes with molasses. (Or so I was told.)

Those tanks became an early family legend. I think I probably did once believe my uncle Pat (Pasquale DiBenedictis) who told me that rain eventually diluted the molasses so thin that local boys used the cellar holes as swimming pools. Had he told me they brought pancakes with them and dipped them in the pools for lunch, I would probably have believed that. There was also a family legend that my father had ridden by there in an elevated train so short a while before the explosion that the back car of his train was splattered with molasses. Imagine: a second earlier and the whole train might have been blown off the track—a disaster! My recollection is that everything about our family legends was given to wonder-seeking with a firm taste for disaster. When later I began to read medieval literature and turned to such compilations of the lives of the saints as de Voragine's *Legenda Aurea*, I found myself on familiar ground. In these tales, as in my earliest tribal legends, the absurdly incredible is never an insult to one's common sense but a simple test of the willingness—in fact, the eagerness—of the medieval mind to believe anything. For though the calendar of my birth (the Fridays always marked in my memory with a vertical row of red fish) asserted the year 1916, I was securely born in the Middle Ages.

My mother, a ritual Italian woman, was born even more securely to them in about 1880 on what I think of as the mountain behind Vesuvius, in a hamlet called Manocalzati, in the province of Avellino, called by the Romans Abellenum. Manocalzati is the Old Italian form of what would now be Manocalzata, meaning "gloved hand," implicitly, a military gauntlet, a sub-insignia of the Legions that signified a *manus* (handful, or squad) of soldiers, and indicated that the town was once a small garrison post for soldiers who guarded the road to Bari. She was about thirteen when she came steerage (a nightmare passage as she recalled it) with her parents, her sisters, and her younger brother, Pasquale.

Medieval women of my mother's time did not think of going to a hospital to give birth. Money was hard to come by: why throw it away on what God and nature would take care of with only a small fee to the familiar and trusted midwife?

That home delivery was not always perfect was well attested by the number of North End kids who suffered from what might likely have been birth damage. My first cousin Mark Accomando, for some reason called Cucci, and later Jimmy Lynch, because that was his ring name in an unspectacular career as a prize fighter, was delivered dead (according to oft-told family legend). With my Aunt Felicella in bad shape, the stillborn bundle was laid aside in a soapstone sink while the women attended the mother, and—so the family folk tale—when they came to pick up the dead boy, he cried. I cannot give a likely clinical explanation of what happened there. I tell the story because something about its combination of unlikelihood and eagerness to believe that God takes care of His own, catches the tone of that first mind into which I was born. I have survived it. I had to survive it toward any remote hope of sanity. And yet the tone of it is an ancient echo. Like the earliest speech sounds one can remember hearing, the sound of a first home. In the *Inferno* Dante walks past the tombs of the heretics speaking to Virgil, and the damned soul of Farinata degli Uberti, a fellow Tuscan, rises from the flames, summoned by the cadences of Dante's back-home speech, filled with a longing for that lost world. I would not, at any choice, go back, and yet, as with Farinata, the echoes of that lost world remain affective. Some of us may yearn more or less for our first of things, but all of us, I believe, are affected by their sounds when they return to us.

My mother, in the custom of her tribe, bore me in the same bed in which she had conceived me in the fifth-floor-front flat of our Sheafe Street tenement, attended by a midwife and by a background flutter of all the clucking matrons of the tribe. The men, in custom, would have been waiting somewhere outside with wine jugs, and since our flat was just below the roof, it was probably on the roof that they waited.

It could not have been other than a festive day. I was the fourth child and the only male. Three times before, that is to say, the woman had dreamed of giving her man—in the near-mystical tribal phrase—"a son to bear his name." Three times he had waited among his friends, and their final toast to him, to the woman, and to the (alas) new girl-child, was ultimately a condolence. This time, in the ancient irrationalities that made the world, the toast rang full, the women wept for joy (they wept for anything), and the new mother must have felt an ultimate fulfillment of her marriage and her womanhood in the act of giving her man his long-delayed sacramental son. I was born, that is to say, over-advertised, but these were certainly the terms of the billing, as they were the terms of my ordination to a stellar brathood. . . .

More than fifty years later when my mother had rambled to her witless end in the nursing home, we were called and told she was dying. We sat by her as she panted her last. When suddenly the panting stopped I could only welcome her death as a mercy. What a sad frayed end of a heroic woman! I bent to kiss her forehead, which was feverish, and I can never forget from how deep in me there came the thought, "It will never be warm again." I was out of tears. I had spent them all in the years of watching her lie in that bed like an unburied corpse. But grief can be mute, too. *Addio, Mama!*

My embalmed father must have been stone cold, a cold that might have breathed into a thousand nightmares, but my kiss came away from nothing with no memory. And so an end, though not an end. I know that was a first memory and not something told to me later. And I can date it almost exactly, for he died July 9, 1919, when I was three years and sixteen days old. . . .

His name was Antonio though I have seen the name recorded as Carminantonio. He had come from Avellino as a boy, from the same mountain on which my mother had been born, though from a different town on it, a tiny settlement a few miles around the bend called, I think, San Potito Ultra, which I have always thought of as "Saint Potty in the Extreme. . . ."

I don't know much about my father. My mother took his sudden death into some inner sanctum of herself and locked him away there. Despite all teaching that there shall be in Heaven neither marriage nor giving in marriage, she spent the rest of her long life waiting to rejoin him, his wife forever. She was never more ritually at home within herself than on Memorial Day when all of the North End gathered at St. Michael's Cemetery, among the slum rows of stones, to honor its dead. She stood me by her beside his stone, once more the man's wife with his son beside her to receive his guests in his last house. It was a meticulous observance climaxed annually by the delegation from I Figli d'Italia bearing a large floral wreath whose ribbon read "Presidente e Fratello. In eterno ricordo." And she stood by as each man in order shook my hand. I was the sacramental son and she was the man's wife once more keeping house for him, though in the long ride back by streetcar to the Forest Hills Terminal, by elevated and subway all across sprawling Boston to Sullivan Square, and in the streetcar again to Medford, she sat silent and motionless, once more a castaway.

Sometimes at night I heard her muttering to him. It was at least twenty years before she let a first touch of color into her widow's weeds. She refused to leave him. Once, fifty years later, in the nursing home, when her mind had rambled beyond recognition of us, I brought her one of the Italian pastries she grew to love gluttonously in her second childhood, and as I was wiping the cream filling from her face she called me "'Ndo." 'Ndo was her fond familiar form of 'Ndonio/Antonio.

But having so locked him inside herself, what passed between them was held apart, as if in a vow, and she rarely spoke of him.

I gathered that he had had some education. Ma could not read and was just able, at need, to sputter her painful signature across a document, but she was proud of the fact that he used to read books—whole books. She must have been awed to find she was the wife of a book reader. Occasionally she would even boast of the many nights he had sat at a table and read. When I turned out to be an avid and indiscriminate reader, she seemed to rejoice in that as if it were one more proof that her husband had been reborn in me. When I got a double promotion from the fourth to the sixth grade, she felt sure it had been partly my father's doing. Was I not the son of a man of learning? It was at that time that a door-to-door salesman called and she bought from him, for God knows how much more than she could afford, a one-volume encyclopedia guaranteed to fill me with all this world's knowledge. I had stacks of tattered dime novels; Horatio Algers, Tom Swifts, Rover Boys, at least a hundred Frank and Dick Merriwells by Burt Standish, I also had from God knows where, Palgrave's *Golden Treasury* and *Gulliver's Travels* which I had read as a funny book, with no sense of allegory, though I recognized Lilliput and the war between the Big Endians and the Little Endians, for what was that but the squabbling between my sisters and me? But THE BOOK, for that was the only name I ever had for it, was a new dimension, a marvel of over 1,500 India paper pages studded with photos on glossy paper, photos of everything: The Bessemer Process, General Pershing, Flags of All Nations, The Roman Forum, Presidents of the United States, Famous Locomotives, Sea Shells—the wonders of the world. I read it till the binding failed and the pages came apart to leave me a box full of loose pages that were finally cleared away when I had other real books, but never another like THE BOOK. I can't imagine where she came up with the money for it. By then, to be sure, the girls were working and bringing home their pay checks, which is to say they had really paid for that, too. But it must certainly have cost more than she could afford in those days when she would take the streetcar and elevated into Boston with ten dollars for the weekly shopping and return hauling four shopping bags and more to where I met her at the streetcar stop, but would not let me go in with her to carry part of the load, because that would cost an extra twenty cents in carfare. I think THE BOOK was the more important to her because she could not really afford it. In one everlasting sense, certainly, it was a gift to her memory of my father as a book reader. I can believe that she explained it to him at night when she went to bed, and that she fell asleep smiling because he approved. . . .

My father had been a laborer and then a tailor at first. Somewhere, probably in night school, he had learned English and basic accounting methods, and had become an agent of the Metropolitan Insurance Company, though as I understand it, his basic work consisted of making weekly rounds of Italian families, collecting from each the nickels and dimes they set aside for simple burial insurance. They were married in Boston in 1906, and the auto accident in which he died happened on a Saturday morning thirteen years later when he was driving with friends to a combined company picnic and sales meeting that was to be held somewhere near Dedham. He was riding in the back seat of an open touring car when it was sideswiped and he was thrown out, his head striking a telephone pole. Five other men riding in the car were not injured aside from minor bruises.

The company claimed that his death was not work-related and disclaimed responsibility, but the Industrial Board of Massachusetts, meeting at the State House, took note of the fact that the picnic was primarily a sales meeting at which quotas were set, and the company was ordered to pay my mother ten dollars a week for 400 weeks. The price of a man.

He made a down payment on a house and a double lot in Medford, six miles northwest of Boston and served by a streetcar line of the Metropolitan Transit Authority, though our relatives thought of it almost in awe, as "out in the country." And the fact is that Medford, now a dormitory suburb, was then almost rural. We got our milk at first from a neighbor who kept a cow. Another neighbor kept bees. We kept chickens and worked a huge vegetable garden. That's far enough "out in the country" for North End purposes. When I was a boy, my cousin Benny, who was about my age, came to stay with us for a week, and he said it all when he saw a dandelion growing through a crack in the sidewalk and exclaimed, "Look! Ciccorias!" In North End patois *ciccoria* with an English *s* did for "dandelions." The wonder was that he had never seen one except in one of the large baskets put out in front of North End grocery stores, and there in Medford, "out in the country," they grew free through cracks in the sidewalk. In a slighter but more edible way it was as if he had discovered that the streets of America really are paved with gold, once you get out of the North End.

Ten dollars a week with four children to feed, the eldest not yet twelve, would hardly carry the mortgage on the house in Medford, but my Aunt Cristina and my uncle Alec joined us as co-owners, he spending his days in a ratty barber shop on Causeway Street under the Atlantic Avenue El in a block since torn down to build piers for an expressway overpass, she working at Schrafft's as a skilled candy-dipper. Ma kept the house and the chickens, worked the enormous garden, gleaned the fields for greens and mushrooms, and sometimes at night, when Aunt Cristina was home, went into Boston to work a late shift as a men's tailor, which is to say in a ratty loft in which lines of sewing machines stood side by side.

Ma's terrible need to make me over into the image of her lost husband was a first oppression I had to survive. I did not know it then, but the Catholic Church was another, and Medford became my escape route in ways I doubt that I could have found had we remained in the North End. I wonder what my father would have thought of that, had he known that the money he was paying down for his house would buy me my way out of the Middle Ages. I dare guess he might have approved. I never once heard that he had been a devout observer, and from hints I pieced from a word here and a word there spoken by his surviving friends, I guessed that he was vaguely a syndicalist-anarchist in the Sacco and

Vanzetti tradition, a man more socially minded than religious, hardly a revolutionary, but a believer in this world first and in eternity only vaguely if at all. But I realize that I may be twisting slight evidence my way because that is the way I would like to believe it. . . .

Misguided by my high school teachers, I took what money I had saved and went to Bates College. Bates is a good small school and more liberal now. It was then heavily Baptist and relentlessly concerned about my character. I had my own doubts about it, but I had dug ditches and saved my money in the hope of acquiring useful information. My character would take care of itself. After three semesters at that moral outpost I had nearly run out of money. Tufts was in my back yard in Medford. There I could live and eat at home. I transferred, and everything seemed to happen at once.

Tufts had a theology school but I never found it to be intrusive and its base was Universalist-Unitarian which left it with a decent tolerance of doubt. I found a larger, more open mind at work there. And best of all I found John Holmes. I signed up for his writing course and almost at once I knew what I was going to do with the rest of my life! I had no idea what I would do for food and shelter, but I was young, toughened to hard labor, and ready to go for broke. Somehow I would earn enough to eat on and to give my mother the little she needed, but what I would live for was poetry! It was a green and arrogant dedication, but better than the thought of becoming a priest, though I was no longer thinking that. Nor had I a choice.

John Holmes was a tolerated junior member of the English Department. The rest of my teachers were Harvard Ph.D.'s, solid and articulate historians of literature, but a closed union that failed even to recognize that John was as learned as they, because he was learned in things they did not know about. If they were historians of music, John was a piano player who knew, as they did not, the things ten fingers must learn to do on eighty-eight keys.

He was himself a poet, the first actually published poet I had ever known. My re-reading tells me he was a far better poet than he has been recognized to be in this age in which reputation is more readily founded on public posturing than on quiet poetic merit. He was exactly the master teacher I had always needed but never found. And of course he became the ideal father figure I had been looking for in the wrong places. I lived on his shoulder. I haunted his house. I read his books. I brought him endless formless poems and he picked them apart for me. I was proud of the times when he was rough with me, for he was always gentle with the hopeless, and I knew when he dressed me down that he was taking my scrawls seriously, perhaps not quite as seriously as I did, but no one could— that seriousness was most of what was wrong with them—for I still had a forest of insanities to survive. John opened doors I did not know were there, and walked me into a larger world than I had known.

When I was graduated from Tufts in 1938, he steered me to the University of Michigan to compete in the Hopwood Awards. Through some professors he knew there, he even got me a scholarship and a part-time job that would take care of my meals.

At Michigan I worked with Roy W. Cowden who became a sort of grandfather figure for me. It was rare luck to find two such teachers, one right after the other. Yet, though I confess it to my shame, I cannot remember a word Cowden spoke to me. At our weekly seminars he droned on over photocopies of worksheets of famous authors, tracing their changes word by word while I fought off sleep. I loved the man. To doze off on him would be unforgivable. And still it was an agony to force my lids to stay open while he droned on in class.

Our weekly manuscript conferences, however, were another sort of trance. We would sit side by side over my last batch of manuscript, his hand hovering above the page as he talked, the index finger extended. Bit by bit, through whatever he was saying, that finger would come down and touch the page—and always, before it lit, I would know where it would light, and exactly why! I have never understood how such a method could work so well. I doubt that anyone else could ever work it in that way. Sometimes I felt as if I were being hypnotized. What I know is that his finger always came down in exactly the right place, and that I knew as it touched—before it touched—what I had done wrong.

And in June I won the Hopwood Award for poetry. There I sat, a Master of Arts, holding a check for $1,200 1939 dollars! It was the largest piece of money I had ever held in my hand! Lucky John was rich! And more doors opened.

That winning manuscript was, alas, a miserable botch, windy, profuse, and founded on verbal indigestion. Later, I, too, served as a judge of Hopwood manuscripts, and I doubt I would have voted for the scrawl I passed in. But the judges, among them Louise Bogan and David McCord, chose to be kinder than I think I would have been; far kinder than the smugness of my assumptions had warranted. To get to Michigan I had borrowed $200 from my godfather, John Follo, who worked in that ratty barber shop with Uncle Alec, and another $200 from my sister Ella; borrowed that money with a firm promise to pay it back in June when (understood) I collected the Hopwood money. It was a tribal pledge and I was honor bound to pay it back in one way or another. Yet in honest retrospect I remain appalled by the arrogance of my assumptions.

(Hopwood rules required that manuscripts be submitted pseudonymously. The pen name I chose was Thomas Aquinas! Was that a far echo from my Middle Ages? It was perhaps, at least in part. But I was reading Dante [is that another echo?], confused by him, but despising the English translations I could find, and determined to try my own hand. If I could not do better than the existing competition, I told myself, it was time to close shop and apprentice myself to a racketeer. St. Thomas be my witness!)

And who needed the rackets? I paid off my debts, gave my mother some money, drifted around for a while, and by January of 1940 I had drifted back to Ann Arbor, broke and looking for a job. But good things had happened and more would follow.

I sold a poem to *Poetry* magazine and actually got a check for it, for maybe as much as ten dollars (if that much), but to me it was the first drop of a great downpour that would certainly follow! Through John Holmes (again!) William Sloane, then trade manager of Henry Holt, had accepted a revised version of my Hopwood manuscript to publish as a book, and he sent me an advance of $100! It was, I was sure, the first ripple of an impending flood of royalties!

The rains did not come and the floodwaters did not cover the earth, but through Bill Sloane, I was offered a fellowship at Bread Loaf in August of 1940. I returned in 1947 as a member of the staff, and every year until 1955, when I became director until 1972. It was at Bread Loaf that I formed friendships, whose memories still ghost me, with Fletcher Pratt, Theodore Morrison, Sloane of course, Robert Frost, and Bernard DeVoto—among many others.

I was on Saipan in 1945 as an aerial gunner on a B-29. I had made some sort of peace with the near-certainty that I would never leave that flowering rock alive, when the war tapered off to what looked like an assured survival, and there came a letter from Ted Morrison to offer me a job as an English-A instructor at Harvard. He even threw in a title: would I care to be a Briggs-Copeland Instructor? So, indirection by indirection, that sad Hopwood manuscript led to seven years at Harvard, marvelous years.

More immediately, in 1940, that manuscript led to my first teaching job just as I was scraping bottom. Louis Untermeyer had been lecturing at Michigan and had packed his puns to go scatter them at the University of Kansas City. When its president, Clarence R. Decker, mentioned that he was looking for an English instructor, Louis mentioned me as the recent winner of the Hopwood Poetry Award and Decker wired to offer me a guest lectureship in Modern Poetry for $900 a semester. It turned out that my duties would be to teach five sections of freshman English, but the title sounded good, and the checks were negotiable. My needs were simple—a few dollars a month to send to my mother, cigarettes, food, an attic room somewhere, and all the girls I could manage to sleep with. Kansas City was a good provider on all points. I was on a university faculty, I was making a living, at twenty-three I wasn't much older than the senior girls, I

11

had time to write, and I was bursting with ignorant energy. I felt that I had survived the dark times and that everything good lay ahead.

What lay ahead, of course, was the war. . . .

In Kansas City, I taught until 1942 and then, terrified that I might be drafted into the infantry and be made to sleep in foxholes, I signed up for the aviation cadets. I even had fantasies of shooting down the Red Baron, but the army saw at once that I did not belong at the controls. At Classification Center in Nashville, Tennessee, I slogged through the mud for ten weeks of testing and was assigned to navigation school. Except that, in the general madness of everything else, there were no openings, and I was sent home to wait week by week for what turned out to be six months—on no pay. For all the army knew, I might have starved by the time I was called late in 1942.

It stayed zany. I finally qualified as a navigator and received an honorable discharge to accept a commission, but the day before commissioning I was called back and busted to private. The Dies Committee of the House, in its hunt for un-Americans, had turned up my name on those Ann Arbor petitions, and I had been designated a PAF—A Premature Anti-Fascist. PAF was then an official Army designation (it may yet be on my service record). In army thinking it meant that anyone opposed to fascism before the declaration of war on Germany was probably a communist or a fellow traveler.

I did not know it then, but I was once more Lucky John. Everyone I had trained with went to the Eighth Air Force in England to be ground up in the daylight B-17 raids against Germany. General Curtis (Iron Pants) LeMay ran the meat grinder. "I can't save these boys," he was once reported as saying, "but if I spend them wisely, I won't have to kill off their kid brothers in a year or two."

Within the year I received a letter from Roger Fredland, my former roommate at Bates, who was in Washington as a Naval Intelligence officer. "You might like to know that I checked your training flight," he wrote. "You were one of forty-four, and every man you trained with is now listed as KIA (Killed in Action) or MIA (Missing in Action)." He thought I might want to send Martin Dies a letter of thanks and sign it Lucky John. Even now I'd be happy to, if I knew his address in Hell.

By the time I got Roger's letter I was at Lowry Field in Denver. I had gone through armament school and had been sent to Central Fire Control School to become a so-called expert in the remote control electronic gunnery system of the B-29's aborted high technology, all of which I forgot almost at once when assigned to an aircrew, for the B-29 was pressurized, with most of the system inaccessible in the unpressurized parts of the plane, and maintenance crews worked on it once it was on the ground. They weren't exactly trained to make certain it would malfunction: it just happened that way.

Nor did I get much chance to use my guns when they did work. The designers of the B-29 miracle must have assumed that the Japanese would fly pursuit curves from the rear, as the Luftwaffe tended to. Had they done so, they would have been sitting ducks. Unfortunately, they came in from dead ahead, which put the wing in my line of sight. The miracle system required time to set in the attacking plane's wingspan and then to track it for two seconds in order to prime the sealed-off computer, but by then any plane that came into view over the wing was out of range.

I did once get a probable hit on a twin-engine fighter called an Irving in the identification diagrams—it fell off, smoking into a cloud and disappeared—but it was not a technological hit. Bud Orenstein was our co-pilot and he and I had worked out a call system for the position of fighters coming in on frontal attacks. When he shouted NOW! I kicked off the computer and sprayed fifty calibres where I guessed the plane might appear. "Probable Irving" flew into the spray from my hose, his smoke was confirmed by other planes in the formation, and so, though restrained by high technology, I became a probable killer. It seemed a long way to go for not much.

The B-29 miracle was, in fact, a botched design. We were trained to go in at 32,000 feet and were assured the fighters could not reach us there—except that as often as not they dove on us. We were there for so-called precision bombing, but on the first mission we discovered the Siberian jet stream blowing at about 200 knots, a wind beyond any calculation the bombadiers could set into their sights. Consequently our bombs blew all over the sky, hitting nothing.

The run across 1,600 miles of Pacific followed by a climb up six miles of air inevitably overheated the engines. Our miracle had always had a nasty tendency to catch fire when the fuel lines vibrated loose and spilled raw gas on a hot engine. In training flights we had had to put out a fire at least once in every three or four flights: the fuel could be cut off, the wind would blow some of it out, the engine could be feathered (usually), and there were $CO_2$ tanks that might help (usually). In combat the B-29 became a high-wing four-engine monoplane with one or more engines afire. But the army, serenely bolstered by high technology, forged on, and every third day at 3:00 P.M. we crossed Choshi Point to keep our appointment with the massed Japanese Air Force to drop bombs that hit nothing. Once the army is geared to stupidity it cannot be deterred. I for one was in it but not of it. I had resigned from the army but I was still on an enlistment with my crew. The Crew was the one unit that mattered.

I was, of course, scared, but that can be lived with, if only at the cost of inventing fantasies. I told myself I would rather be dead than live to see a Japanese battleship sail into San Francisco Bay with the surrender terms. That would be worse than dying. It seemed certain that I could not get back alive, but despite army stupidity, there did seem to be a reason. I wonder what I could have told myself had I been in Vietnam being asked to die with no reason even to invent. In Vietnam I think I would certainly have cracked.

But it all fell into place once the plane had taken off on a mission. The bad times were the nights before a mission when we were sent back at last from preflight preparations to get a few hours' sleep that would not come. I lay there telling myself Hell, I had died last week and it was too late to worry about it. But then the thought would come, "By this time tomorrow you may have burned to death." I wasn't over-dramatizing, but reading evidence.

The obvious next question came inevitably. "And suppose you do; what would you like right now?" I never had any trouble with the answer to that question. I wanted a woman, whiskey, and a good T-bone rare, in that order. It seemed the least a benevolent government could offer before sending me out to die, but the high-tech army was beyond basic benevolence. The Hell with it. I could still take some solace in knowing I had survived the last shadow of Catholic guilt. My relatives were absolute in their assurance that I would turn to God on my death bed. It was a grim sort of comfort to know that I might damn well be on it, and that my last hunger was for this world.

In the end it was luck—and poetry—that saved me. I came in from a mission more scared than I ever had been before. Our crew had been pulled apart and reassembled. My original pilot was promoted and reassigned. My original co-pilot was given his own crew. My original flight engineer, an old hand, was sent to Wing to instruct new flight engineers. I flew a few missions with new hands at the controls and they terrified me. Every landing seemed to be an adventure. And then, returning from a bad one, I was ordered to report to headquarters.

The colonel in charge of personnel needed what he called a grammarian and he wanted a man with combat experience. He had searched civilian background files of crew members looking for a writer, and just then an issue of the *Atlantic* appeared with some poems of mine. It obviously made up his mind, for it was on his desk as he talked to me.

I had, he told me, been transferred to him. I was to pick up my gear and report to Headquarters Company or Squadron or whatever the clerks were called. I was to be in charge of Awards and Decorations. Since I would be flying back and forth to Guam to report to the Twentieth Air Force Board there, I would be kept on flight pay, a far from negligible 50 percent over base pay.

What he handed me was an empire. In that medal-happy army, I was the man who processed all the papers for awards. Soon even full chicken colonels were stopping by my desk to chat and leave me an extra fifth of the bad whiskey they got for $1.10 a month on officer's ration, and for which GIs of the high-tech army paid $35.00 on the black market. But fair is fair: hero-makers need heroic spirits.

My additional duties consisted mostly of writing letters of condolence to the next of kin of lost men, letters showing an intimate acquaintance with the dead man, for, of course, General Rosie O'Donnell's signature. As part of his public relations image of himself, the General meant to pose as a close buddy of every man in his command. And for slathering on the adjectives, I was almost immediately promoted to technical sergeant. I couldn't make it for getting shot at, but maybe Stephen Spender had been right after all and words are the ultimate power.

Or luck. Three missions after I went to headquarters, the crew I had been on took a direct hit over Tokyo Bay, the plane exploded in midair, and all hands were reported lost. It was a fluke. We had stopped taking the heavy losses of the first six months or so. My former crew was, in fact, the last one our squadron lost in combat. Yet I knew that had I been on it, and had I been left time to think, my last thought would have been a simple grim acknowledgment of what I had been sure of all those sleepless nights before missions. Except for an adjectival fluke, my number had been up.

So before long I found myself writing the general's phony letters of condolence for my own crew. By that time there wasn't a clean adjective left in the English language, but I turned the crank and let noble sentiment flow. Worse yet, the parents or wives who had sent those boys off to die probably cherished those letters. I have visions of them on family walls by photos of the hero, a gold star hung above the shrine, his Air Medals, his DFC, his Purple Heart, his service ribbons, and his wings, ranked under the photo, and beside it my letter reeking of mimeographed nobility for the general's signature. I even got my own letter, a commendation for my services as a grammarian. I am not sure whose mimeograph cranked that one out, but My General signed it. I have served!

And in August of 1945 the A-bombs went off. Douglas MacArthur delayed the official peace signing for almost two weeks so that he might sail into Tokyo Bay and pose in view of a thousand cameras on the deck of the *Missouri* riding at anchor above the fish-picked bones of what had been my crew. But nothing on earth belongs to the dead, the war was over, I had enough rotation points to go home, my original pilot, now Major Robert M. Cordray, gave me a job on his new crew, and late in September we flew home via Kwajelein and Oahu, and by the fourth of October I was turned loose on the streets of Sacramento as a civilian.

And a rich civilian. Part of my pay had gone monthly to my mother, an enemy alien—which I suppose made me guilty of providing aid and comfort to the Axis. For my first ten months on Saipan I was broke within two hours of the start of the payday crap game. Then in September, the eleventh month, I won almost $4000, almost doubled that on our stop at Oahu, and so with terminal-leave pay and travel allowances, I hit the street with over $8000. The job at Harvard was waiting for me and I could have started in February of 1946, but I wrote Morrison that I would report in September. I had most of a year in which to become a civilian again, and I had enough money to do as I pleased. As a promising start, it took me two months to get home on a coast-to-coast tour of friendly girls I knew.

Once home, however, I was bombarded by Clarence R. Decker. He urgently needed an English instructor, so urgently that he even offered to approximate a living wage, a measure he would never have resorted to except in desperation. He wrote, wired, phoned, and sent people to ask me to dinner and arguments in favor of my prospects in Kansas City. By the end of the year I was becoming restless. And I had a prospect of my own. I had stopped in Kansas City on my way home and there I had researched a dancer I had known before the war. She was given to talk about live food and dead food and about "getting into tune with the rhythm of the universe," but when I stopped listening and concentrated on the way her ass swayed when she walked, I was all for universal harmony. It was a better rhythm than any that reached me in Boston.

So in late January I was back in Kansas City, but not to the harmonies I had had in mind. Decker sent me to the journalism teacher, Miss Judith Hostetter, to be interviewed as a returning hero, and he told her to watch out for me as a brash young man. Miss Hostetter dutifully watched out for me all through the interview, and that night at dinner, and the next night, and the next, and through the semester, at the end of which she made a Country Club Christian of me. I still have a photo of the wedding party under a sign that says Country Club Christian Church. It wasn't truly a golfing date: the Country Club is a district of Kansas City, and the sign is the equivalent of something like Shady Grove Druidical Coven. In any case we left for Boston—or should I say Cambridge? (or should I say Medford?)—together, and if there was a brash young man in all this, his place has long since been taken over by a husband and father in no hurry to survive the arrangement. I was thirty years old and I was in the Garden of Eden!

I felt that my last shadows were behind me and that I had become luck's golden boy. Harvard kept raising my salary and asking for no more than I could get done in two days a week. I began to pour out poems of love and celebration. It was a celebration simply to be in pajamas at noon. *The New Yorker* began buying my poems almost as fast as I turned them out. Before long I was under contract with them, nearly doubling my salary in the process. In 1947 the Atlantic Monthly Press & Little, Brown published my war poems, *Other Skies*, and though most of them were still formless, I find I can still read a few of them without embarrassment. By a wry quirk of history I finally found some sort of voice as, of all things, a war poet, though the poems were written in haste, in the time between missions, when they had to be finished because I might not live to finish them. The book sold more than three copies in the United States alone, and I still have a carton of remainders in my attic, but it had been a start. And even the lecture circuit was opening before me. To begin with I had been eager to go anywhere for fifty dollars, until Judith insisted I was doing too much. So I doubled my asking fee only to find I was getting more and more invitations, whereupon I doubled it again and again, every increase leading to more invitations.

But luck and joy are not in themselves a sure remedy for idiocy. I contracted a case of malignant decency. I had fought and nearly died for the United States. As I saw it, that left me with an obligation to work for good government, and with no hope in the political establishment of Republicans and Democrats, I found myself in a splinter group called the People's Party, which soon became the Progressive Party in support of Henry Wallace's presidential campaign.

Ted Morrison opens his novel, *The Stones of the House*, with the question, "What good does it do to do good?" I didn't know, but I was sure I was doing some. I became a pitchman at fund raising rallies. Soon I was traveling with Wallace's running mate, a man named Taylor from Idaho—was his first name Glenn? His rhetoric was as inane as mine with fewer flourishes and a poorer sense of timing, but no one expects much from a vice-president, and less from a candidate v.p. I spouted, money came in, and as a reward for frenzy I began to travel with the great man himself, though I was never allowed to make any of the major fund pitches. I did find myself in a few evenings when Wallace talked in chambers in a relaxed way, and by mid-September I had come to see him in a new light. I thought he might have done well at a small college discussing Emerson and Thoreau with underclassmen, but that he was a disaster as a potential president. I rather liked the man but he seemed to be so fuzzy that I doubted he could have kept the White House furniture from being stolen. I needn't have worried for he hardly showed up in the final balloting, but I did worry, for I had been filling myself with the spurious rhetoric with which insiders convince themselves that they are going to win when everyone else knows they are dead and buried. I had more than enough to worry me. I was persuaded that the man was dead wrong and I was still committed to nearly seven weeks of nightly appearances in which I was required to be fervent after I had lost all conviction. Nor did I know how to cancel for I had made my commitments with local people I had come to think of as friends.

Not even in writing Rosie O'Donnell's graveside PR had I been as miserable as I was during those seven weeks. On election day, alone in the confessional of the voting booth except for the ghost of Tom Jefferson, I cast my vote for Harry Truman and went home from cause forever. If I was too stupid for politics, I was not too stupid to know it.


Was it Yeats who wrote "Words alone are certain good?" They have remained so for me. Love, time, friends, words. I had survived my tribal shadows, the ghost of my father reborn in me, guilt, God, arid poverty, mad adolescence, combat, and even the grammar of the USAAF. In those mad years of campaigning for the wrong ghost, I finally survived the fuzzy notion that an excited sense of social decency could lead to a social good. Let us, by all means, win through to a flowering society for all, but I do not know how to get to it.

I still had to survive ambition, which may be the worst trap of all, but insofar as a man may say so in reason, I think I am beyond it now. I no longer dream of writing big, important poems. What is big and important will probably end by blasting the race off the face of the earth. I cherish what is liveably small. If I can make it small enough, that may remain life-size, and what other size shall I think to?

My life reads back to me as a history of stupidity blessed by love and luck. Some of it has been blind luck in which I had as little choice as I had in deciding the accuracy of Japanese flak or the efficiency of USAAF ground maintenance of our flammable engines. Muriel Rukeyser once wrote that there were no heroes "to withstand / Wind, or a loose bolt, or a tank empty of gas." I wish she had mentioned rivets rather than bolts and that she had said "empty tank" instead of "a tank empty of gas," but the sentiment is one I have lived in. Once over Japan the plane on our right wing took a hit and began to smoke and fall out of formation, the Zeroes waiting to swarm on it once it was away from our covering fire. I was at the right blister as it passed under us. There was a boy in the top blister of the stricken plane. I was probably the only man in his direct line of sight. He waved to me, and I waved back. A least exchange forever. He waved there at the end of his luck, I waved and went home, and nothing either of us had ever done had any voice in deciding which of us was which.

When I did seem to have some choice in things, part of my luck has been that I could put by what my life was finished with. I have never been tempted, as the

18

confessional poets have been (really the couch poets) to dredge my psyche and to hold all its debris in awe because it once belonged to sacred me. I tend to look at this autobiographical note somewhat as an evolutionist might look at a collection of fossils. "Christ!" I think, "the things we have to have been before we get to be whatever we are!" I have never been proud of the various messy stages of my evolution into whatever. If I were to meet the boy I was at, say, twelve, I don't think I would like the sneaky little brat.

There is a residual ape in me, as there is in all of us. It is through that ape that I still share part of the brat I was. It is a stupid ape but I forgive him and even cherish him, for it is from confrontations with him that poems often come. Let him yammer. I am half-ready to believe I have him caged.

The actuarial tables give me plus or minus ten more years, perhaps a little longer if I stop smoking, but having been a chain smoker for almost fifty-five years now, I am satisfied to die of my own bad habits and pray only to escape my death as a result of someone else's. Beyond prayer, I claim survivor's rights, at least some of the rights that would in any case have been mine had I been the one to wave from that smoking bomber forty years ago, or had Martin Dies not cherished my name, or Rosie O'Donnell, my adjectives. I am an obsolete word freak with all debts paid up and a little time left—my time. It need not come to much to be all there is. I wouldn't have missed it.

# John Ciardi: The Many Gifts

## Vince Clemente

In "The Gift," Josef Stein, poet and survivor of Dachau, as his final journal entry recorded "three propositions":

> That Hell is denial of the ordinary. That nothing lasts.
> That clean white paper waiting under a pen
>
> is the gift beyond history and hurt and heaven.

Like Stein, John Ciardi was a survivor: of the forty-four young men he trained with in navigation school, he alone lived to see the end of World War II; later, stationed on Saipan, three missions after he had been assigned to headquarters as writer-clerk, the B-29 on which he had served as aerial gunner went down over Tokyo Bay. All were lost. It was Ciardi's duty to write letters of condolence to the next of kin of his own crew. It rent his large heart.

Stein's precepts may well sum up Ciardi's life: he was, above all, poet of the quotidian, of the very "ordinary," who insisted one keep the poem "life-size." Has anyone ever written better about marriage, or raising children, or bird watching from the patio, or mourning a mother, or burying a father—or growing up poor in America?

Never one to be conned, he was a realist, a skeptic, accepting—even embracing—life's impermanence, its arbitrariness, who, like his old friend Robert Frost hoped only to leave behind a few good poems "that would not go away." He expected nothing more of life. Finally, he was a writer who taught by example the holy calling of the writer's vocation. This most skeptical of men was dedicated to his craft with the constancy of medieval monks illuminating parchment manuscripts. And like them too, he was a miniaturist.

I was privileged to know this man, to visit with him and his family in Metuchen and in Key West, to enjoy John and Judith as our house guests the spring he was poet-in-residence at the Walt Whitman Birthplace, where I serve as a trustee. (That perfect Sunday in June, I introduced him to the standing-room-only audience at Sweet Hollow Hall, West Hills, Long Island. It was the proudest moment of my life.) I have been blessed, serving as editor of a John Ciardi Festschrift, a book we had hoped to have ready soon after his seventieth birthday on June 24, 1986. *John Ciardi: Measure of the Man* is an attempt (borrowing from Stanley Burnshaw) "to see Ciardi plain," to celebrate a writing career that logged in over fifteen volumes of poetry, among them *Lives of X*, an authentic American classic, and *Selected Poems*, a major achievement; a career that produced three etymological dictionaries as well as a definitive translation of Dante and the ghosting of one of the great jazz autobiographies of all times, *Treat It Gentle*, life of Sidney Bechet; a career that for twenty-one years helped shape a nation's tastes in poetry, from the editorial offices of *The Saturday Review*; a career that found time for directing the Bread Loaf Writers' Conference from 1955 to 1972, where Ciardi insisted, simply, that people write well, remain worthy of the "clean white paper waiting under a pen." What prodded me to press ahead with *Measure of the Man?* Norman Cousins says it best in his essay "Ciardi at *The Saturday Review*": "We are all in his debt and it is important that we say so."

I saw "Ciardi plain" in January 1986. Annie and I, along with our daughter Gina, were guests at the Ciardi Key West home. The cottage was ours for two weeks while John and Judith were at Miami for one of John's speaking engagements. Gina had been ill for much of the year. John felt the Florida sun would do us all much good. Of course he was right.

John Ciardi was no cartographer, but his earliest military training was in navigation, so he alerted us to the perils of Florida driving with a half dozen maps, warning me, that were I to take a wrong turn, I would find myself in an "old cemetery, never to be found." Right again! I did, however, extricate the family and soon found the cottage.

On the kitchen table, propped under a vase of flowers, was a long note, John insisting that he was "not the best of housekeepers." (He was alone at Key West; Judith would leave Metuchen and meet him in Miami.) He went on to caution us of the "greedy cats" that stalked the compound, and to say that we should "use *anything* in the refrigerator," especially "the large smoked turkey breast and the bags of rock shrimp in the freezer . . . one of my favorites, and I hope you would like it too."

And he was right about the cats—all the cats. They too found Ciardi a soft touch. They were there every morning—an army of them. I added two bags of catfood to the large one he had in the kitchen corner.

Attached to the note was a handwritten postscript: "Please don't tell Judith I mismatched the sheets and pillow cases. She'd scold me." Not only had he gotten us there safely from Setauket, Long Island, tidied up the house, stuffed the fridge with enough good food to take us into summer—the man had made our beds. I recall now what John Williams says in his "Looking for John Ciardi at Bread Loaf," that "the salient quality of the man's character is loyalty." He felt responsible for us, like the night he called from Metuchen, after the evening news reports of the devastating hurricane damage on Long Island, imploring us to "pack a bag" and stay with them—"and for as long as you want, Vince," he added.

Annie and Gina had the twin beds in the master bedroom, and I had John's study, size of a monk's cell, really, but enough for the likes of me. First night there I dreamed of John: we were both young men (John was sixteen years older than I, a kind of "older brother"), playing football in a meadow below a mountain. He was a blocking back and made my runs over center easy. (It is only now that I realize how Karl Shapiro's description of John in *The Bourgeois Poet*, "heart like a halfback," informed that dream.)

I spent hours in that room, certain not to disturb anything—all the works in progress: a mound of new children's poems on his desk, etymological notes for *Browser's III*, drafts of new poems for a volume after *The Birds of Pompeii*, sketches for lectures, letters to publishers and editors and friends. And all this spilled out of the study and into the cottage. Every corner was a writing station. And every corner held the man who carried with him, always, the earth trace, and for all of us in his debt, a way, a rhumb line, a path of surefooting.

John is gone now. Three days ago on Monday, March 31, 1986, Judith called from Metuchen: "Vince, is that you? Now, I want you to sit down. Are you sitting down, Vince?" I thought John had been nominated for a National Book Award or for a Pulitzer, but her voice told me otherwise. "John is dead, a massive heart attack—last night." And the world I had been carrying with me since I was twenty, a trainee in the 716 MP Battalion, reading John Ciardi for the first time, ended. I felt as if someone had driven a Mack truck through my ribcage.

But the man has left me so many gifts: thirty of his books inscribed, each with a holograph poem. I also have a collection of letters—about eighty—I'm sure one day to give to his beloved Tufts. I've manuscripts for our *Poesis: A Journal of Criticism* interview as well as manuscripts for his Walt Whitman Birthplace visit, including his Whitman essay for *Starting from Paumanok*, the Birthplace in-house publication. And I've his own collected Whitman, with his notes reading the "Big Bang": the ten-volume Paumanok Edition, edited by Bucke, Harned, and Traubel, published by G. P. Putnam's Sons in 1902. He gave me the collection three years ago as we walked through his attic study in Metuchen, saying simply, "Here, Vince, they'll do better with you."

And, of course, I have the joy of working on this book. In fact, in his very last letter, dated March 26, 1986, just four days before he died—his final words to me—he wrote, "I hope your work on the Festschrift will bring sweet rewards, in addition to those that you and Annie have with one another. Love, John." Yes, such "sweet rewards," all these many gifts. But the man is gone forever.

# John Ciardi's Early Lives

## X. J. Kennedy

"Here's a letter for you from my cousin John," the mailman greeted me on an afternoon in the mid-1960's. I was coming out of a three-decker house on Curtis Street on the opposite slope of that same steep hill down which a young John Ciardi, to prove a point to a friend, had whizzed like a bat out of hell on a bicycle whose brakes soon failed, inspiring motorists to climb the sidewalks to avoid him until he hit a curb, smashed the bike, and landed in a hedge.

"John Ciardi?" I said skeptically. "He's your cousin?"

"Sure. My name's Ciardi too. John, he's a big man now, isn't he? A poet. But when he was a kid nobody was sure if he'd grow up to be a poet or a gangster."

Our house was in West Somerville, Massachusetts, where Ciardi (the mailman) plied his route. Just across the street rose the campus of Tufts University, John Ciardi's alma mater. A few doors up the street, Medford began. At the top of the hill Curtis Street changed its name to Winthrop, and if you followed it downhill all the way to the Mystic River you ended up in the boyhood neighborhood portrayed in the *Lives of X*. If memory serves, Ciardi (the poet) was writing because he had accepted an invitation to visit Tufts again, and I was tending to the details. When Tufts called on him, as it did often, he would generally do a reading and sessions with students, and combine the trip with a visit to his family. One time, when the Tufts administration wanted to make him a college trustee, he begged off, pleading loyalty to another love—poetry.

Almost a gangster? I suspect the cousin of overdramatizing. Still, it would seem that as a boy, when he didn't have his nose in a book, John Ciardi was an *enfant terrible*. At least, as he tells us in the *Lives of X*, his precipitous bike ride down the hill won him a lasting reputation among the local police force as "the freshest kid in Medford." Later, noticing some bruises on him from a fight, the cops picked him up and threw him into a cell temporarily, to try to throw the fear of God and the Law into him.

His crimes appear to have been minor. As a youth he worked on a fishing boat that pandered to stag parties, taking members of the VFW out into the Bay for an evening of lethal moonshine and hard-core exhibitions. Hardly enough to get a man arrested for today, but at the time the skipper had to keep an eye out for the harbor patrol. Ciardi recalls, too, how he served as "bird dog / for the last organized gang of pheasant poachers / to operate" in Forest Hills, Boston's wooded cemetery. This misdemeanor was a family affair. Money was scarce and meat costly. A raid on a game preserve would bag a Sunday night's dinner.

All these reports rest on the evidence of *Lives of X*, if we are to take it as autobiographical fact. I assume we are. No one will sum up John Ciardi's work without reckoning with the *Lives*, a personal memoir and meditation in thirteen sections that cohere as one long poem. Let me offer a few background notes, at least to the poem's earlier parts. These deal with Medford, where Ciardi grew up and attended school, and Tufts College; the *Lives* goes on also to tell of the Army Air Corps and later life. As in most autobiographies, scenes and persons of childhood and youth appear to have carved the deepest notches upon the author. I would offer the book belated admiration. *Lives of X* is Ciardi's finest poem, a high accomplishment—a resummoning of "Ghosts a ghost lives by. Gone from but not left." One of these ghosts is that of the Mystic River:

> Is there a longer death than rivers die
> out of the sainted valleys of their first,
> following the mist-blown tribes and their dim totems,
> and the congregation of saints beside the water
> that came and went, and still came and still went
> where black stumps of the rotted shipyards stubbed
> the sewer-slimed edges of the rotted river?
> Where, through the same green cumulus, the spire
> the saints appointed as their arm to God
> lifted its four clocks to the rose of winds
> that took the captains out past God,
>
>                                         down river,
> clearing Hull point, aslant to Provincetown,
> and on to the Azores and Canaries.
> Until the Trades grew wicked with their south,
> the cargo was still God and Medford Rum,
> with barter as it came.
>                         But before landfall
> on the Gold Coast, God's corpse went into the hold

and chain and shackles rigged them out as slavers
triangling to Jamaica in their stink
to trade what flesh had not gone to the sharks
for kegs of black molasses, and then home,
the hold scrubbed out with soda, God broken out
like a new flag to fly above the Square
where God's distillery waited for the syrup
to start a new firewater its three ways
from God, past God, to God again one Sunday.

This speaker has no illusions about the glory of a history that surrounded him as a boy. In a neighborhood through which Paul Revere had sounded his alarm, the smudge of the slave trade had lingered. Like the Mystic River, the glorious past had died and rotted. In "The Benefits of an Education," there's a memorable profile of a Yankee captain of that same Boston fishing boat used for stag parties, who in an earlier age might have commanded a whaling vessel.

Unlike a European town, which would have made the most of a broad calm river flowing through its center, Medford does its best to ignore the Mystic. Even today, shops on the town's main business street turn their backs upon the river, like merchants who will have no truck with natural charms. One enterprise, now vanished, was a Chinese restaurant John Ciardi liked, called the Peking on the Mystic. (How Wallace Stevens, so fond of minglings of reality and imagination, might have savored that name!) But it too faced the high street and merely set out its trash on the riverfront. Although the Mystic has wide banks, the Town Fathers, instead of encouraging outdoor cafés, seem to have made little effort to use its shores for the commonweal. On the north bank they left the choicest land to low-income blacks who kept chickens and fortunately enjoyed one of the pleasanter river vistas in Middlesex County. The south bank, where Ciardi lived, they abandoned to builders of two-family and three-family homes sold or rented to an Irish and Italian proletariat. *Lives of X* recalls not only the river but a furious traffic artery that parallels it, the Mystic Valley Parkway. At its intersection with Winthrop Street so many accidents took place that young John, curious to see spilled blood, could run from his house at the sound of a crash. Usually he could beat the ambulance to the scene.

The poet's raising tuition money, attending Bates College for an unsatisfying time, and transferring to Tufts back home in Medford are sparely chronicled. Literally "The Highest Place in Town," as a section of the *Lives* calls it, Tufts campus sits atop a hill, one of the few in Boston. County Unitarians founded the college, lest their sons be schooled for the ministry by Harvard city-slickers; but the bonds to the Unitarian church have weakened over the years. From one brow of the hill you can see all the way to Harvard Square and Bunker Hill; from another, to Medford's shops and residences. This situation makes Tufts by nature a bit standoffish. It looks down on Medford much as (in a less physical sense) Harvard looks down on Tufts. Most Tufts students shun Medford and at the front gate of campus catch buses to Harvard Square, twenty minutes away. As a result, Medford Hillside has never developed collegiate business of the kind that borders most thriving liberal arts colleges: no restaurant whose menu isn't enclosed in a plastic case, no decent bookstore, no film house with intellectual pretensions. Driving along Boston Avenue on Medford Hillside, a stranger who didn't know the locale would not suspect that a college stood near. By and large, the people of Medford regard Tufts with a certain deference. Its position is not unlike Kafka's Castle, the object of a gaze from the town below. Growing up beside the Mystic, John Ciardi now and again must have looked up the hill to Tufts' short but overweening towers. On the day he first ascended Winthrop Street and climbed the hill to register, he must have felt himself rising in the world, in more ways than in altitude.

John Holmes, a central figure in the *Lives of X*, became his mentor. A Tufts graduate who taught there for most of his career (except for a brief interlude at Lafayette, where he formed a lasting friendship with Theodore Roethke), Holmes touched the lives of generations of students and New England poets and is still locally revered. When I came to Tufts to teach in 1963, the year after Holmes died, I inherited the courses he had established and named ("The Forms of Poetry"). From reports a modest, soft-spoken pipe-smoker, Holmes was the kind of teacher who chose to spend his evenings during World War II writing newsy letters to old Tufts grads at the front.

Awed tales preserve his ways of teaching the writing of poetry. Saying little, but that little pointed and wise, he would fall into long silences which at last the squirming student would feel impelled to break. As Holmes looked at him and puffed, the student would find himself staring intently at his poem, criticizing it, finally breaking down and realizing where it had gone wrong. Ciardi recalls Holmes' incisive comments on his early efforts, among them a remark that helped him turn into a poet himself. He has told the tale more than once; here is its metrical version:

> The first poem I turned in for Holmes to praise
> (what else do we mean when we ask for criticism?)
> was about seeing sharks in Long Island Sound

and being haunted by them—by anything.
"A sense of process, a name of the hunting sea
haunts me," I wrote. Holmes wrote back in the margin:
"All right, you're haunted. When does it haunt me?"

I was never pretty again in any mirror.

At Tufts, Holmes apparently led a life to try a saint's patience. For years he toiled in a fiendishly rigid freshman writing program, held down in rank by his lack of a Ph.D. Only late in his career was he promoted to a full professorship. (In 1950, I see from the jacket of *The Double Root*, he was still an associate professor after having published seven books and having taught at Tufts for sixteen years.) A former student, Cid Corman, has called him "a minor poet, but genuinely driven to poetry." Ciardi praised his natural and intuitive knowledge of the making of poems, and from all reports Holmes worked hard to communicate it. I suspect that he vented feelings of his own in "The Old Professor":

. . . sometimes I walk the college streets at night,
Hands rammed into topcoat pockets, collar up,
Kicking the leaves before me, cursing the College,
Cursing the dull dear young indifferent damned,
The boys and girls who never wanted to know,
And never will, but can be passed in the course.

For extra money Holmes taught nights at the Boston Center for Adult Education, where the most celebrated of his poetry workshops included Anne Sexton, Maxine Kumin, Sam Albert, George Starbuck, and Theodore Weiss.

His life off campus was severely troubled. An alcoholic, Holmes succeeded in swearing off, only to drink again in his last years. His first wife, suffering from mental illness, took her own life, and Holmes discovered her body, "three walls of books torn down to rubble round her," as Ciardi records in the *Lives*. Holmes married for a second time, happily, but a throat cancer went undetected, and spread to his chest and shoulders. Maxine Kumin remembers his "talking about a shawl, a cape of pain." A John Holmes room now commemorates him in Tufts' Wessell library. Ciardi came back to town and helped inaugurate it. On the brow of the campus that affords a condescending look over Medford stands a stone bearing a quotation from one of Holmes' poems, implying that Tufts is all the world a man could ever desire.

With characteristic loyalty, Ciardi brought about the posthumous publication of Holmes's *Selected Poems* (Boston: Beacon Press, 1965) and supplied an introduction for it, assessing Holmes' work clearly and fairly and lovingly, without making outlandish claims for it. Holmes wrote a generous handful of poems that deserve memory. Many strike me as the work of an old-fashioned Romantic with an obstinate streak of tough-mindedness. Holmes' correspondence with Robert Frost still rests in Tufts Library; I never succeeded in persuading any doctoral candidate looking for a thesis subject to blow the cobwebs off it. A biography of this close friend of Frost and Roethke, the mentor whom Ciardi, Kumin, and Sexton all found inspiring, still remains to be done; it would be valuable.

Ciardi's *Lives* is never better than when it draws true characters, like Holmes, and scenes. This is one of Ciardi's prime strengths; he has the first credentials that ought to be required of any author of a long poem: he is a first-rate portrait artist and a spellbinding storyteller, for which reasons *Lives of X*, for most of its length, holds the reader riveted. You will not know where Ciardi came from as a poet until you read the account of one Cataldo, nicknamed Sputasangue ("Spitblood")—

> the one artist
> I ever knew to stretch a roaring curse
> a full ten minutes and not run out of figures
> nor use the same one twice. Religious poetry
> lost a fountain the day he was kept from school
> to weed his first dry ledge. The man could start
> at the triune top and work the hagiography
> down to St. Fish by strict anatomizings,
> to frottery, battery, buggery, rape, plain mayhem,
> and on to atrocious-assault-with-intent, compounded
> twelve generations back and twenty forward.

Sunday nights, drinking wine in the kitchen, Sputasangue would reduce his listeners to helpless admiration. Memorable, too, is the account of how, sent to grade school dressed in white stockings, young John had to defend his honor against "a pug-nosed Irish snot."

Vivid, complex, ironic, the portrait of Ciardi's mother discerns that she found in young John a reincarnation of her dead husband. Though she beat the boy for misbehavior, says the narrator, "Sometimes I think she was beating him for dying." This determination to keep alive the husband in the son Ciardi was called, in an interview with Vince Clemente, "a hysteria she lived with, partly a madness, partly a martyrdom." To rise out from under her dominance, the boy had to assert himself like his father.

She was sitting in the kitchen

like a stone sybil hissing, the leather cat—
it was my day for cattails—on the table
like a dried familiar, dead but hissing back.
I let her work me over till the welts
bled through my shirt and wouldn't make a sound
except to say, "You having a good time?"
It broke her fit. She was the one to cry.

But everyone played his part in our asylum.
She dropped the cat and stood crying. I picked it up
and tossed it into the garbage. And she kissed me.
And both of us knew it was my confirmation.

A great story, told with rare economy. The idea of each family member playing his part is vital here: elsewhere, the narrator of the *Lives* calls his family "a family of actors" and tells how he once detected his histrionic mother in a pretended swoon and accused her of bad acting. She must have been a mother difficult to love; somehow, the narrator succeeds, and compels our respect for her as well.

Among scenes in the *Lives,* none is more colorful than the account of Ciardi's summer job on the fishing boat, captained by the down-on-his-luck Yankee. The best story is that of the first money Ciardi ever made out of education: by his rescue of a drunk on the stag show boat, poisoned by the bad whiskey sold on board. The first mate, worried at the prospect of a corpse on his hands, tried to bribe young John into sticking fingers down the drunk's throat to make him vomit; revolted, Ciardi instead hit upon the bright idea of tickling the back of the man's throat with a feather. The first aid worked. Asked where he had learned the feather trick, the lad had to admit he had got it from reading Roman history: how patricians made themselves throw up in vomitoriums, that they might feast anew.

In a recent issue of *Poetry* appeared a wide-of-the-mark attack on Ciardi's *Selected Poems,* charging that Ciardi in his poems never developed any distinctive voice. If a critic wanted to go for Ciardi with a vengeance, I suppose he could find some ways to do it, but I can't imagine any wilder, less effective way than that. If any poet of our time has firmed himself a voice, it is John Ciardi. The voice is so distinctive that it is like the "sound of sense" Frost cultivated, whose tone could be understood though the words came to you only half-intelligible through a closed door. It is a vigorous, gutsy, no-nonsense voice of authority: a voice of passion unfeigned, and absolutely devoid of sentiment.

I saw God squeeze my friend into a fist,
then drop him blue-pale in a sleep of weeds
till the black grapple stirred him, not awake.

It is this tone we hear continually in Ciardi's best short poems, and in *Lives of X*. Reading this large, powerful poem, we understand how, out of such a childhood, could have developed a tough individualist whom no father's ghost, no priest, and no policeman could scare, a man who would grow up to speak his mind. I have met poets of tender hide who for years have nursed the scars of some remark he once made to them. The first time Ciardi talked with me, at Bread Loaf in 1960 where I held one of those fellowships that required a young writer to eat with and be nice to the paying customers, he warned, "Don't get too smart around here—I've read a lot better stuff than yours"—which hurt at the time, but which on reflection seemed merely the obvious truth.

From *Lives of X* we can understand the reasons for one of Ciardi's favorite themes: making money. It is hard to write a good poem about making money or not making money; offhand, I can think of only one poet who has done the trick: Philip Larkin in "Money" in *High Windows*. In Ciardi's *Lives*, the narrator's delight in how much a poem has earned results in a passage of banality, in pure prose. But it is hard to resent an honest delight in having made money, when we find that delight in the author of the *Lives*, who tells us how he grew up as a poor widow's kid in the Depression, in a family where you'd shoot a robin and throw it into tomato sauce for a meatball you didn't have to buy.

Like so many of Ciardi's shorter poems, *Lives of X* is cast in a loose line that decides from moment to moment whether to use an alexandrine or a blank verse line as its base, a line flexible enough for all purposes. More tightly written than it looks, the poem, like most long poems, has a few stretches of low intensity (which Yeats argued are essential to a poem, so that the higher moments may shine). But *Lives of X* is the most readable long contemporary poem I know. Parts of it endure in the mind far more vividly than anything in *Paterson* or the *Maximus Poems* or the *Cantos;* and as those alleged masterworks never have done, Ciardi's immense poem has kept me bolted to my seat, clasping the book, determined to see what happens next. Negations may loom in it, but its central thrust is to affirm: "Let what I love outlive me and all's well."

# *Thanks, John, for Being*

## Richard Eberhart

I remember John vividly when he was a young man discovering poetry with John Holmes at Tufts. He had great energy, force, and was a brilliant, unforgettable presence. He was handsome and charming. He had discovered poetry, which had such a powerful claim on him that he said if he had not discovered its enlightenment for good, he might have become a criminal. This shocked me and I have remembered it ever since. Ancient Greeks sometimes held that poetry itself was criminal because it was too grand for the commonality of mankind. I felt that this idea was new to me, and I admired young, enthusiastic Ciardi as a new American. He had been here only a generation or two. I felt I was an old American since my ancestors had come here around 1720. This gave me sober and somber thoughts. I assumed America was best in newness not oldness. I watched the career of John Ciardi ever since his youthful days and am glad to be able to honor him now.

His *Mid-Century* anthology was one of the best of its time, and I owe John thanks for understanding and promoting the work of his then still-youthful elders. We used to go to John's house in Metuchen and enjoy the lively talk. We followed the growth of his and Judith's children. Only last year he published a fine poem to his splendid wife. When I first went to the University of Florida in 1974, John was the first to greet me. I then went to a lecture of his in Gainesville. We saw the Ciardis from year to year as they stopped en route to Key West. He was always amiable, open-minded, knowledgeable.

I learned from his early poetry something about the newness of our country. I was astonished later on when he said he wanted to make a million dollars. That was newness. I had a graveyard full of ancestors in Lancaster, Pennsylvania or Austin, Minnesota. John went into business with his usual energy and daring. I never found out what figure he got to—but like to report the Americanism of his efforts. His mind was always eager-spirited and open to possibilities. He was not afraid of life but willing to throw his weight into the fray, whether as a gunner in World War II, into poetry or prose, or into business. His work always had the integrity of truth-seeking and honesty.

In 1980 he wrote a poem called "An Inscription" to me in a Festschrift published by *New England Review,* edited by Sydney Lea, Jay Parini, and M. Robin Barone. For his own Festschrift, why not let John Ciardi speak his own words:

> I do not intend the people I know to believe me
> outside themselves: belief is inside the self.
> "It is the not-me in my friend delights me,"
> Emerson wrote. It is my friend in me
> that lets me see my friend. —These are convictions
> one sleep this side of poetry. But in time,
> with sleep dissolving from me like a mist,
> I find the shape of a scimitar still in my hand
> and know what holy wars I should have gone to
> in the right season. When I say to my friends:
> "We are that invisible war," they smile
> with a smile I know from myself. It is so we learn,
> one from another, our difference is no war
> but the delicate jointure of the parts of a skull.
>
> But is the articulation of bones a meeting?
> I have slept on ruined Rome and wakened green
> with the squeal of birds and the power-hum of the bees
> sealed in the air like amber. In the atrium,
> a laborer was eating bread and cheese
> in the noonday of his wine. I watched his ease.
> It was longer than the ruin. "*Buon appetito!*"
> I cried like God in the Sunday of my pleasure.
> He raised his wine flask and called back "*Salute!*"
> Then did he turn to stone? Or the stones to him?
> Something stayed fixed in time out of that meeting:
> a signal from my friend in me, a placement
> of holy banquets in their atrium,
> a vision of the bones that speak themselves.

Thanks, John, for being.

# Ciardi the Taler

## Lewis Turco

Over the years one of the things I've most enjoyed about John Ciardi is his storytelling. He was a grand master of the art of the narrator as well as the craft of the poet. When you've finished reading one of his story-poems you feel as though you've come as close to the poet as to an old friend. Reading his work is both an entertainment and an education.

Take "A Knothole in Spent Time," for instance, from one of his finest—and most neglected—books, *The Lives of X* (1972), as an example of Ciardi's ability to catch and hold the attention of the reader in the same way that a novelist or short fictionist does.

Like nearly all his work, this is a verse-mode, not a prose-mode piece. It begins with two thirteen-line stanzas in which the poet reminisces about his wedding—the poem is typical in this regard, too, for much of his work is autobiographical and nostalgic. Ciardi often reaches back into his past to pull out of the shadows moments dappled by the sunlight of recall, to consider them in the leisure of time, and to take out of them lessons learned, epiphanies achieved.

Ciardi begins by talking about his bride-to-be showing him where her school once stood in the southern woods, how they picked blackberries there and Judith got poison ivy. Then, the trip to Chicago and an itchy honeymoon, Ciardi sneezing through the cold he caught—the tone of humorous recollection is set, as is the prosody, normative accentual-syllabics, for Ciardi has always been a formal poet, if one can catch him at it. His meter is going to be iambic pentameter blank verse in this poem, but he will allow himself enough freedom to give the impression that he is writing prose: one finds, if one scans a few lines, that there are going to be hexameters among the five-foot lines, and even in the normative lines there will be reversals and substitutions of feet.

A third "stanza" appears to continue the story of his wedding and its aftermath; instead, however, Ciardi launches into a series of rhetorical tropes as he asks how Wordsworth or Tennyson might have reacted had they gone back to their childhood haunts: "All change unghosts / something we change in leaving." What would they have done had they discovered "Super Mkts, / cloverleaf ramps, and ten Drive-In Self-Service / Omnimats—"? The "stanza" extends itself for an extra line and three-fourths, then it drops down to the next space and turns itself into a strophe instead, a strophe and a verse paragraph that begins with "Craddock School"—and Ciardi has dropped with it into the farther past, to his small-boyhood in Boston.

It is Ciardi's first day in kindergarten. Although "It's out of focus now," he remembers the elms synesthetically, "a whispering sky that spattered sunlight through" like rain. The roof of this world is closer, yet it is still high above his head. Indoors are "walls like the sides of a ship," an "ark" full of small creatures that need to be tamed and civilized. Indoors the hallway ceilings appear to be as high as the trees outdoors, "lost in their own dusk."

Ciardi piles similes upon descriptions—the hallway "smelled of chalk / the furnace room, and sneakers. It creaked and breathed / as if there were giants sleeping in its attics." The poet has done what a good talespinner does—he has introduced his hero, set the scene, pulled us into the story, for we remember these things too, even though we may not have lived through them ourselves. We are experiencing the school as the small boy does. The senses of smell, sight, hearing have been brought to bear upon these evocations, but literacy itself is not ignored, for he springs an allusion on us, an allusion out of school:

> If heaven needed a barn for better beasts
> than any of us were, the Craddock School
> would have done for Apollo's cattle.

The poet-to-be sits down. We are ready to be introduced to our first antagonist in the shape of a woman characterized by nomenclature and simile: "Miss Matron-Column" who "stood pillared / over our heads like a corseted caryatid / spilling out of her corsets on a scale / of two of anyone's mother. . . ." The second antagonist is not far off:

> Ma meant the day to be ritual, and had made me
> a jumper-something called a Buster Brown,
> and bought me new school shoes, and long white stockings
> that buttoned, or tabbed, into my underwear.
> I wasn't exactly comfortable but I took it
> until a pug-nosed Irish snot behind me
> —Tom something-or-other—got his needle in

> to let me know white stockings were for girls
> and that I was not only a Dago but a sissy.

Which portended the inevitable after-school fight, but not until his teacher called him "John Sea-YARD-i," which was to stick until he was old enough and far enough away to assert the correct pronunciation of his name.

Ciardi is very good with textures, characterizations, imaging, but he can go deeper, and he does. After the fight he must go home to his widowed mother who will likely be waiting with a strap to discipline the reprobate who has not lived up to her expectations. The boy spends time worrying about it:

> Ma would be waiting with that strap. My tail
> would come away from it ridged. Then *she'd* cry,
> and I would have to stop bawling to comfort *her.*
> I've never thought far enough back—not for trying—

[he says, thinking back,]

> to understand how we came to that arrangement.
> I know it had something to do with my being ghosted
> into her husband and he into her son.
> Sometimes I think she was beating him for dying,
> and me for not being enough of what she'd lost.

That is complicated psychological analysis simply stated.

When Ciardi wants to paint a scene into the reader's memory or to drive home a point, he can do so with more than imagery or rhetoric, he can do it with sound. Though there are no end-rhymes in this verse tale, there is plenty of music. When he is promoted to the next grade, he meets Miss Absolute Void whom he cannot remember at all except as an absence in his personal history. What he does remember is the *sound* of emptiness:

> I droned fly-drowsy sun its leafy day
> down through the elm's own daydream into mine.

The image has its tunes as well as its associations—alliteration (droned-drowsy-day-down-daydream), internal rhyme (I-fly), repetition (day-daydream), consonantal and vocalic echoes (r's, l's, i's and y's), consonance (droned-sun-down-own). The meaning of this passage resides in *how* it sounds as much as in "what" it says—it's no coincidence that Ciardi once edited a textbook titled *How Does a Poem Mean?*

Ciardi's mastery of the sonic and sensory levels of a poem would be enough for many bards, no doubt, but this one wants his stories to have point as well. In all of them, he is going somewhere. This is where he had been heading all the while with "A Knothole in Spent Time," whether we or he knew it or not, for this poem is a voyage into the land of epiphany, of self-discovery:

The lad has been daydreaming. Suddenly, the teacher calls on him to pick up the oral reading in the book before him, the book where he has lost his place. "The book was on my desk but I'd lost the page. / I got to my feet. Somewhere in a separate haze / I remembered a girl reading and her last words / still floating in the elmtops. I held the book / and said from memory whatever Blind Mice / or Chicken-Little came next, pretending to read. . . ." And he pulled it off! Elation! He had fooled his teacher, who was made of clay after all. What an amazing victory!

> Then hit on a truth as if I'd cracked my skull—
> they wouldn't believe me! Ma wouldn't understand.
> My sisters wouldn't care. Miss Absolute Void—
> well, how could I tell her? I was alone
> my first time into the world, at an edge of light
> that dizzied like a dark; my gloat, half fear,
> my eye at its first peephole into heavens
> where Teachers were only people and could be wrong,
> and all Ma's stations and candles could be rounded
> by a truth I'd caught and held, and couldn't tell!

Yet here he is telling it after all, and we believe it! Not only that, it isn't, in context, at all a trivial incident, though perhaps it would have been had Ciardi told it in any other way. The poem is not quite over—there is a denouement in which the author, like the professional raconteur he is in person or in his role as poet, winds up the loose ends and ties them into a neat knot, but that is the climax and the point of the performance, for that is what it is, the performance of a work of language as relevant to our world as it is to the teller's. "This is the room. / The first place in the world where I was alone / with more than I could tell of what was true."

On this level of the ideational Ciardi has taken his subject, growing up, and cast it in the form of an autobiographical narrative. He has mixed his viewpoints to correspond—egopoetic and narrative—so well and subtly that one has a difficult time telling opinion from description, narrative from discourse. His syntax, likewise, has been a blend of the subjective and the objective. The level

37

of diction he has chosen is the conversational, and his style is literate but not overly literary. The major genre of the poem is clearly the narrative, but there is an undercurrent of the didactic as well—all good stories are but illustrations of lessons learned about life.

Sometimes Ciardi's stories are tossed off—they have the quality of throwaways. I remember one in particular that stuck in my mind until I had to do something about it myself. Early in 1965, when I was teaching at Hillsdale College in Michigan, John came to talk to us at Chapel in the morning and to read some of his poetry in the afternoon. At the morning session he said, "To quote Emerson, 'It is the *not-mes* in my friend that delight me.' But Emerson didn't go far enough—I have discovered that there are no *not-mes*."

He went on to tell a story illustrative of this theme. To the best of my knowledge, he never put that story into verse, so some years ago I took the liberty of doing it for him. He saw this—I sent him a copy of my chapbook, *A Cage of Creatures*, in which it appeared in 1978, so it would have come as no surprise, but let me hang it upon this peg as my tribute to a great teller of tall tales and true:

## Sasquatch

### *with apologies to John Ciardi*

After the wind-tempest, when
branches lie in crambles upon the clearings
and neighbors at far distances phone
down the foothills under the mountains

to ask if all is well still,
the answer is "Yes" and, sometimes, "But have you
seen anything of a shambling man
dressed in furs running before the birds'

"chirming just before the sun
was wiped out of the slate sky and the rain erased
the trees, made them slop and wiggle like
pines in a fingerpainting?" And, "No,"

is the answer, "not this time,
but now you mention it, last time we thought we
saw a bear at the edge of the woods,
and when we went to look there were prints

"in the mud—footprints the shape
of a big man's, a huge man's bare feet. They put us
in mind of the manse of the films,
the girl in the chiffon gown walking

"down the hall to stop under
a portrait whose eyes move. And then, you know, it
slides aside, and a hairy arm comes
reaching out toward the maiden, and

"we scream, don't we, for the girl
in the white gown, but you know, what must it be
like to be the thing the arm belongs
to? What wouldn't we want, and wouldn't

"we hide in the walls and woods?
And if a storm blew up, wouldn't we wander some,
down from the timberline to where the
houses started, to look in windows

"at firelight and carpets,
to think about chiffon and wish the folk would
understand somehow, somewhen, that there's
a bit of hairy arm in everyone?"

The last eight words are a quote from the old master taler from whose whole
cloth I stitched these verses. Yes, John, what you said is quite true, but especially in your own case—it appears there was a little of everyone in you.

# John Holmes and Roy W. Cowden:
## Teachers of a Teacher

### Vince Clemente

Looking squarely at John Ciardi's achievements—and they are formidable—we tend to forget he was a remarkable teacher. In fact, his mentor at Tufts, that good man, John Holmes, wrote in 1955 that Ciardi's "teaching, like his writers' conference work, and lecturing, is forceful, brilliant, and a rare combination of scholarship and earthly humanity. He was voted by the students the most popular professor at Harvard." Even after leaving Harvard and Rutgers, in a sense, he *never* left the classroom, as the nation at large became his classroom. Entering his seventh decade, he became a kind of wandering medieval scholar, like those who carried in their skulls whole libraries and civilizations, passing through sleepy cathedral towns.

In "'A Man Is What He Does with His Attention': A Conversation with John Ciardi," published in *Poesis: A Journal of Criticism*, Spring 1986, I say, "In a letter dated April 25, 1983, you write, 'I was blessed by good teachers, and at times even great ones.' I'm sure you had in mind John Holmes of Tufts and Roy W. Cowden of Michigan." He went on to speak of these "great" teachers:

> I transferred from Bates to Tufts in the middle of my sophomore year, and so in early '35 I signed up for John Holmes's writing course. Almost at once, I knew what I was going to do with the rest of my life, if I lived that long.
>
> John was the first real poet I had really met. . . . My other teachers at Tufts were good men. . . . But they were historians of music. . . . John was a piano player; he knew what to do with ten fingers on eighty-eight keys. I knew at once it was the kind of learning I was hungry for. Of many good teachers, he alone talked about the insides of a poem. His

sort of technical analysis is common enough today . . . but it was rare then.

John, moreover, was a loving teacher . . . indulgent with the hopeless. He did me the honor of being tough with me. . . . Time after time, he nailed down what I had done that was false, weak, dull, random. He didn't have to hammer: his last nudge told me. He knew how the piece should be played and which piece was worth playing. . . . I lived on his shoulder like a forty-four pound monkey, and he accepted me, though the addiction was mine rather than his. I read his library, I haunted his house, I sat while he pulled my poems apart.

And in the interview he remembered Roy W. Cowden of Michigan as "a grandfatherly man with twinkly eyes, a monotonous voice, and a taste for pouring over the worksheets of great novelists, especially Hardy." Of the actual class sessions, he could recall little—just the sheer "agony of fighting sleep." Cowden was the kind of man who taught best *out* of the classroom. The manuscript conference made all of the difference:

We would sit together over the manuscript of one of my poems. He would begin to talk, waving his right hand in air, index finger extended. As he talked that finger would wave over the page, finally coming down on some detail. And always, before it came down, I knew where it would land, and why.

I have never understood the process. I cannot remember a word he said to me. I remember that magic finger in air, and what it was going to point to when it came down, and somehow he made me understand not only what but why. . . . Nor was he ever wrong. . . . I don't think anyone else could teach that way.

Ciardi's first book, *Homeward to America* (1940), was dedicated to John Holmes, his second, *Other Skies* (1947), to Roy W. Cowden, his *Selected Poems* (1984), published in his sixty-eighth year, is "for John Holmes and Roy W. Cowden in loving gratitude." Only fitting then that his first books and what may be his crowning achievement as a poet be gifts for two "gifted" teachers.

It is right, also, that both men add their voices to this Festschrift, and appropriate that they speak from the pages of the *Tuftonian*. I'd like to thank the Tufts University Archives for furnishing copies of Roy W. Cowden's "A Note on John Ciardi at Michigan," *Tuftonian*, Vol. IV, No. 3, Fall 1944, and John Holmes's "John Ciardi, Tufts Poet," *Tuftonian*, Vol. VII, No. 1, Fall 1955.

# *John Ciardi, Tufts Poet*
## (from the *Tuftonian,* Fall 1955)

## John Holmes

In the fall of 1938, after his graduation magna cum laude, from Tufts, John Ciardi went to the University of Michigan for an M.A. and some of the Hopwood Prize money. He wrote that, being short of funds, he would send me a standard-form telegram if he won anything, "May Easter bless you many years," for fifteen cents. But when the awards were made, a straight wire said, "Ring out wild bells twelve hundred bucks." It was the largest Hopwood prize ever given for poetry. *Homeward to America* was published in 1940, dedicated to me, a satisfaction all the greater when in 1947 he dedicated his second book, *Other Skies*, to Roy W. Cowden, his professor of writing at Michigan. Thus Ciardi saluted the two universities that had given him his formal and higher education.

John Ciardi was born in 1916 in the North End of Boston, of Italian immigrant parents, and his father died when the boy was too young to know him. His mother brought the son and several daughters to Medford, and he grew up within sight of Tufts, and went to the Medford schools. He cheerfully threw away a freshman year at Bates College. A kindly professor of Latin told him, however, that he had the highest grade of those who had failed the course. He was given one more chance, at Tufts, because it was near home. He lived at home, on South Street, which runs parallel to the Mystic River, the water a hundred feet from the house.

He took part in campus activities only by writing for the *Tuftonian*, and acting for Three P's. He played a grim Troc in Maxwell Anderson's *Winterset*, as if he had lived the part. His free daytime hours he spent in the West Hall rooms of some regional scholarship men, two of whom are now professors of English, and two others scientists. They happened to be in his courses, and he happened to discover that the kind of fierce pleasure he had found in other ways, they found in literature, and in ideas, and in high grades. Loud and long the talk ran on in the rooms in West, and into the early morning. Competition, and challenge, in studies, became exciting to him, though poetry finally proved more so. He missed election to Phi Beta Kappa by a few tenths of a point, and was not happy that his friends made it. But his wild drive had already become channeled in a creative and intellectual direction, and though no one then or now could call him a conformist, the drive deepened to a powerful force, and the wildness concentrated to a flame of energy both physical and mental. He found himself at Tufts.

Or better to say he found that he had brains and could write. There had been an earlier finding, of another part of himself. Until he was twelve, he might have taken any of several turnings, for good or not, but never for the ordinary. It happened when, as he says in "Elegy," he began the dream of his father, when he knew he wanted to be man of the family, father-son, son-husband, and himself. "I have done nothing as perfect as I dreamed him," he says in the poem, of his father. But he has, and a triumph of growth into wholeness began then. The casebooks would have given him no odds at all, none; but there is more to the dreams of a fatherless twelve-year-old boy than any casebook says. There was a later finding, when in 1946 he married Judith Hostetter, when he returned to Missouri after the war. But by that time all his discoveries were right; the love poems, some of the most passionately beautiful of our time, affirm this.

He found the great satisfaction of writing poetry in his years at Tufts. He would bring not one, but five or six poems to the advanced writing class. We did not finish with his, but at the next class he was not interested in those. He had new ones; and better, he said. He began then to be a prolific, an eruptive writer, but one who grew fast, who advanced in skill with every new poem, ranging wider and further for new forms, new subjects, new metaphor, new vocabulary. Though he assembled a book for the Hopwood prize, and rewrote a great deal of it between award and publication, he took with him from Tufts the essential poetry of that first volume.

After the year at Michigan, he made a trip to the west coast by car, discovering America for himself, as he says in a poem his parents had had to for themselves. A visit at the University of Kansas City brought him an appointment there as an instructor in English, from 1940 to 1942. He is still on the editorial advisory board of the *University of Kansas City Review*, one of the best quarterlies. From 1946 to 1948 he was an instructor at Harvard, and then a Briggs-Copeland assistant professor until 1953. The Briggs-Copeland appointments are for young men of already distinguished literary achievement, and have a limit of five years, without reappointment to the Harvard faculty thereafter. Since 1953 he has been a lecturer in English at Rutgers University.

When the war began Ciardi wanted to be in the Air Corps, and served from 1942 to 1945. He trained first as a navigator, but for reasons that had nothing to do with his ability, did not receive his lieutenant's bars. He was retrained as a gunner, and flew some fifteen missions in the B-29's from Saipan. His USAAC ranks were those of private and technical sergeant, perhaps one of our most expensive non-coms, considering the months he spent in training. But poetry profited. *Other Skies* is almost entirely made up of his war poems, among them some of the best by any American poet in World War II. They are remarkable, among other excellences, for using so much of his air-base experience, as for example "On Sending Home My Civilian Clothes," "Reflections While Oiling a Machine Gun," "Death of a Bomber," and then "Elegy Just in Case" and "V-J Day." The poems use, too, his return to civilian life. The training in navigation, which gave him no job as such, gave him striking metaphor, and enlargement of understanding. All experience became his poetry, from the bitterest to the most beautiful.

Ciardi's position in the literary world, his achievements, influence, recognition, and service in it, were extraordinarily rich during his years in Cambridge. He was publishing in all the best magazines, all the time. *Poetry*, in Chicago, gave him its Blumenthal prize in 1944, the Tietjens prize in 1945, and the Levinson in 1947. He delivered the Phi Beta Kappa poem at Harvard in 1952 and was elected to the Alpha chapter there. He was elected a Fellow of the American Academy of Arts and Sciences. He traveled widely in this country to take part in summer-time writers' conferences, and reviewed books in *The New York Times* and other periodicals. He became poetry editor for Twayne Publishers, of New York, and initiated the Twayne Library of Modern Poetry, which began by the publication of eight new books of poetry a year. His present executive position with Twayne keeps him reading mountains of manuscript, and pushing through new publishing projects.

In the summer of 1947 he was a member of the staff of the Bread Loaf Writers Conference, the oldest in the U.S., and has continued to go there ever since. This fall he was appointed its director, succeeding Theodore Morrison. Morrison, a poet and novelist, has been a professor of English at Harvard for a quarter century, and was chairman of English A there. Ciardi was an instructor in the department, and being also a Briggs-Copeland appointee was a natural candidate for the Bread Loaf staff. His teaching, like his writers' conference work, and lecturing, is forceful, brilliant, and a rare combination of scholarliness and earthy humanity. He was voted by the students the most popular professor at Harvard. It is impossible to recount his wide and warm acquaintance among the living writers of fame, or to account for his influence, direct and indirect, on writers younger now than himself.

His third book of poems, *Live Another Day,* was published in 1949, and in 1951 came *From Time to Time.* He edited *Mid-Century American Poets* in 1950, an anthology in which he brought together fifteen poets whose work seemed to him in full swing at that time, and got each of them to write an explanatory preface for their own selections of their poetry. His own introduction to the book is a valuable piece of working criticism.

Just as his wartime experiences became poems, all his human experiences become part of his books. One of the richest elements in his poetry is provided by his family. His poems to the father he never knew recreate him, or in fact create him, a most moving performance, a triumph of understanding or identity, warm with longing, some pity, some laughter. Again and again his mother in her garden, his mother in her house, his nieces and nephews around him as his family, make figures in the poems. His third book is dedicated to Judith, his wife, and from there on her presence, and that of their three children, a daughter and two sons, is added and felt, a further enrichment of his life and poetry. His love poems are among the best of that kind, passionate and wise, and his family and household poems are also. Poems to one's father, mother, wife, and children can be and most often are painfully bad. This is very sad and very true but it is neither true nor sad with Ciardi. The subject of the family in poetry is one that no one has yet dared to evaluate and anthologize, and would be a risky thing in any hands. But were it to be done, Ciardi would appear in the first excellence, as in fact he would, and does, in poems of love, war, satire, and commentary.

Last year John Ciardi's translation of Dante's *Inferno* was published by the Rutgers University Press, and it appeared simultaneously in paper covers. He had been at work on this great task for some years. He had grown up hearing Italian, though not at first speaking it much. He could easily read it, though, and brought new interest to bear when he undertook the translation. From a summer in Rome he brought home valuable books and close impressions of his land and Dante's. Translations of major works in world literature are not done often, and by no means with high success though the labor is long. Fortunate is the generation that produces a first-rate, enduring new translation, and because of John Ciardi, ours is fortunate.

"A major contribution to the resources of Dante in English," says Edmund Fuller, in *The American Scholar,* the Phi Beta Kappa quarterly. "What we have is Dante," says Richmond Lattimore in *The Nation,* "translated with fidelity into an English poem which swings along at a good pace, which is plainer than most English verse, and easier to understand." Dudley Fitts, himself a leading translator of the classics, says in *The New York Times,* "Here is our Dante, Dante for the first time translated into virile, tense American verse; a work of enormous erudition which (like its original) never forgets to be poetry; a shining event in a bad age." And the poet and editor and professor, John Crowe Ransom, says, "Fresh and sharp. I think this version of Dante will be in many respects the best we have seen."

In his brief and masterly translator's note, Ciardi says, "When the violin repeats what the piano has just played, it cannot make the same sounds and it can only approximate the same chords. It can, however, make recognizably the same 'music,' the same air. But it can do so only when it is as faithful to the self-logic of the violin as it is the self-logic of the piano." He is speaking, of course, of the eternal problems of the translator. Scholars and plain readers look at every new translator to see what he has done differently and well, the same as before and not so well, or perhaps differently and extremely well, as Ciardi has. Dante wrote his long poem in groups of three lines, triplets, the first and third rhymed, the middle line picked up in the first and third of the next triplet. This is called *terza rima*. In Italian it is far easier than in English, because there are many more rhyming sounds. The versions in English, in trying to follow the *terza rima* mechanically, inevitably pad, distort, or dull the effect. Ciardi realized that Dante nevertheless wrote in sentences and thought-patterns that most frequently filled three lines and stopped. So he made a bold decision to use a triplet in which the first and third lines rhyme, and the second does not. This is in itself a major step. It freed the American poet to make the utmost use of "a language as close as possible to Dante's, which is in essence a sparse, direct, and idiomatic language, distinguishable from prose only in that it transcends every known notion of prose . . . it is what common speech would be if it were made perfect."

This translation was made when Ciardi was in the fullness of his powers—to say the height implies that he might not do a better *Purgatorio* and *Paradiso*, the second and third parts of *The Divine Comedy*, at which he is now working— and he brought to it all the force of his nature, his inheritance, and his skill, fused now into a fine and single balance. The book is provided with a long historical introduction by Professor Archibald T. McAllister of Princeton. And the huge circulation of the paper-book edition has put it in every city and town in the U.S., and in many in Europe. It is in wide use as a text, and copies of it may be seen in Tufts classes.

John Ciardi's newest book is *As If*, his poems new and selected, published this year. It is a rigorous selection of only sixty-four titles. There are a hundred and sixty-one titles in his four previous books. There are only eight of the many war poems. He rightly makes a section he calls "Tribal Poems." Two other aspects of his work are in "Poems Looking Out" and "Poems Looking In," and there are groups of prayers, scenes, and fragments from Italy.

"As If," says Ciardi, "strikes me as the enduring mode of poetry. *Is* is the mode of prose. Poetry is *As If*'s reality. When one has imagined ('lived as if') all his possibilities he may begin to guess who he is and what world this is."

Commenting on this summation of almost twenty years of Ciardi's poetry, Archibald MacLeish wrote, "Ciardi is a poet of remarkable vitality and this book is alive in a way that few books of modern poetry can be said to be. There is a man here and a voice speaking—a unique voice." Dudley Fitts observes the completion, though he could not have known that is what it is, of the story of the making of a whole man—the story that really began in Italy, had as second chapter his birth in Boston, and as one of the most important the years from 1934 to 1938 at Tufts. "For me, the central quality of Ciardi's style is tremendous violence joined to tremendous control. I find delight in the acid, humane, earthy, and hard-bitten stance, in the richness of the *melos*, in the assured handling of the whole poetic apparatus. To sum up the achievement of Ciardi's mind and style in a single poem, I would cite the Elegy to his father."

### Elegy

My father was born with a spade in his hand and traded it
for a needle's eye to sit his days cross-legged on tables
till he could sit no more, then sold insurance, reading
the ten-cent-a-week lives like logarithms from
the Tables of Metropolitan to their prepaid tombstones.

Years of the little dimes twinkling on kitchen tables
at Mrs. Fauci's at Mrs. Locatelli's at Mrs. Cataldo's
(*Arrividerla, signora. A la settimana prossima. Mi saluta,*
*la prego, il marito. Ciao, Anna. Bye-bye.*)
—known as a Debit. And with his ten-year button

he opened a long dream like a piggy bank, spilling the dimes
like mountain water into the moss of himself, and bought
ten piney lots in Wilmington. Sunday by Sunday
he took the train to his woods and walked under the trees
to leave his print on his own land, a patron of seasons.

I have done nothing as perfect as my father's Sundays
on his useless lots. Gardens he dreamed from briar tangle
and the swampy back slope of his ridge rose over him
more flowering than Brazil. Maples transformed to figs,
and briar to blood-blue grapes in his look around

when he sat on a stone with his wine-jug and cheese beside him,
his collar and coat on a branch, his shirt open,
his derby back on his head like a standing turtle. A big
man he was. When he sang *Celeste Aida* the woods
filled as if a breeze were swelling through them.

When he stopped, I thought I could hear the sound still moving.
—Well, I have lied. Not so much lied as dreamed it.
I was three when he died. It was someone else—my sister—
went with him under the trees. But if it was her
memory then, it became mine so long since

I will owe nothing on it, having dreamed it from all
the nights I was growing, the wet-pants man of the family.
I have done nothing as perfect as I have dreamed him
from old-wives tales and the running of my blood.
God knows what queer long darks I had no eyes for

followed his stairwell weeks to his Sunday breezeways.
But I will swear the world is not well made that rips
such gardens from the week. Or I should have walked
a saint's way to the cross and nail by nail
hymned out my blood to glory, for one good reason.

# A Note on John Ciardi at Michigan
## (from the *Tuftonian,* Fall 1944)

## Roy W. Cowden

Early in October of 1937 I received the following letter:

> I write to request information concerning the Hopwood Awards.
>
> Since I do not know what personal data might be pertinent at this time, I will burden you with no account. You may, however, find it serviceable for purposes of classification to know that I am a senior in Tufts College, the Department of English, and that my interest in writing is entirely given to poetry.
>
> I shall be happy to hear from you, and shall submit further information as soon as I know what would best guide you.
>
> Respectfully yours,

The name signed was John Ciardi. I pondered over the word Ciardi trying it this way and that and wondering how to pronounce it. I noted too that he called his writing poetry rather than verse, and I was aware that he was either careless of his language or had strong convictions about his talent. From the details of his letter I inferred that if he came to Michigan he would enroll in the graduate school. I sent him our current Hopwood bulletin, and checked the pages which described our seminar in English composition leading to the master's degree. The description of this course stated that candidates should submit manuscripts of their own composition as evidence of their qualifications for the work. October came again before I received an envelope containing writing from John Ciardi; and when I opened it and turned the pages, I realized that, as his letter had indicated, he was interested only in what he called poetry.

For many years I have done much of my reading at home and the evening of the day I received John Ciardi's manuscript, I sat across from my wife in the living room, and took the envelope addressed to me out of my case. The ten or twelve short pieces of manuscript were typed on sheets of paper differing in weight and quality, and some of them were worn and wrinkled to such a degree that I felt the writer must have had them in his hands many times.

It may well be that only a teacher can understand the feelings that come to one who for the first time is looking at the creative effort of a young writer; the eager desire to discover a talent, the hope upon hope that this time one is going to find something he has never before known; and also, it must be admitted, the dread born of former experience that one is going to hear only the voices already familiar to his ear and the clichés through which no new voice can be heard. I read John Ciardi's manuscript through to the end, and then read it again, and then with growing excitement I went back through the pages, and at last I interrupted my wife in her reading and said, "Listen to this. Have you ever heard lines like these before?" and I read several passages here and there. She too felt the vitality and the freshness of the language. I read the lines again aloud and then I said, "I think this year we have a poet coming here to Michigan."

Other members of the committee that passed upon manuscripts for the seminar agreed with me and eventually John Ciardi was enrolled in the course. When I first saw him I was startled at the quiet, deliberate bulk of him. He might have come from a year before the mast, or from a business where heavy lifting was the task. No one would have guessed him to be a poet.

Six students were in the seminar that year all working on book-length manuscripts. As the weeks passed and John began to do the poems that were finally to make the volume entitled *Homeward to America* I became deeply interested in his development. In the introduction to Edwin Arlington Robinson's *Jasper*, Robert Frost raises the question of how a man comes on his difference, and how he feels about it when he first finds it out. John Ciardi's growing awareness of the quality of a line that belonged to him and growing recognition of the lines in which he fell from his own way into the paths of others was for me one of the most notable experiences of the year. The other members of the class soon became aware that they had a poet in their midst, and at least one of them, Iola Fuller, whose novel *The Loon Feather* won the Hopwood fiction prize that June, must have been stimulating to John.

During this year at the end of which he was awarded our major prize, John was studying poetry as only a poet can study it. Eventually he left Michigan. The war came. Today he is called the central control gunner of a B-29, but in truth he is a poet.

Several months ago he sent me a piece of prose in which he had set down his mature creed. I quote two paragraphs:

The time to worry long about style and form is the time one lives through while writing that first thousand poems for the waste basket. In that time one acquires a reservoir of tricks, opinions, tendencies. After that he should write completely as he pleases, drawing from that reservoir wherever the mind taps it at the moment of writing, and revising by instincts developed out of every earlier piece of writing. He should write as he pleases because he has trained himself, and whether he is well or ill trained he must rely wholly on that judgment. What other is there?

But style and form are only adjuncts to the human problem the poet must face: how to find a semblance of order in a world plundered by the contradictions of its political system. Style and form are simply ways of making the human statement more complete, and more true by loading it with the impact of emotion. Otherwise they become mere embroidery.

# English C, 1947

## Donald Hall

In October of 1947, John Ciardi published his second book of poems, *Other Skies*. Two afternoons a week I watched the young poet stride into the classroom with a green bookbag over his shoulder, a lock of blackest hair falling across his forehead. He was vain and he mocked his vanity; he told us he had insured the black lock with Lloyds of London.

With his furry voice, he read us poems by others of his generation; I remember him passionately advocating the poem by John Frederick Nims which begins "Clumsiest dear, whose hands shipwreck vases. . . ." Young poets that autumn were Nims, Ciardi, Moss, Kees, Nemerov, Viereck; Berryman and Jarrell began to be heard of: New Directions had published them. *Lord Weary's Castle* was published in 1947; *The Beautiful Changes* came out a year later, and soon enough the names of "Wilbur and Lowell" were loud in the land. But in 1947 the most eminent of the younger poets was Karl Shapiro, who had won the Pulitzer Prize in 1944 for *V-Letter*, and Auden was the great influence.

William Carlos Williams, Wallace Stevens, and Marianne Moore were *elder* American figures, members of the Generation of the Twenties. When we heard that the editor of *Poetry* rejected a pile of Stevens, it was with the mild *frisson* of scandal; Williams was writing a long poem, which seemed a contradiction in terms. Ransom and Tate formed a conservative opposition to the experimental generation—and most of us wrote iambic pentameter. Ezra Pound was at St. Elizabeth's, and *The Pisan Cantos* had not yet appeared. Eliot was unimaginably eminent, albeit suspect for his politics.

At Harvard in 1947 the thirties returned from the war intact, and leftwing groups competed for attention and membership. Brahmins sold *The Worker* at peripheries of the Yard. Many of us hung around the American Youth for Democracy, popular front alternative to the Young Communist League, and joined Marxist study groups and read Christopher Caudwell. We knew that Truman was

—52

a cold warrior implacably hostile to our old ally Stalin, and Dewey—who would be elected in 1948—was worse. Therefore, many of us flocked to the banner of Henry Wallace and the Progressive Party; we rang doorbells in South Boston to petition to put Wallace's name on the Massachusetts ballot. We students were aware of John Ciardi's politics (F. O. Matthiessen was another Wallace man) and most of us cheered when John delivered the fund-raising speech at the Progressive Party's convention in Shibe Park in 1948.

And before I graduated in 1951 the Korean War had started, the un-American Activities Committee prepared the way for McCarthy, the AYD and the John Reed Society turned invisible, F. O. Matthiessen jumped out of a window, and at Eliot House the subject was no longer the Cold War but original sin.

Ciardi was a superb teacher, at the same time working on his own poems with great energy. (One day I remember him coming to class and telling us he had just sold eight or twelve poems to *The New Yorker*—I don't know how many; some unimaginable figure—and had made a down payment on a new car, his first, and if he didn't watch out, the next election he would vote Republican.) He took our writing seriously enough to give us a bad time. Creative writing was not a racket in 1947. This course combined poetry and prose, and to my recollection the prose writers were better than the poets. Of course most of us stopped writing; but one of us was a story-writer who turned into the poet Frank O'Hara.

Frank sat up front next to the window on the left, beside his roommate from Eliot House, Ted Gorey—since by metamorphosis become Edward St. John Gorey, artist, designer, author of limericks. When Frank spoke up in class, he was forthright, witty, and camp. I was a freshman and could not *believe* the way people talked around here.

John scheduled conferences. I remember him liking one thing I wrote: "Mirror, mirror, on the wall,/Who is Donald Andrew Hall?" (Doubtless I was influenced by "Elegy Just in Case," with its reference to "Ciardi's pearly bones. . . .") John was natural with us. Once I talked to him about Bread Loaf; I had gone there at sixteen while he was in the Pacific. Two and a half years later I was ridiculing or lamenting my sixteen-year-old behavior: *What a fool I was. . . .* I remember John saying, "We were always a fool, two and a half years ago. . . ."

In general he listened to me with patience. Once he said something irritable, doubltess in response to my unbearable pomposity: "Oh, Hall," he said, "why don't you stop trying to be great and just be good?" Here I guess I disagree, much as I understand the provocation: I doubt that you are likely to be good if you don't want to be great.

While I was still an undergraduate, John began advising Twayne Publishers. It was his idea that I make an anthology out of the pages of the *Harvard Advocate*, reprinting the juvenilia of old editors and contributors like Wallace

Stevens, E. E. Cummings, two presidents named Roosevelt, T. S. Eliot. . . . This is the sort of book which is conceived with enthusiasm, which is widely reviewed, and which sells nothing. My *Harvard Advocate Anthology* was noticed in the daily and Sunday *New York Times, Time, Newsweek*, etc.—and sold four hundred and twenty-four copies.

It was thrilling to edit a book that appeared in December of one's Senior Year. While I finished the editing, in the spring of 1950, John and Judith invited me to the house for spaghetti, along with Frank O'Harra and Ted Gorey, whom I had come to know better at Eliot House. (They gave the best parties.) It was an affectionate, humorous occasion, John's wit and Frank's different and complementary. Late in the evening Frank was lamenting that he was about to graduate and had no idea what to do. He wanted to write: Who didn't? And what to do in the meantime? Of course Frank would settle into the Museum of Modern Art and rise in the hierarchy making poems in his lunch-hour. But this was the spring of 1950.

John suggested, with absolute casualness, "Why don't you go to the University of Michigan and win a Hopwood?" After all, that was what John did after he finished Tufts, before the war. With equal casualness, Frank allowed that the suggestion sounded all right. . . . John cleared a space at the table and wrote a letter to Roy Cowden of Michigan's English Department, soliciting a scholarship for Frank, and Frank spent a year at Ann Arbor, won his Hopwood, and thereafter remained committed to the art of poetry. It is also true that he never left New York or came near a campus again.

Sometimes still when I taste a good spaghetti sauce—oregano, garlic, basil, anise—I remember that night around the Ciardi table, young John and Judith, young Ted and Frank.

# *Letter to an Old Friend*

## Dan Jaffe

Dear John,

More than thirty-one years ago I first encountered you as a professor at Rutgers. You were the new poet on campus, the first writer of consequence I ever met. I was ready to be awed. You knew how to do it. I had a basket of clichés. You dumped it out and stomped on each one. I had false notions that needed to be challenged; you embarrassed me enough so I had to challenge them. Now I know that what I write and what I help others to write has followed from your influence. But I pride myself in not sounding like you. I thank you for pushing principles and discipline more than self. Your first impression on me was so great that had you done the latter I might have ended up sounding like a faded carbon.

Maybe this sounds a bit overblown. I guess I could go on in this vein and give the impression I was writing ad copy. I won't. Over the past few weeks I've thought back over the thirty-one years I have known you. I've asked myself what has made us friends for such a long time, despite distance and the inevitable intrusions of life, all those necessities and interruptions that so often get in the way of friendship. Those thirty-one years have been punctuated by moments during which you were more than just a profound teacher or a hard taskmaster, moments during which you affected my life in ways I couldn't have anticipated when I signed up for your creative writing course at Rutgers.

I remember talking with my father about you during those early days. You weren't really human to me yet, just an archetype of what I wanted to be. My father was wary of what seemed to him my exaggerated enthusiasm. That was before you and he struck up your own friendship. I can remember the two of you chatting in a coffee shop on Longboat Key, discussing the inadequacies of the younger generation. I thought to myself, "I wish you guys would stop trying to build my character." But that was long after my father had warned me that "all men have feet of clay, even John Ciardi." Sometimes I think he was a bit jealous. Later he would share my admiration and recognize many of the reasons for it. Of course, he was right about your clay feet. I've seen you impatient, petulant, abrasive, even intolerant; a few times you've even been wrong. But though I came to realize you had flaws, that has not diminished you in my eyes. Thank God you are not a saint. That would be absolutely unbearable. This way I'm capable of empathizing. For just a man, John, you sure have lightninged your way into my psyche.

I remember that sonnet of Shakespeare's, number 130, with its catalogue of false, stereotyped virtues, all of which are undermined before the recapitulation of the closing couplet:

And yet, by heaven, I think my love as rare
As any she belied with false compare.

I am afraid to say too much about you, John, for fear of seeming to forget what that sonnet is about. But my friendship, love, and admiration are not lessened thereby.

One night in 1957 or '58 after Robert Frost had read his poems in Kirkpatrick Chapel on the Rutgers campus, I ran into you and Judith outside the chapel. You invited me and my date to President Lewis Webster Jones' home to meet Frost. I was a Targum journalist at the time, full of a romantic notion of what journalism was and what it could accomplish. During the evening Krishna Menon, the Indian ambassador to the United Nations and an old friend of Mrs. Jones, came up in conversation. The discussion stressed the unfairness of the press, how disreputable and inaccurate it was likely to be. John, you said nothing, just kept grinning in my direction. I was sure you knew that I would finally erupt and challenge our hosts as I did. I think you enjoyed it, and that made me feel good.

You see, sometimes it was what you didn't say that mattered most. I came up to you shortly before I graduated, not knowing we would stay in touch. What I wanted was some assurance about what the future held, at least an easy promise that I would succeed as a writer. "John," I said, "do you think I have a chance?" You looked at me as you started to walk away. Then you threw it back over your shoulder. "How much do you want it?" That's a hell of a question to ask someone to ask himself.

After Rutgers I wrote to you from Washington, D.C. I was stationed there courtesy of the U.S. Air Force. I never expected a reply. But you answered at once. So I risked another letter. You answered that one, too. I complained about the military and the city. I think I described Washington as one of the circles that Dante forgot. You told me it was time for me to decide "what you mean to be and what you mean to be against." That was sufficiently abstract to give me lots of leeway but somehow monosyllabic enough to be insistent and solid.

While I was in the Air Force I visited Bread Loaf. I was on leave and that helped me to be wide open. The conference in Vermont drenched me in all sorts of things I needed to learn. You greeted me as a friend and gave me a lesson in craft. I'll never forget you looking at a poem of mine and saying "That's all right, Dan, but Dylan Thomas said it all in one phrase, 'the crossed sticks of war.'" I went back to Washington, D.C., with a better sense of what I was about.

After my discharge I visited you a number of times. You suggested that I try for the Hopwood Prize at the University of Michigan, as you had. You even gave me some sound advice before I left. "Don't take Reinhardt," you said. Believe me, I avoided his course and proved to be one of the lucky ones. Not long after I was on the Michigan campus I learned the Hopwood speaker in 1958 would be John Ciardi. Great news, I thought at first. But then I was terrified. I had a vision of you sitting down after your lecture, watching the winners of the Hopwood prizes parade to the platform. I wasn't one of them. You would be up there thinking, "Too bad, Dan didn't really have the stuff." As the rules prescribed I submitted my manuscript under a pseudonym. I waited for the last-minute letter. I was to learn later that the judges were John Hall Wheelock and Marianne Moore. Somehow, despite my vision, I was one of the winners. John, I'll never forget that I received the Hopwood check directly from you, not from Arno Bader, the Hopwood chairman. You made my winning a celebration of friendship. That was surely one of the good moments.

After a fellowship at Bread Loaf, which you arranged, I visited the Ciardis in what I think was your first house in Metuchen. As I remember you kept complaining about the workman you had hired to redo the kitchen. He was an artist you said. Everything had to be absolutely perfect. The damn kitchen was taking forever. I spent a long afternoon eating, listening to limericks, and waiting, waiting for you to say something about the manuscript I had sent to you a short time before. I thought you would never get to it. I was still riding high on the Hopwood Prize and the Bread Loaf fellowship. I couldn't wait for your approval. "Well, Dan," you said. "You're not Yeats yet." Thanks for that one, John. It lasted a long time.

This is a strange letter, personal and public as it is. There is so much I don't have to say. You know all about the intervening years: My two-year stint at the University of Nebraska, where you stopped to change a flat tire for Karl Shapiro; my brief spin into Oregon and my return to what was then the University of Kansas City, where you had begun your teaching career. I'm still there, but it's now the University of Missouri-Kansas City. I survived some hard times in Kansas City, but you helped me out during the hardest. I won't make too much of this because you will be embarrassed by it. But on one occasion, when things were particularly shaky here for me, I was offered another job elsewhere. The timing was perfect. I was shocked by the offer to take the place, even temporarily, of a Pulitzer Prize-winning poet. Unfortunately, although the university was a fine one, it was located in a city where I didn't want to be. Nor did I want to dislocate my family. But I shook the telegram offer in the right faces, got a raise, some attention, and enough momentum to get tenure. I couldn't believe my luck. How did that happen, I asked myself? I found out later that you had dropped my name in the right corner. Of course you never said a thing about it to me. Not a word.

Just a few years later my first marriage disintegrated. I was numb, depressed, absolutely without vigor or self-esteem. I had preached alertness to my students but had not seen what was happening in my own life. I was raising two children, six and three, alone, trying also to keep myself together. I stuck my thumb with needles, scorched clothes, burned the eggs. But somehow it never seemed like a situation comedy.

One night about 10 P.M. you called from the Muehlback Hotel. You were on your way from a reading to a reading. Would I meet you for a drink? You didn't know anything about my circumstances. My voice must have sounded hazy. I needed to call a baby-sitter before I could drive downtown. An hour later in the bar of Muehlback I laid my confusion in front of you. I can only imagine what I must have sounded like awash with guilt, doubt, melancholia, and full of my own bad cooking. Anyway, you never equivocated. You never questioned me about how I had behaved, never treated me like an unfinished poem. I was full of doubts, but you never doubted me at all. "Hell," I thought when the evening was over, "John Ciardi's my friend. I can't be a total mess." So I started to crawl out. I will never forget the strength of your friendship when I was most vulnerable.

There are many other moments I could remind you of, John, far back and recent. Some are amusing, as when one of my students came up to you after a reading at the Kansas City Jewish Community Center's American Poets Series. You had come to help get the series off the ground for just plane fare for you and Judith. The student commented that you had said some of the same things Professor Jaffe had told her class. You didn't even tell her who was the source of what.

When the University of Missouri-Kansas City decided to run a writers' conference on Longboat Key, I contacted you, John. I felt presumptuous; maybe I was taking advantage of our friendship. You came each year, stunning as ever, and never made me feel I shouldn't have asked. I vowed I'd never let distance or disaster keep me from making regular contact again.

I still feel the shine of the evening not long ago when the University of Missouri-Kansas City presented you with an honorary degree, long overdue I might say. It was an extraordinary ceremony, after which poems by both of us were sung, by soprano and chorale. An enormous respect and affection for you filled that auditorium. And I was enriched by sharing the moment.

I've introduced you a number of times, John, always inadequately. But I've stopped blaming myself. I don't know anyone who has been so devoted to making poems, to the notion of craft and creating. You haven't sold out to easy causes, to the fashionable thrusts. You haven't degraded the best side of yourself by getting soft on the mediocre. At this point I'm not going to talk about your work, its variety, intensity, candor, multiplicity, wit, and skill. There's a wide open field for critics of sense and patience. There is a prayer in the Passover *Hagadah* with the refrain, "Dayenu," *It would have been enough.* If you had simply been a poet I read, John, that would have been enough. If you had simply been my teacher, that would have been enough. But you have been my friend, and I am grateful. You named our six kids the Ice Cream Bandits. They still call you Uncle John. Robin, my wife, joins them and me in sending our love.

### Afterword, May 1986

Chekhov supposedly said no one would remember his work five years after his death. It is a special greatness that underestimates itself. How unlike political memoirs. So John Ciardi came to distrust the dimensions of his own achievements, came to call himself obsolete before his too early death. But even his first poems catch us and reverberate. If one reads John Ciardi, his poems, his translations, his commentary and criticism, his definitions and his footnotes, one realizes how rare his mind was, how tough and graceful his style, how generous his instincts. No, he never won the Nobel Prize or the Pulitzer. Nevertheless, he became a widely popular figure, but one who did not sell out to fads or causes, who held his art in all its complexity sacrosanct. If John Ciardi held to any cause it was the notion of precision, to an uncompromising excellence, to the notion that to strive was in itself not enough, that one needed to judge honestly, to assess courageously, and to respond without flinching. He had firm standards, the same for friends as for those he disliked. He expected to be judged by those same standards. If he seemed harsh at times it was because he meant to push writers, audience, and students to something better, because he believed it was a matter of character to distinguish "any shriek from a true high-C." Ciardi himself, at his best, sang that sweet pure song, sometimes lyric, sometimes comic, sometimes ablaze, sometimes sudden and revealing, sometimes subtle and suggestive.

He had a reputation as a rough and tumble curmudgeon. Such an oversimplification! Travel through John Ciardi's work and you will find America, not sentimentally, not abstractly. He looked into himself, into his own experiences and feelings, and found what was common to his countrymen but so often hidden. Reading John Ciardi one comes to realize one goes deeper than one thought. That is why he was so loved and is already so missed. He did not talk down to us; he did not pander to our weaknesses; he assumed we had talent to use and the character to use it. The history of criticism, it is said, is the history of error. In his own time John Ciardi was awarded a certain honor and fame, even riches enough to make jealous those who courted assiduously what gravitated to him so naturally.

But time will reward him more generously. He would deny it, even as he hid his generosity. He was a man of love. Walk through America, from San Francisco to Kansas City, from Georgia to Boston; you will meet someone he helped, someone he moved, someone he inspired, someone he awakened. So many ate at his table and did not even know it. He goes out with the comet. You will not meet such a man again soon.

D.J.

# *From Dissertation to Friendship: The Joy of Knowing John Ciardi*

## Jeff Lovill

What I had to go on was a twenty-year-old picture in the Twayne Series edition of *John Ciardi* and an equally vintage description from Norman Cousins: "John Ciardi looked like a combination of a Hemingway big-game hunter and a charging fullback who had carried half the opposing football team on his back in a successful plunge for the touchdown."

During those moments when I was not trying to visualize an updated, composite image from these sources, I was convincing myself: "This only happens to other people. Other people get to visit and stay with famous writers." Yet there I sat, flying from Tempe, Arizona, on my way to the graduate student's Land of Oz.

I must have had my usual lost look, because it was Ciardi who found me in the luggage carousel area—and luckily so, for it was apparent that the fullback physique I was looking for had long ago been put on waivers. But the wit was there: "If I'm not illegally parked I should be." These first words confirmed Cousins' praise: "John Ciardi had absolutely no talent for ambiguity." Only part of the car was slightly on the curb; the rest covered the yellow-striped area. We had a short walk.

I had first written John Ciardi shortly after starting the doctoral program in English at Arizona State University. My chairman, Professor D. G. Kehl—how blessed to have had him, the man who gave focus and form to my Ciardi work— encouraged both the dissertation and my working with Ciardi. My first letter arrived:

> Dear Jeff Lovill:
> I am moved that you should want to and I will help as I can.

Two years and an ASU Graduate College grant later, I was having my quickest terminal-to-car jaunt ever.

It is only a slight exaggeration to say I remember everything about my visit. John Ciardi had opened his home and graciously accepted me. How thrilling for this wide-eyed Ph.D. student to share the daily life of one of America's authentic men of letters. We gulped morning coffee, which by the time I left I was able to tease Judith about its being "jet oil," to which she bantered: "But it's guaranteed to jump-start John's heart." We gulped it over conversation and over the noontime meal, as John observed his "9:00 impossible . . . unbearable . . . paralyzed o'clock A.M." We shared this time at the kitchen table over *The New York Times* crossword (I remember "gridiron zebra" was an easy "toots" for John) and over John's letting the cat in and out, which I recall with each reading to my children of "My Cat, Mrs. Lick-a-Chin":

> The thing about cats, as you may find,
> Is that no one knows what they have in mind.
> And I'll tell you something about that:
> No one knows it less than my cat.

John indulged me with over five hours of taped interview. His voice was so rich and resonant he could have read *The New York Times* want ads and I would have kept the tape recorder going. As I stumbled through questions, he supported me with consummate answers. The pure romance of the interview was that we held it in a place that up until then I had thought was only a mythic region: the writer's garret. John had granted me complete liberty to prowl about up there during my stay. I was the kitten let loose with a lion's ball of string. What a wonderland of book-lined rooms, halls, desks, floors, closets, and chairs. His *Browser's* room was bulging with dictionaries, as the whole upstairs bowed under lecture circuit, *Saturday Review,* Bread Loaf correspondences. Two presidential-size desks had already been evacuated, and the third, where we sat for most of the interview, supported a teetering act of books, manuscripts, and letters. I remember a cluster of letters that prompted something John said would do for an epitaph: "Archibald MacLeish was my friend. I did not do everything wrong in life."

I have two favorite memories from my stay: one is a drive back home after a brief tour of the Rutgers campus and a few errands in Metuchen. It was getting dark, the day colder, the roads slicker. The snow was out of a Frost poem, and John's car out of Detroit: the defogger was not working. This made it nearly impossible to see where he was going, under already unsure conditions. As he wiped a pie-size space on the inside window, John epigrammatically uttered: "This is a situation I'm familiar with—like life."

As I look back on it now, this was more than a classic Ciardi line (delivered with his singular chuckle); this touched the very heart of his poetry. John's poems are not grand pronouncements, nor are they imposing edicts on *what* life means; rather, they are honest observations on *how* life means. They transform the "inconceivably ordinary," the "miraculous commonplace" into *This Strangest Everything*. In addition, I found myself growing close to this man who had few of life's answers (as he wrote to me later, "If we could only be born with a little experience in how to be a human being"), a man unsure of his own world, yet still in love with its mystery: "Thank you / for the experience which I, lovingly, did not / understand." I was growing close to this man who teaches: "A man can survive anything except not caring."

A second memory incised in my mind occurred the night we watched *Yes, Giorgio*, with tenor Luciano Pavarotti in the role of a young lover trying to win his lady's hand. Giorgio had bought out a restaurant for a night as he wined and dined her, trying desperately to impress her, insisting how everything was marvelous, so larger than life. "No, Giorgio," the young maiden replied, "life is only life-size."

John glowed in the lady's retort and continued to revel in the reply, as the comment surfaced throughout the interview:

LOVILL: I like that you write only "unimportant poems."

CIARDI: What else! It is the opposite of Giorgio's view that life need not be just life-size. I think life has no choice, that everything comes down to life-size.

John even drew on the line to salvage yet another unfocused question from his house guest.

LOVILL: What do you see as your weakness in poetry?

CIARDI: In reading and rereading the poems, you discover weaknesses, and that is why you have a wastebasket. If I have worked well, I have chucked the weaknesses into the wastebasket. That is one of the good things about writing: you can make your mistakes, and then if you are lucky, you get them thrown away before you get them published. Another weakness might be that I am too ordinary—but so is life. Back to *Yes, Giorgio*. "Life can be more than life-size": that is a wonderful romantic assertion. But once it is larger than life-size, what do you do with it? How do you get it into a pair of pants, for example? Do you have to wear togas?

The line traveled south with John and Judith during their yearly migration from the cold.

Dear Jeff,

We finally made it to FLA. Jan. in NJ was hardly a pleasure. As Giorgio would not have liked it, it was less than life-size. I'm not sure what life is, but it fits more conveniently into winter in Key West.

The line summarizes what I revered most in the man: his uncompromisingly compassionate account of the human condition. This stance permitted John to take life not always so seriously, allowing him to chide himself about perplexities—even like growing old. Parts from two letters tell it better: "I hope your energy holds out. I remember having had some and even what fun it was to spend it, but my memory begins to fade. I cling to an evil mind, but how can you be evil when you can't remember the steps?" and "I become increasingly tottering on my pins. Whattahell! So long as you keep your health, who minds being dead?"

Even death is kept life-size, and toward the end of the dissertation, I found myself focusing on the lines:

The trick is
Not to die
A little longer.

The thought of John's not being here hurt, so I sent him his lines and my advice: "Get that trick down, John. Get it down." He wrote back immediately: "Don't be sad about the fact that I am old enough to drop dead. I've already spent a year practicing to be dead back in 1944–'45. I did not expect to make it off Saipan alive. That leaves me with 40 years of good gravy."

I found John's repugnance of those who pose as larger-than-life equally delightful. I eagerly memorized: "I like everyone but important people being important/And academic people being academic." Even in the interview John said, "I think it is a waste of energy to try to be important. Important people bore me. I give them to one another." Unlike big, important someones, John sums himself up this way: "I did not choose to be gross, fumbling, small, inept and subject to gravity: I found that I was, choicelessly." Even my children (insisting on nightly "John Charlie" readings) enjoy John's jabs at self-inflaters. (Though for now, it is pure fun for them; there is time later for them to learn about life's Giorgios.) From "Poor Little Fish" they love:

There was a fish who was born in a cup
He grew and he grew till he filled it up.
Then he sang all day, "Just look at *me*!

A bigger fish you will not see!"

Poor little fish—he took his cup
To be a sea. When he filled it up
He shook with pride from head to tail.
He *really* thought he was a whale!

And how they insist on double (even triple) readings of the "BOOMS" from "A Loud Proud Someone":

Someone I knew was very proud.
But all he was proud of was—being loud.
When he said "Hello" it went BOOM-BOOM-BOOM
Like guns going off in a very small room.
He told me his name, but all I heard
Was BOOM-BOOM-BOOM—not another word.

John insisted that such a person is one who is "a whole lot of nothing."

I am convinced such an attitude made him the surefooted, generous and large-hearted man he was, secure enough both to realize and to laugh at his own limitations (reflected even in the title "On Leaving the Party after Having Been Possibly Brilliant for Certainly Too Long") and to accept happily his own humanness.

I first discerned this acceptance during my visit, listening to John (or as he proclaimed himself, "the richest poet on the block") tell how the *Inferno* went well enough that he would be translating the next two books, aware that he might translate the whole *Comedy* and come up wanting for a rhyme on the third, final "star"-ending couplet. He made me privy to his option:

At the end stands Ciardi handing out cigars
By the Love that moves the Sun and the other stars.

Another glimmer was during a return visit to Phoenix. Before an overflowing auditorium at Glendale Community College, John was given a five-minute stellar introduction. Looking like one who is going to reveal a secret, John walked to the podium and mentioned that whenever he receives such an introduction (one listing his accomplishments) he likes to remind the audience of his "brief and unbrilliant TV career," one in which CBS promptly replaced his nationally televised *Accent* show with *Mr. Ed:* "They went from one end of the horse to the other."

Finally, I recall a limerick John wrote for my wife, Debbie. Midway through our dissertation journey, he penned the following:

> Said Debbie to Jeff, "Seems to me
> There's not much to this stuff by J.C."
> Said Jeff, "Though it stinks
> I can stand it, methinks
> —At least to a certain degree."

It is precisely this kind of compassion, shared humanity and fun that led me to thank (inadequately) John on the acknowledgment page: "I would like to thank John Ciardi for his willingness and graciousness in working with me. I have cherished the letters and the visits that have given such a joyous immediacy to my study."

Along with my working with the poetry, it was the pleasure of seeing John make good on a promise: "I look forward to seeing you in a couple of weeks. Tell Ryan I am eager to meet him. In case he happens to like ice cream—which he probably doesn't, of course—he and I have a date to go to the best ice cream place in Phoenix, and he is invited to order the biggest dish of ice cream and goo his parents will allow." He took Ryan to Carvel's Ice Cream, where the two of them spent ponderous moments selecting just the right ice cream cake. The moment is frozen for me: America's cultural headwaiter and my son selecting dessert, settling on a cake shaped like a mighty blue whale. On the ride back to our house, Ryan was pretending, wondering what the Blue Whale had done at sea. I gave a bland "Nothing," but John was intent on pretend too: "Nothing of the sort. He was a ne'er-do-whale." (In letters, John continued the fun, playing with Ryan's name: " nayr-do-whale.") He later commissioned Debbie and me over the miles "to harpoon a Ryanic whale: a boy that needs a blue whale damn well needs a blue whale."

It was the warmth John shared with Adam's birth: "All best to you and Debbie and the child to be"; "That first felt kick! What a moment that is!"; "The son is handsomely named Adam Christopher"; and "A warm welcome to this world from a friend of the family." With Logan: "Happy thoughts to you and Debbie and Happy Increase. Joys to you all in it."

It was the support John gave when my father died the summer after my visit. I told him about Dad, his excitement that I was working with John Ciardi. John wrote back: "To bury a father is a numbing experience. He does sound like a loving man, but how could he be proud of the fact that you were working on my writings? He was proud of *you*, sharing your enthusiasm for what you were doing. Teach his good to your own boys and they will have a legacy."

There is a kind of joy that is too deep for tears—as on John's first night in Phoenix, when I picked him up at the airport and took him to his hotel, where we stayed up and visited out beyond time. Driving home, I felt like a man many times blessed by the kindness and love John had lavished on me and my family.

Knowing John Ciardi was a life-enhancing process. If, as John suggested, "Purpose/is what a man uncovers by digging for it," then it has been nothing but delightful digging. Since that first "Dear Jeff Lovill," it has been all gravy. Thanks, John. Thanks beyond all thanks.

# The Mid-Century *Fifteen, a Memoir*

## Philip Booth

1950. Thirty-five years ago. The Second World War just over, the new jets about to take off for Korea. Thirty-five years before that, the first biplanes flying combat in France. And now, having reached the moon, we have Star Wars on somebody's drawing board. And where we once had Quiller-Couch's *Oxford Book of English Verse* to cover 1250 to 1918, we now have William Heyen's anthology of younger American poets, *The Generation of 2000*. What terrific optimism on Heyen's part, to believe he can predict not only the poets, but the very prospect of a new century.

Only forty-seven years after the Wright brothers first flew, the world at least *seemed* more simple. The war was over, a sustained time of peace felt almost palpably predictable. It isn't hard to recall how it felt to be home from the Air Corps, to have exhausted the GI Bill with a quick M.A. from Columbia, to have tried teaching, to have aborted a novel, to have finally given in to trying to write poems. But it's immensely hard now to return one's self to the optimism of that pivotal year in which Truman was halfway through his full term, and the jets hadn't yet taken off for Korea, and Twayne was publishing John Ciardi's *Mid-Century American Poets*. That publication may, in this sequence, seem anticlimactic; but it was, in fact, a measure of optimism and a small-scale event of more than small importance.

What courage to come up with any anthology of only fifteen poets. And what remarkable judgment to have made *then* the selections that John Ciardi did. Donald Allen's *The New American Poetry 1945–1960* would ten years later counter the ease with which Ciardi dismissed the vision and energy of Whitman and Pound, and his neglect of poets who had learned from them and from Williams. But this was still 1950, and the ground Ciardi staked out measures well when compared with Untermeyer's standard-brand choices and Oscar Williams' politic *potpourri*.

All that's easy to see and say, now. Poetry anthologies collect *ex post facto* Furies the way football games collect Monday morning quarterbacks. But *Mid-Century American Poets* was, from the start, a high risk / high gain anthology: the risk was in Ciardi's comparatively narrow focus, the gain was in how deeply that focus was illuminated by his choice of poets and poems.

In his *Mid-Century* introduction, Ciardi wrote that "the poets presented in this book are all part of what will be recognized as a poetic 'generation. . . .'" And he went on to say, "Already, in fact, there is a younger generation, no doubt influenced by some of these poets, but as distinct from them as these poets are from those of the twenties." Only twenty years after the end of the twenties, these were Ciardi's choices:

> Richard Wilbur
> Peter Viereck
> Muriel Rukeyser
> Theodore Roethke
> Karl Shapiro
> Winfield Townley Scott
> John Frederick Nims
> E. L. Mayo
> Robert Lowell
> Randall Jarrell
> John Holmes
> Richard Eberhart
> John Ciardi
> Elizabeth Bishop
> Delmore Schwartz

It's easy, these thirty-five years later, to wonder how M and N made the anthology when O and X and Y apparently went unnoticed. It's even easy to assume, in 1985, that Wilbur and Rukeyser and Roethke and Lowell and Jarrell and Bishop were inevitable. But such assumption neglects simple history: that Wilbur had thus far published only one book and was still under thirty; that Roethke, only a two-book poet even at forty-two, was far from being well known; and that Bishop's first and only book had been mildly honored but had not yet gained the attention she already deserved. At least several poets on Ciardi's list are all but totally unknown to readers today. But that fault is not Ciardi's nor, in at least one good instance, the poet's. Try John Holmes if he seems obscured by time. Better come late than come never.

Various as Ciardi's fifteen poets were in age, and varying as they may yet prove to be in staying power, his choice of individual poems remains remarkably astute, and his whole anthology still confirms his focus on "a poetic 'generation.'" In long retrospect, it's possible to see now that what distinguishes these poets from the then "younger generation" was not a wide gap in years but a terrific gap in experience. All of Ciardi's poets, including himself, had earned their majority *as poets* before or during the Second World War.

I sense this distinction still, insofar as I was, or am, part of that next generation, and insofar as I surely was influenced by "some of these poets" in first coming to know them through John's anthology. I was twenty-five in 1950, so innocent that even the lesser of Ciardi's fifteen seemed notably "modern." Untermeyer's anthologies had been standard in the two "poetry courses" I took in college; what I didn't then know I needed, but found first in *Mid-Century*, was a sense of poetry as *being* contemporary; and in that immediacy, of being necessary to my life. I was still in New Hampshire then, a carpenter's helper, a ski-book salesman, an apprentice to my own need to write. What John had put together, including the poets' prose responses to the questions he had set for them, was not for me a textbook but a catalyst, a source of energy that gave impetus to my own.

Save for two poets I knew in Vermont during those first years I was writing poems and beginning to publish, I was happily alone. Before I moved south from the North Country to start teaching again, and there met John Ciardi's own teacher John Holmes, and poets of my own age like Anne Sexton and Donald Hall, Ciardi's fifteen were the poets I most truly "knew." Eliot and Frost and Williams I had studied and had already heard read; I'd been stunned temporarily by Thomas, and I'd long since found Jeffers for myself. But *Mid-Century American Poets* was my sustaining introduction to Wilbur, Roethke, Jarrell and, most importantly, Bishop. Who's to know, now, the number of the "younger generation" of poets who were influenced by John's *Mid-Century* fifteen, or know how they were influenced? To such unanswerable questions I only know to say this: without the presence and immediacy of John Ciardi's anthology—a right book at a right time—some of us might not be here to remind ourselves how much it mattered, and to speak long overdue thanks.

# Ciardi's Dante

## W. S. Di Piero

One of the distinctions of Ciardi's translation of *The Divine Comedy* is that its quality makes it dangerous for the reader who has no Italian. Dangerous because, unlike most versions of that poem, Ciardi's is a sustained act of invention in an American English that is neither too blandly international nor too provincially idiosyncratic. Between Singleton's useful prose trot (we go to his edition of Dante, at any rate, mainly for the commentary) and Ciardi's American Dante, there is that wide middle ground occupied by translations, many of them the products of the postwar years and of the expansion of the graduate schools, which are tonally uncertain, donnish, too familiarly colloquial, or pedantically "faithful." Each has, I suppose, some kind of classroom use, and the erudition carried over into these translations has something to teach us all. The difference is that Ciardi's translation is all of an imaginative and inventive piece, and for the reader with no Italian, Ciardi's language is so "naturalized" as to be nearly too persuasive, the figural presentation too sharp and foregrounded, the outlines of the actions—like the draughtsmanship in a Giotto fresco—too definitive and charged. Other modern versions of Dante that I admire are William Carlos Williams' "The Descent," which translates the opening movement, the pitch downward into memory, of the opening cantos, and Seamus Heaney's version of the Ugolino episode. But these are brief visits to the poem. Ciardi, taking on the whole enterprise, working in the volatile mood of arrogance and humility that translators need to do their job well, performs the act of sustained psychic emigration that Cesare Pavese spoke of.

In good translations I think one learns to be alert to, and enjoy, the serial decisions made by the translator which register like faint scorings on the completed work. These are part of a translation's "finish." For me, the part of the inventive vitality of Ciardi's Dante—especially his *Inferno*, the most fully realized of the three canticles in his version—is bound up in the decisions that were made in composing (or recomposing) some of the crucial encounters that Dante has in hell. The Master Adam episode, in Ciardi's retelling, is at once ludicrous and shameful, and Virgil's chastisement of Dante's fascination has the cuffing effect of moral intelligence momentarily acted out as anger. When Ciardi describes Brunetto Latini's leave-taking, he gets remarkably well the swiftness and lightness but also, and more importantly, the velocity of despair *down there*. In practice, of course, a translator proceeds piece by piece, word by phrase by line by stanza. And if a translator's decisions are a necessary part of the inventive matrix of his work, he hopes they will be visible not because of their uncertainties or failures but because of their resolutions. As a translator's manual, Ciardi's work is a kind of chronicle of mostly successful resolutions.

Ciardi seems to have had in mind from the outset the whole shape and integral structure of the poem, and knew that he would also translate *that* (and not assume, as many translators do, that it would take care of itself). Dante's poem cannot be fully re-imagined into English by any modern writer; it was the product of a complex political, social, and rhetorical matrix which is already too far from our own, and too disjunctive, thanks in part to the huge and permanent intervention of psychological realism in the nineteenth century. Dante's allegorical procedures, the processes his image-making faculty followed, make him much less our contemporary than we pridefully like to think. And so each translator has to decide to translate, in effect, one kind of Dante, or at least to allow one kind of Dante to emerge more forcefully and more finely articulated. Ciardi's, I think, is nearly a historical counterforce to the nineteenth century, because he chose to translate above all the Catholic realist whose allegorical figures need to be presented in hard outline of personage and action, and, at the same time, in their processional rhythm. And this returns us again and again to the essential action of Dante's poem, that the act of memory that remakes the Christian experience is a Way, a journeying, a *cammin*.

If Ciardi's lines are clearly the result of careful deliberation, learning, and the kind of luck that occasionally visits translators when they are doing their work well, those line-by-line resolutions never stink of the lamp. One might quarrel with plenty of his decisions, but one can't fault the natural intensity that he sustains over the three long canticles. Perhaps the single most persuasive characteristic of his version is its insistent veracity: Ciardi translates that Dantesque fact that ine journey *records* a sequence of actual events. Dante wrote down what he saw. That conviction, that imaginative veracity, is somehow carried over in Ciardi's version. I mean to say, he translates the feeling of the conviction. I do not know how he managed this, but I recognize and appreciate one of its effects: the tercets are not little doors slammed in the reader's face.

Closures in Ciardi's version are safe-conducts, assurances of continuity, as they are in Dante's poem.

I said earlier that Ciardi's translation is, in a sense, dangerous for the reader with no Italian, who is liable to memorize Ciardi's lines and think he is memorizing Dante's. But this is also the power of an exceptional translation, which is a new memory infused with the memory of the original poem.

# Form and Style in Ciardi's Dante

## Charles Guenther

The translator has two purposes, to learn and to communicate. Ultimately, the latter may be more important and far-reaching, but during his lifetime the learning process is more urgent and meaningful. Perhaps no translator of Dante's *Commedia*—from Henry Boyd (1802) and H. F. Cary (1814) to John Ciardi and, more recently, Allen Mandelbaum—has undertaken the task for simple enjoyment, but rather as a major learning experience.

The *Commedia* has always posed special challenges to both scholars and translators: in language, interpretation, and length. As a teenager I had bought the Salani edition (1938) of the *Commedia* but I found even that edition, with its many commentaries, almost too formidable. I used it as a text to savor the original where the original was lacking in the best (but often prosaic) English versions then available. It remained for a poet of Ciardi's stature to "reconstitute" Dante.

The *Commedia* is the summit of summits to translators, who tackle the job because "it's there," like a mountain, and for more important reasons. The rewards lie in making the journey oneself with Dante's circle, painstakingly in the thousands of lines, in one's own language. And the journey is intimate, from pit to paradise, with the first person immediacy of Dante, sharing that poet's experiences of sin, reparation, redemption and beatitude in another age.

So Ciardi lowered himself into Hell with Dante, proceeded through Purgatory, and emerged from Paradise with a wondrous new poem for us. New, but authentically Dante. Not to be diverted by exegesis, Ciardi went right to the heart of the poem, combining his skills with the scholarly tools available and concentrating on the poetry: its form, structure, music and meaning. Ciardi gives us a few insights on his method in the translator's notes to *The Inferno* and *The Purgatorio*. In the first he points out the paucity of resources of rhyme in the English language, and why he deleted that third, "all-consuming rhyme" in his own rhymed, metrical version of the *Commedia*'s three-line stanzas. (Any poet who has tried pure *terza rima* in English, at least in any long poem, realizes the maddening, distracting challenge of that third rhyme, which subjects the poem to artificial and archaic inversions, distortions and padding.) Ciardi's decision to use two rhymed lines in each stanza seems not only adequate but also a perfect compromise in English which, with few exceptions, must accept compromise in translations of long poems from the Romance languages.

In prefacing *The Purgatorio*, Ciardi gives us one concentrated example of his craft and method, a stanza from Canto VIII describing two angels that descend with Dante and his companions into the Valley of the Negligent. The rough literal version might read:

> Well was I discerning in them the head blond
>> But in the face the eye dazed itself
>> Like a virtue that at too much confounds itself.

Ciardi shows his progress with that single stanza, and how it evolved into this, his final version:

> I could see clearly that their hair was gold,
>> but my eyes drew back bedazzled from their faces,
>> defeated by more light than they could hold.

A splendid transformation, of course. Yet some readers may take exception to the word "bedazzled" with its rather archaic prefix, despite the antiquity of the original text, and to the slight ambiguity of "they" in the third line, which of course refers to "eyes." But these small points only serve to illustrate the translator's difficulties of re-creating meter and in using English pronouns which are less apt to be ambiguous in the Romance languages.

Present and future generations may take exception also to Ciardi's occasional use of Tudor English, for example, in translating the Lord's Prayer at the opening of Canto XI of *The Purgatorio*—an embellished, poetic version of that prayer as we know it. But we must remember that Ciardi's translation was made twenty-five years ago and it has only been in the last decade that Christian churches, generally, began adopting a more contemporary idiom. (But not all parishioners, we should add, approve of the revisions of Scriptural texts and hymns.) In Ciardi's Dante, in fact, the occasional use of archaic language seems appropriate in those passages and gives a marvelous change of pace to the whole poem.

Whatever the language or idiom, the *Commedia* is enjoyed most by reading it in long sections, at least several Cantos—and this includes a study of the notes to each Canto. But the notes should not bog us down. Like much of Whitman and St. John Perse, the poem should be taken in great drafts. For this purpose several recent translations, especially Ciardi's, are eminently superior for the reader who hasn't mastered Italian. Throughout all three volumes, from the first descent to the highest enthronement, Ciardi shows a consistently high quality of verse-rendering. One passage, chosen almost at random, may suffice to illustrate why Ciardi's translation in rhyme and meter seems more authentic and readable than earlier prose versions which, ostensibly, were intended to communicate the "story" better to readers who eschewed poetry. These lines—again from *The Purgatorio*—describe Dante's vision of Beatrice (Canto XXX)[1] in the Carlyle-Okey-Wicksteed translation, one of the standard versions popular before Ciardi's appeared:

> Ere now have I seen, at dawn of day, the eastern part all rosy red,
> and the rest of heaven adorned with fair clear sky,
> and the face of the sun rise shadowed, so that by the tempering of
> the mists the eye long time endured him:
> so within a cloud of flowers, which rose from the angelic hands
> and fell down again within and without,
> olive-crowned over a white veil, a lady appeared to me, clad,
> under a green mantle, with hue of living flame.
> And my spirit, that now so long a time had passed, since,
> trembling in her presence, it had been broken down with awe,
> without having further knowledge by mine eyes through hidden
> virtue which went out from her, felt the mighty power of ancient
> love.[2]

This was an adequate translation perhaps for readers who wanted to get the sense and "feel" of the poem without confronting rhyme and meter. But compare that passage with Ciardi's version which approaches, strikingly, the clarity and authenticity of the original Italian text:

> Time and again at daybreak I have seen
> the eastern sky glow with a wash of rose
> while all the rest hung limpid and serene,
>
> and the Sun's face rise tempered from its rest
> so veiled by vapors that the naked eye
> could look at it for minutes undistressed.

Exactly so, within a cloud of flowers
    that rose like fountains from the angels' hands
    and fell about the chariot in showers,

a lady came in view: an olive crown
    wreathed her immaculate veil, her cloak was green,
    the colors of live flame played on her gown.

My soul—such years had passed since last it saw
    that lady and stood trembling in her presence,
    stupefied by the power of holy awe—

now, by some power that shone from her above
    the reach and witness of my mortal eyes,
    felt the full mastery of enduring love.

Purists may take issue with the few discreet interpolations and embellishments of Ciardi's style. Still, a poet-translator, just like a poet, aims to make poetry. Were that not so, without the poet any computer might do the job.

The question of metrics is another matter, but I think it was imperative that Ciardi adopt the 10- and 11-syllable line with five stresses (basically the iambic pentameter, so often misunderstood and maligned in our time), following Dante. It is still *the* line of English verse (with its infinite variations) from Chaucer to Hart Crane, who gave it a swaggering syncopation ("Tintex, Japalac, Certain-teed Overalls—ads") and new respectability. It isn't for all poets, of course, but those who understand its subtleties and appreciate it hold the key to most of the greatest poetry in our language.

Ciardi's *Commedia* may not be "definitive" (but what translation is?); still, it's likely to hold its appeal for a long time to come. Ciardi freed our age of the Victorian gingerbread which had encrusted so many earlier translations, and gave Dante back to us. While Eliot had tried to tell us that the poetry of Dante is "extremely easy to read," Salvatore Quasimodo points out that the "simple style" of Dante is really a very difficult style (and he quotes *Inferno* XXXIII, 67–74 to make his point). As Quasimodo further adds, Dante's is the "language of great poetry." And that language, well assimilated and rendered by Ciardi and certain others, is always understood.

# Notes

1. The original Italian text reads as follows:

Io vidi già nel cominciar del giorno
la parte oriental tutta rosada,
e l'altro ciel di bel sereno adorno;
e la faccia del sol nascere ombrata,
si che, per temperanza di vapori,
l'occhio la sostenea lunga fiata:
cosi dentro una nuvola di fiori
che da le mani angeliche saliva
e ricadeva in giù dentro e di fòri,
sovra candido vel cinta d'uliva
donna m'apparve, sotto verde manto
vestita di color di fiamma viva.
E lo spirito mio, che già cotanto
tempo era stato ch'a la sua presenza
non era di stupor, tremando, affranto,
sanza de li occhi aver più conoscenza,
per occulta virtù che da lei mosse,
d'antico amor senti la gran potenza.

(*Purgatorio*, XXX, 22–39)

2. Alighieri, Dante. *The Divine Comedy.* The Carlyle-Wicksteed translation unabridged. (New York: Random House, The Modern Library, 1932), p. 373.

# Bibliography

Alighiere, Dante. *The Inferno.* Translated by John Ciardi. New York: New American Library, 1954.

——. *The Purgatorio.* Translated by John Ciardi. New York: New American Library, 1957.

——. *The Paradiso.* Translated by John Ciardi. New York: New American Library, 1961.

# *John Ciardi and* Treat It Gentle

## Richard Elman

John Ciardi's work on the Sidney Bechet "autobiography," *Treat It Gentle*, has gone largely unnoticed, ever since its publication in 1960. Jazz circles are notoriously "tight like that," to use the profane, and Ciardi was never one of the inner cognoscenti. He loved the music, and he visited the clubs—52nd Street, abroad. When he heard Bechet playing live in Paris in 1950–51, in sweet Sid's last great swan song, he was moved and went back, and got to know the man, and helped him to put down his story which some have called a life and others a work of consummate fiction.

Jazz critic Gary Gilder has called *Treat It Gentle* "one of the three great jazz books of all time, quite in a class with Milton (Mezz) Mezzrow's *Really the Blues* and Charley Mingus' *Beneath the Underdog*." When I read Gilder's remarks I went out and special-ordered *Treat It Gentle* in an expensive Da Capo Press reprint edition, and was pleased to discover Bechet's reedy sibilance carried over to print: "No one had to explain notes or rhythm to him," Bechet expatiates on his grandfather, a slave, Omar: "It was all there inside him, something he was always sure of. All the things that were happening to him outside, they had to get there to be measured—there inside where the music was." It was also an astonishment and a small wonder to discover a short preface to one edition which acknowledged the editorial contributions of John Ciardi.

Ciardi now tells us that when he met Bechet face-to-face in the clubs of Paris way back then he knew he'd stumbled on a storyteller. He also insists his major editorial effort was in removing the fussy rhetoric of the young woman to whom Bechet had originally dictated his memoirs. "Do what Orey say," the old New Orleans tailgate tune reminds us in monosyllables, but this woman thought she could improve on, "O I can be mean, I know that. That's a thing you gotta trust."

Initially, it seems, Ciardi did a certain amount of cutting and pasting and blue penciling, but he also tape-recorded Bechet's accounts of the old times, the life

79

on the plantation and in New Orleans. Then there developed some sort of controversy, a falling out over who owned what literary rights, and the original edition, though 90 percent Ciardi's, was brought out by Hill and Wang under the name of another ghost; and he lost track of it, or interest, right about this time. As Bechet might have put it, about Ciardi's labors, "He hadn't any bowing to do to anybody." The *Treat It Gentle* republished by Da Capo Press contains some opening chapters on rural black life in Mississippi in the generations preceding the birth of the soprano saxophonist which is of narrative power equal to some of Faulkner's writings.

Here Bechet evokes the first meeting of his grandfather, a slave, with his slave grandmother, near Congo Square, one Sunday on the Plantation: "She was standing sort of off by herself, just standing and well . . . it comes over him, it was one of those things. She was standing there a little off by herself, and he just fell in love with her. Suddenly, everything he was doing, he was doing it for her. The girl, she must have been 13 or 14, all full of a kind of dream, like in the morning when no one's seen it. . . ."

The full narrative involves an attempted rape by an overseer, and the flight of Bechet's future grandfather; it is lengthily dramatic and evocative. As Ciardi has continued to tell us, Bechet was a "fascinating storyteller with a powerful and vivid native idiom." Of the overseer incited to the point of rape, Bechet writes, for example, "She'd done murder inside him (all that kind of picture he had inside himself of the way she moved, all slow, all full, like some day in the middle of summer when its got no hurry). . . ."

Whenever I've read that story to creative writing classes, I'm forced to point out how Bechet, the saxophonist and monologist, puts in so much that they always leave out: action, texture, fresh language. In reminding you now that Ciardi, a sophisticated reader as well as a poet, may have had some hand in its construction, I wish to take nothing away from Bechet's imagination, and talent for language and recall.

Just as he was able to sustain such extraordinary ever-varying obligatos on the soprano sax while playing in ensemble with the Dixieland greats of his era, so, it seems to me, Sidney Bechet's musicianship with words was validated and sustained by his collaboration with Ciardi. Ciardi's praise is best: "A back-country Wallace Stevens," though it's not clear if he refers to Bechet's horn-playing, or his memoir-making. It seems to me Ciardi and Bechet were both lucky that time in Paris to each meet up with the "emmes," which is jazz and hip and also Hebrew for the truth, the real goods.

Ciardi's career has been rich and varied, but he was wise never to have placed himself beyond collaboration. He must have realized much was to be gained from his collaboration with other sensibilities. They say Charlie Parker once appeared at Edgard Varèse's door and offered to serve as his butler in return for composition lessons. "It should be the other way around," Varèse, a Parker fan, insisted modestly. So it always has been with the truly creative artists in our midst. They read scholarship but write poetry, or, as in Ciardi's case, know all they can about Dante's world to translate *The Divine Comedy*.

Ciardi told Vince Clemente* about his time with Bechet, that he was looking for the words to make a characteristic Bechet sound. He tape-recorded, but he probably wrote a little, too. That's what collaboration is like. To find the color of Bechet's Creole with words as well as music, to make into it all the drama and exhilaration of a man's life, a man's voice. Ciardi had to know "Tin Roof Blues" and "Clarinet Marmalade" to help Bechet write this book. He had to dismiss what was florid and banal for what simply was and to know what it was to be a "real walkaround man," as Bechet calls Billy Bolden in these memoirs.

*Treat It Gentle*, though minor to Ciardi's canon, is a major memoir of the popular culture, and an enduring account of the jazz life in New Orleans, New York, Europe, etc., during the first four decades of this century.

*See the letter following.

# *Writing* Treat It Gentle:
# *A Letter to Vince Clemente, September 22, 1985*

## John Ciardi

I met Sidney Bechet when I was in Paris in 1950–51 and he was playing at the *Vieux Columbier.* I don't qualify as a jazz buff but I found the man to be impressive. We met and talked a number of times in cafés, usually at the Deux Magots. Someone told Sidney I was a writer whereupon he said he was writing his autobiography. At the time I was doing some editing for Twayne Publishers and said that I'd love to see it for our list.

It was a curious manuscript and Sidney turned out to be a fascinating storyteller with a powerful and vivid native idiom, but whenever in the manuscript Sidney stopped talking there came a burst of high-lilac College English. When I asked Sidney about those vaguely scented purple passages he said they were by a girl named Joan Something (I forget the name) who was his secretary. He had dictated his recollections to her and she had set them down with her fancy little additions.

I think Sidney lied about the arrangement, though I took his word for it at the time. I think Joan (Reed?) was not being paid as a secretary but interviewing him for an "as told to" autobiography. Sidney, as I began to sense in time, could be shifty. . . . I have heard he could even be mean, but I found nothing to justify that rumor.

Taking his word that Joan X was only a paid secretary, I went through the ms. red-inking out her fancy little touches and doing my best to get it all into Sidney's own voice and idiom. I interviewed him further, took my notes home with me to the U.S. and spent about six months transcribing and setting in order my new notes. When he came to Boston to play at Birdland, I interviewed him again with a tape recorder developing some questions I had made while editing, and also some new recollections. (I must have lost those two tapes when we

82

moved from Harvard to Rutgers. I have searched through every corner of my study, and they have not turned up. Ralph Ellison tells me they should be in an archive, and I agree, but they have disappeared.)

At any rate I worked over those tapes, added them to the ms., and sent the ms. to Sidney, who approved, and to Twayne for publication. I thought it was a good book, and even that it would pay for itself and show some profit. But as soon as Twayne announced the title, Joan Reed (is that the right name?) claimed as her own the ms. she had botched so miserably and threatened to bring suit to recover what she claimed was her property. So threatened, Twayne backed out, and the whole project died until about ten years later. I was no longer with Twayne then, but I gather they made a deal with Hill and Wang, a new publishing house. H&W gave the ms. to a new man (I have forgotten his name, too) who added an account of the last ten years and published it over his name. I shrugged, having other things to think about, but as I recall it the first eighty-five or ninety percent of the ms. is just as I had set it down, with only the last clip as his writing.

By then, as I recall, Sidney had died, and so had my interest in the book, though I retain a happy sense of Sidney as a presence, as a musical genius, and as a voice. He reminds me in fact of a back-country Wallace Stevens. He had blown all his life into a horn, recognizing it in the way it sounded back to him from the music. Like Stevens' "Blue Guitar." And though Sidney said it in a half-Creole country idiom, what it came to was a perception of life very much like Stevens'.

Sorry I can't detail it more closely. I was fascinated by Sidney's story and by his way of saying it in idiom, but the work I did was sandwiched in between other things. I suppose I could have sued Hill and Wang for stealing my work, but why bother? The story is told, it is a good one, and I told myself that what work I did was sufficiently rewarded in the doing.

Writing this makes me want to go back and read the book again. Hill and Wang did send me a copy and I have it somewhere in my messy attic, but like those tapes, I can't seem to find it. It will turn up some day when I am looking for something else. It's a messy filing system but nothing ever gets lost in it—not forever. It's there somewhere. And it's in my mind.

# A Blade

## William Heyen

In 1961 I was a student home on Long Island for spring break from college. I would be graduating soon, but was confused and unhappy. I'd started out in physical education, had lost interest, and had switched to English education only because I liked to read and because I didn't have the math to go into astronomy. I'd have to leave Brockport in a month or two, and didn't know where I'd be going. While she finished college, I'd have to part from the girl I'd been going with for three years, and this time, after being hurt my freshman year almost to the point of breakdown because my high-school love had met and married someone else, I was afraid that if I lost Han I'd lose myself. I remember that at home I took long walks, trying to become tired enough to sleep, trying to figure out where I was headed. I was twenty years old, had never been able to take life lightly or put things into perspective, and was close to the edge.

This all comes back to me now because I'm holding a particular book I found in a now defunct antique shop-used bookstore on one of those gloomy days when I couldn't have been paying any attention to the budding of the Island. According to an inked-in price, I paid thirty cents for the book. And I inscribed it, as though twenty-five years later I would want to remember: "Bill Heyen—purchased over Easter vacation, 1961, St James, L.I., New York." I've had this book longer than any other except for some high-school yearbooks.

It's a copy, a first edition still in its now tattered red and white jacket, of John Ciardi's *I Marry You*, which had appeared a few years before. I'd myself tried to write a few poems my senior year in college, but wasn't especially interested in poetry, and I'm sure I hadn't bought any book of poetry, even for thirty cents, before this, but *I Marry You* found me. I did know Ciardi's name from a world literature class in which we'd read his *Inferno*. I must have given my hand to *I Marry You* as Frost's farmboy must have given his hand to the saw that cost him his life. Or the book leapt out at me as the saw, Frost's canny speaker seems to think, may have leapt out at the boy. (I know what I just said, and am tempted to revise, but when I think my figure through, it holds.)

I'd go on to know Ciardi's *Saturday Review* columns, his important *Mid-Century American Poets* anthology, and other books of his poetry including *Lives of X* in which I recognized myself again and again; I'd write a paper on "Men Marry What They Need. I Marry You" during graduate school at Ohio University where Ciardi's friend and Bread Loaf colleague Hollis Summers taught and sometimes referred to him; I'd fill my book with notes and think of doing my master's thesis on Ciardi; I'd write him a letter filled with the Great Questions, and he'd be gracious and patient enough to reply. I remember, in part, "Death is everything, nothing"—this would all happen later, but before that, during that spring in 1961, I needed to give my life to something more than I'd been, and that book was there for me, a blade.

*I Marry You* was the first book of contemporary poetry I read, and I read it often, trying to understand it. I didn't know how a poem meant, but I was moved by many of these, including the prologue lyric from which the book's title came. It spoke to the condition of my need: "I marry you from time and a great door / is shut and stays shut against wind, sea, stone, / sunburst and heavenfall. And home once more. . . ." I wanted to have a home with Han, my wife now of twenty-five years. I loved and needed her. I needed to hear the family loyalties of this book. Before even that, under consciousness, I needed its music, its language unlike any language I had known. I remember being struck by Ciardi's descriptions of two egrets "like two white hands / washing one another / in the prime of light," but I was also amazed by the less logical "lemons and bells of light, / rails, rays, waterfalls, ices— / as high as the eye dizzies" in the same poem, the impressionistic flow and spill of the words themselves. On another note, I remember feeling the melancholy fact of death-in-life in this book, too. "I have no time. I love you by despair." I can trace now, as I hold this book again, the beginnings of my own abiding desire to write poetry of my own experience, wanting to "sit by pond scums till the air recites / Its heron back. And doubt all else. But praise." The book came "from the shapeless waters under time" for me, and gave shape to my feelings.

The pages of this Festschrift for a distinguished poet, a man of strength and integrity, should perhaps be reserved for those who have known him longer and more intimately than I have, but I am thankful for the chance to say that the sheaf of love poems that found me in 1961 helped me find a way to here, where I am now found, within this life of poetry, and I am thankful.

# *John Ciardi: Heart Like a Halfback*

## Karl Shapiro

An odd coincidence; I woke up that morning thinking about him, got dressed and went out for the daily *Times*. I turned directly to the back page or section where they have obituaries and saw the young Ciardi. Here is a prose-poem I wrote for John Ciardi which I included in my prose-poetry book called *The Bourgeois Poet*.

When they ask about your poems I say: He writes like a truck driver (if only you did). Your idiom coarse as Indian hair, you click along on Union Pacific meters. You tell your rhymes like beads; you ambiguate as well as the gobbledegooks. Honor bright. We all came out of the same army and joined the same generation of silence. Each took the territory of his choice (yours is the biggest). You handle Dante like a Cadillac. (Our colleague drives a Mercedes-Rilke. Our serious one can't tell the names of cars.) Good social conscience, lover of gab and gag, you're known in every dimension, heart like a halfback—

One time you beaned the lady-poet, I scratched my head. What the hell were you trying to do? People attack affinities. The gurus call you middlebrow; you shrug it off. You feel at home in the poetry lab, a manual or two under your belt. This isn't an ad or a tax return. It's a Chanukah card with Haitian angels. The Christmas seal says Help Fight Gongorism. You weave across the country like a trend. Have you lost the essential bum? It's not what you sit on. The busted image has melted back together, as hot as cooling glass. Now that the Bishop's got his ashes hauled.

# John Ciardi and "Jabberwocky" in the Indiana Cornfields

## Norbert Krapf

It was almost twenty-five years ago that John Ciardi's *How Does A Poem Mean?* (1959) served as one of two texts for the second half of my freshman English course. This was at St. Joseph's College, then an all-male school of about a thousand students sequestered in the flat cornfields of northwestern Indiana—a long drive from the hills I grew up in to the south, near Kentucky. As I recall, my plan was to become a high-school English and Latin teacher (the one I loved, the other I liked and was told it would provide "security"); and I entered my second college semester somewhat shaken because I had not done well in the first half of Composition or World Lit. I worried that I had made the wrong choice for a "career." Even in my wildest hallucinations, I could never have foreseen that I would eventually take a Ph.D. in English and American literature, teach college English, including poetry courses, and write poems that would come together as volumes.

I still have my tattered paperback copy (I paid $2.00 for it) of the blue Ciardi anthology. I have had to scotch-tape the front cover, on which a few undistinguished doodles are preserved, but the book has remained with me this quarter of a century through college, graduate school at nearby Notre Dame, and a move to Long Island, where I have taught and written poetry for just over fifteen years. Whenever I have had the good luck to be knee- and waist-deep in the poetry of the past and the present, I have often reached back for the tattered blue book to see what Ciardi says about a given poem or aspect of poetry.

I could not have seen or phrased it this way as a college freshman, but the Ciardi anthology—I too have my misgivings about such textbooks, usually shy away from them—seems a model of hard-edged lucidity and common sense. Above all, I continue to see the book as a treasure-trove of fine poems. Leafing back through the chapters, faintly bird-tracked with my cryptic juvenile markings, I recall with pleasure experiencing for the first time, at least in any conscious way, a number of favorites. There is evidence that we read many others, but I remember best Frost's "Stopping by Woods," still perhaps my all-time favorite, and his witty "Departmental"; De la Mare's magical, alluring "The Listeners"; Eliot's monumental "Prufrock," a poem that stunned me and baffled the class into silence, prompting the frustrated instructor to move on to something else. "Lord Randal," which I asked a Scottish colleague to tape for my classes when I taught in England over a decade later, transported me to a world that was remote yet somehow familiar; whereas Robinson's "Mr. Flood's Party" sobered me into reflecting on the dangers of growing up in a hard-drinking town where teen traffic fatalities were almost commonplace. There was the joy of gazing into Shakespeare's "my mistress' eyes" (the Great Poet could make good fun of "poetic" poetry!) and the more somber "bare ruined choirs" sonnets; and then leaping into Donne's worldly, skeptical falling-star "Song," a charge to the heart of any green backwoods teenager, before settling into the depths of "Valediction" and "The Flea." I distinctly remember also Stephen Crane's wonderfully bitter "I Saw a Man" and MacLeish's "Ars Poetica," the text of which still bears comments in my scrawl, in pencil and red and blue ink—strange fossils of myself as a college freshman. I can't decipher exactly what I thought about this poem then, but I do remember it made me think seriously about poetry.

I frankly don't remember reading "The Ancient Mariner" at that point in my life, but a curving slash of green ink beside the "He prayeth best" stanza proves I did. As a college freshman I was not far from the woods and fields I still occasionally hunted during vacations, and it's not surprising that I would have responded to the "All things great and small" religious sentiment of that stanza. I was also not far removed from the high school gridiron and diamond and memories of epic World Series games flashed on a relative's TV, and can remember, as clearly as I would the first frost of each year, the delight with which I entered Rolf Humphries' "The Polo Grounds." I can still hear the Irish-American instructor read in that husky, rich voice the "boomlay boomlay boom" of Vachel Lindsay's "The Congo."

One more poem must be added to this admirably catholic group of poems I experienced so richly in the Ciardi anthology that twenty-five years later I remember reading and discussing them. My most vivid memory of that long-ago semester associated with Ciardi, whom, I soon learned, my professors were reading in the columns of *The Saturday Review,* is of the day we discussed Lewis Carroll's "Jabberwocky." Again, I hear the instructor *reading* the poem to us; his reading of poems may have been his outstanding gift and most successful technique. (To this day, I cannot discuss a poem with a class without first reading it to them, then reading it again after we have had our say.) On that winter day twenty-five years ago, there was something astonishing, almost sinful, about deriving such pleasure from the communal sharing of language that didn't "make sense." Here I was in the middle of the frozen cornfields with a small group of fellow Catholic teenagers, many of us the first in our families ever to attend college, all of us aware that, in the eyes of our parents, a college degree would have the practical advantage of helping us "get a good job." And John Ciardi, son of Italian immigrants, and an Irish instructor were piping us away with poetry! To change the metaphor, I can still taste "brillig" and "slithy" and "Jubjub" and "vorpal" as if they were spoonfuls of forbidden pudding.

When my daughter, now five, was growing into the pleasure of words, she celebrated having a father who seemed as much a mother by calling me "Mapa." My son, now two, opens the door of my study as I write, walks toward the turntable, points, bounces up and down, and chants pleadingly for "Moo-cat! Moo-cat!" When my children grow up, I hope they too shall have jabberwocky wherever they go.

Most of *How Does a Poem Mean?* is not, however, a defense or celebration of the kind of "nonsense" language that appeals to all children and a poet like Lewis Carroll. In fact, Ciardi does not hestitate to introduce the critical terminology which helps us to discuss poetry intelligently. I'm sure that my understanding of such basic, essential terms as *symbolism, imagery, tone, diction, denotation, connotation, rhythm,* and *meter* comes from the Ciardi anthology.

What distinguishes the book, though, is Ciardi's tough insistence on balancing the head with the heart, the intellect with instinct, technical know-how with common sense. At the beginning of the "Burble Through the Tulgey Wood" chapter, there is a masterpiece of a paragraph. I did not underline or annotate it back then, but I wish that everyone who reads, teaches, or writes poetry would commit it to memory:

> Everyone who has an emotion and a language knows something about poetry. What he knows may not be much on an absolute scale, and it may not be organized within him in a useful way, but once he discovers the pleasures of poetry, he is likely to be surprised to discover how much he always knew without knowing he knew it. He may discover, somewhat as the character in the French play discovered to his amazement, that he had been talking prose all his life, that he has been living poetry. Poetry, after all, is about life. Anyone who is alive and conscious must have some information about it.

I don't imagine that such a cleareyed classicist as Ciardi would care to be nudged into bed with a wild-eyed romantic like Emerson, whose poetry he does not include (Whitman, who advanced Emerson's American romanticism by several leaps, is represented by only a "catalogue" from "Song of Myself"); but when I think of Ciardi's insistence on the connection between poetry and life, I can't help but recall a sentence from "The Poet": "The people fancy they hate poetry, and they are all poets and mystics!" Whether we are classicists or romantics or, like most of us, a combination of the two, we must surely applaud the editor of an anthology who asserts:

> If the reader cared enough for poetry, he would have no need to study it. He would *live into it*. As the Milanese citizen becomes an encyclopedia of opera information, and as even retarded boys in the Bronx are capable of reciting endlessly detailed baseball statistics, so the passionate reader of poetry becomes alive to it by natural process.

Some of us, however, do need the influence of an inspirational teacher and a memorable book to help us rediscover the jabberwocky of our passions.

# *John Ciardi: The Many Lives of Poetry*

## John Frederick Nims

It is not easy to know, when about to explore the poetry of John Ciardi, where to enter so diverse a region and how to proceed when once there. It is hardly too much to say that here—as Dryden said of Chaucer—here is God's plenty. There are similarities with Chaucer: the record of a pilgrimage, the many interests, the amused warm tolerance for human folly so long as it is neither cruel nor pretentious. Chaucer too was a man of affairs, worldly wise in a time when men were inclined to be more spiritual than now. We may think of the poet as being maladroit, like Baudelaire's albatross, once he leaves his airy realm and comes down to earth. But many have been effective when dealing with things of this world; we would have to put John Ciardi among them. If you wanted advice on the stock market, he could give it to you. If you wanted to know about real estate values or the best buy in a used car, he could tell you. If you wanted to know how to raise roses or get rid of moles in your lawn, he knew that too. If he had inherited the mom and pop grocery on the corner, likely enough he would have developed it into a worldwide chain. If he had gone into politics, he might have been our Governor Cuomo. Only a strong commitment to poetry prevented him from realizing some of the abilities he sacrificed for it. The multifarious interests, the many lives he led, account for the variety of his poetry, and for the difficulty of covering it in a hasty survey.

"The many lives of poetry." In an early birthday poem he speaks of

> An album of myself . . .
>         . . . seen year by year
> Posed in the changing fashions of its skin

and a quarter of a century later he confesses

> I was not able to make one life of all
> the presences I haunted . . .

At every age he was, like Montaigne, a student of himself. He was a soldier and then a householder, observing a quieter world from his patio. Through these observations he became a naturalist and particularly an ornithologist, the very Audubon of poets. Always he has had a sharp eye for what is authentic and what is pretentious in the human creature; watching it, he could hardly fail to be at times a satirist. Books were part of his life from his earliest years; he was known as a scholar, a word-watcher, an adventurous and entertaining etymologist. He was a translator, a teacher, a lecturer, an editor, the author of a dozen or more books for children. A citizen, a political commentator. "I am an actor too," he says in *Lives of X*. He calls himself "a missionary bee/sucking for souls." He even says, "Were I to dramatize myself,"

> I'd say I am a theologian who keeps meeting
> the devil as a master of make-up . . .

A missionary? a theologian? It is a little hard to see Ciardi wearing, together with his twenty or more other hats, the kind of biretta worn by the priests of his childhood. If he ever had worn one, we can be sure that he would have transformed it into a cardinal's hat, and been active in running the Mafia out of Sicily—unless indeed he had become head of it.

Before we come to his poems, some remarks about the bibliography are in order. Where do we find these poems? There are thirteen books of them. A few poems, but not many, appear in more than one volume, up to the *Selected Poems* of 1984. There was not much revision of poems once they were published; most appear without change over the decades. Whereas some poets have done extensive rewriting of early poems, Ciardi simply rejected—or at least refused to reprint—what he came to consider imperfect work. In the *Selected Poems*, there are no pieces at all from his first book, *Homeward to America*, though poems in it won the coveted Hopwood Award in 1939 at the University of Michigan. Of the forty-two poems in his second book, *Other Skies*, he has taken only three for *Selected Poems;* of the forty-one poems in his third, *Live Another Day*, only two. Yet of the poems in this book eleven had appeared in *The New Yorker* between 1946 and 1949. Many young poets would have given anything to have been published there even once. Not one of those *New Yorker* acceptances is in *Selected Poems*, which is very selective indeed.

Changes in the published texts are so few that we will never need a variorum edition. The poet wrote with such assurance that the poems succeed, or in his mind did not succeed, as wholes. There are not many changes of even a word; when there is a change we can see the reasoning behind it. In "S.P.Q.R." he originally wrote

> A thousand kings have held Rome; none, the Romans . . .

Warned against hyperbole by the muse of history, he changed this to "Hundreds of kings. . . ." In "The Invasion of the Sleep Walkers" he wrote

> Once on Fifth Avenue I watched five miles
> Of faceless cops march on St. Patrick's day . . .

But again Clio, with a mind for facts, remonstrated; what we have in *Selected Poems* is the more likely "two miles." Textual trivia; but they are a sign of the poet's respect for reality.

A couple of changes show that with the years came a mellowing of the more aggressive spirit of youth. In the earlier version of "Dialogue of Outer Space" the poet "claims" mercy; in the later version he "begs" it. In the earlier version of "In the Hole" he concludes with

> Damn my neighbors. Damn Brewster Diffenbach.

In the later version this is softened to

> Forgive me my neighbors. Forgive me Brewster Diffenbach.

These are changes of attitude, not of technique.

The few technical revisions are all in the direction of conciseness. Only once in the *Selected Poems* does he add lines to an earlier version. But he does cut. The fourteen stanzas of "Poem for My Twenty-ninth Birthday," in *Other Skies,* had been cut to eleven stanza when it was published in *As If* eight years later. One of his best known poems, "Elegy Just in Case," has twelve stanzas as it appears in *Selected Poems,* having lost three over the four decades. The poem is strengthened not by extensive rewriting but by the omission of three weak stanzas. In *As If,* it begins:

> Here lie Ciardi's pearly bones
> In their ripe organic mess.
> Jungle blown, his chromosomes
> Breed to a new address.

Progenies of orchids seek
The fracture's white spilled lymph.
And his heart's red valve will leak
Fountains for a protein nymph.

Was it bullets or a wind
Or a rip-cord fouled on Chance?
Artifacts the natives find
Decorate them when they dance.

What his wiser eye omitted is the stanza about the progenies of orchids, the heart's red valve, and the protein nymph. They do seem to be in fancy dress between the starkness of the pearly bones and that of the bullets, the wind, and the rip cord. In the last two lines quoted above we have one of the few examples of rewriting to be found in *Selected Poems*. In *Other Skies* he had written

What artifacts the natives find
Failed and left no tomb . . .

Decorated with parts of the fallen plane, the natives step forward more vividly, ready to be photographed for *National Geographic*.

But the equally famous companion poem, "On a Photo of Sgt. Ciardi a Year Later," remained unchanged over forty years. That does not mean that it did not go through many manuscript versions before being committed to publication. The chances are that it did.

What this bibliographical summary suggested is that the poet wrote with conviction and power from the beginning. If a poem was worth keeping, it was kept, almost always, in its original form. When there are variations in the printed versions, very often the poet restored the original wording for the text of *Selected Poems*. Having made our dutiful bow to bibliography, we can now return to the work itself.

Through the *persona* of Leonardo da Vinci, Ciardi once wrote:

You know how or you don't. But to know how

is first to be born of a people, to be
the bearer of their seed—son, husband, father.

These are the lives—those of son, husband, father, with the sense of being born of a people—that we will glance at first in what might be thought of as our Ciardi sampler, our little anthology of the pleasures his work affords us.

The poet finds what are probably the deepest and truest sources of his work in the emotions that give us poems of three generations. All are *dynamic* relationships—I wondered briefly if *dynastic* would be too pompous a word. The author of *A Browser's Dictionary* would know that both words come from the same root—and that there is *dynamite* in that family. I was reassured to find that he himself had used *dynastic* in his "Letter to Mother," the first poem in his first book:

> And it is good to remember that this blood, in
>     another body, your body, arrived.
> There is dynastic example in a single generation
>     of this blood, and the example good . . .

In fact, more than three generations are present. There are poems that go back to a grandfather in Italy,

>         . . . Father's father,
> photographer- and Sunday-scrubbed and scarved,
> Sorrento painted behind him . . .

and to a grandmother who

> in *her* tribe's dark, kept herbs and spells
> and studied signs and dreams . . .

The first section of *Selected Poems* is called "Tribal Poems," as was a section of *As If* almost thirty years before. Several members of the tribe are as colorful as Aunt Mary, who "loved us till we screamed," and who "died of eating twelve red peppers," fried in oil, "after a hard day's work," thereby undergoing

>         . . . red-hot transformation
> from gluttony into embalmer's calm.

Dominant in the poems of family feeling is the mother. Thirty-five years after that early "Letter to Mother," *The Little That Is All* was dedicated to her "in loving memory." But from the very beginning the love between mother and son is never without tension. "Letter to Mother" can say, "it was good, it was all good." But it can also say, "Mother, I can promise you nothing." Passionate and simple, from a hearty peasant background, the mother was "instinctual," says her son, "as peasantry breeds in any Apennines. . . ." He was just as passionate, but without her background—growing up as he did amid books, classes, the excitements of city life in a new land. He found he could not continue to share, for one thing, the unquestioning fervor of her Catholicism.

> . . . Once on a shelf
> a candle lit a plaster saint
> and I knelt in a blaze of self.
> The reek of guilt would leave me faint
> where my mad mother stretched my soul . . .

Nor could his mother share all of his interest:

> By flashlight under the covers
>            . . . there
> in the cave safe from Mother,
> I read my eyes out of my head . . .

Some of her practices would have seemed superstitious to the citizens of her adopted country, although their own ancestors had been just as superstitious not so many decades before.

> . . . When we poured
> concrete for a new house, she leaned over
> the half-filled forms muttering,
> and dropped in a penny, a crucifix, a key,
> then pricked her finger and shook out
> a drop of blood . . .

> She was using everything she knew anything
> about, and she knew she was using it.

"That," her son comments, "is my kind of savage," for her superstitions were based on blood and bone and the vitality of her beliefs, not just on the number 13 or black cats or ladders or the meaningless obsessions of people walking the street—"ritualists," the poet calls them, "without conviction."

The love between mother and son was complicated because husband and father had been killed, when the child was only three, in a traffic accident—a loss that "maddened the woman, and then wasted her witless," a loss

> . . . that had been the blood
> and error and evil of all my Mother's tears . . .

More and more she saw the father in the son; more and more he saw that his "best chance was to play the husband" and (especially on those occasions when she was punishing him) to win her love with his rough affection. "Then *she'd* cry,/and I would have to stop bawling to comfort *her*." He came to be protective not only as a husband might have been, but even as a father. As she grew weak and fey with age, he could say, "I think perhaps this woman is my child." Again he calls her "my abdicated matriarch and my daughter."

Two poems show her at the extremes of her life. In "Bridal Photo, 1906" we see how

> Pompadoured and laced and veiled for giving,
> the woman sits her flower-time at his side
> badged with his gifts—gold watch on a fleur-de-lis
> pin at the heart, gold locket at the throat—
> her hand at total rest under his hand.

In "Epithalamium at St. Michael's Cemetery" we see her at another kind of bridal, as she is laid to rest next to the husband dead for fifty years—she now

> the hag end of his lost bride, her wits shed
> some years before her light . . .
> 
>                       . . . The bride is dressed
> in tissue, ten claws folded on no breast.

"And there's a life, God knows, no one would choose," he says of her last years. And yet that life is shown bathed in a kind of radiance. Perhaps her son's best tribute to her is in *Lives of X:*

>         . . . history's daughter
> tall from her root of love, my comic source,
> my radiant witch of first-made lunacies,
> and priestess of the tongues before a man . . .

The poet can hardly have remembered his father, who was felt, however, as a powerful presence: "the deepest grave I know." In "My Father Died Imperfect as a Man" we read

> My mother lied him to perfections . . .
> 
> So history lied my father from his death,
> she having no history that would let him be

imperfect and worth keeping vigils with.
She made a saint of him. And she made me

kneel to him every night. When I was bad,
he shadowed me. And always knew my lies.
I was too young to know him, but my bed
lay under him and God, and both their eyes

bored through the dark to damn me as I was

Much of what he remembered was an imaginative creation, as when he described how his father, out of his savings, had bought "ten piney lots" in the
country, which he liked to visit on Sunday and make plans for:

when he sat on a stone with his wine-jug and cheese beside him,
his collar and coat on a branch, his shirt open,
his derby back on his head like a standing turtle. A big
man he was. When he sang *Celeste Aida* the woods
filled as if a breeze were swelling through them . . .

—Well, I have lied. Not so much lied as dreamed it . . .

In a time when the vogue was for children to enjoy composing, and profiting
from, exposés of their parents, Ciardi, though aware of shortcomings, could regard his own with admiration, respect, and love; it is with something like exalta-
tion that he proclaims

I am the son of this man and this woman.

In *Selected Poems*, the "Tribal Poems" are followed by a group called "I
Marry You" (title of the 1958 volume, subtitled "A Sheaf of Love Poems"). In the
last of the group, the poet returns to his tribal memories:

My father did read some. But it was
his mountain he came from, not the mind
of man. He had ritual, not ideas . . .

Such ancestral pieties also inform the love poems: marital love as consecrated
by ritual is the theme of more than one of them. "Epithalamion After a War"
begins

Now by a ritual of legality
You are my flesh's darling, my mind's encounter . . .

Of the dozen or so love poems in *I Marry You*, only four are reprinted in *Selected Poems*. Is that because love poems are harder to write, and for that reason less likely to succeed, than other tribal poems—particularly when they are poems of happy love, as these are? When Keats babbles about

> More happy love! more happy, happy love!
> Forever warm and still to be enjoyed

he is looking not at flesh and blood but at ceramic figures, their imagined emotions far above "all breathing human passion." We must all have noticed that there are fewer poems—though more verse!—about blissful lover than about love star-crossed or unrequited. The lover who feels fulfilled has other things to do than moon over his typewriter. As Yeats says, had he been happy in love, he

> . . . might have thrown poor words away
> and been content to live.

The difficulty is that poems of happy love, having few ironies to invoke, may seem not only simple-hearted but simple-minded. The poems to Ciardi's mother, also poems of love, are gripping because they are not simply poems of "more happy, happy love"; they are poems about the interplay between love and what threatens to destroy it. But the poems of *I Marry You* seem to offer the most untroubled and luminous vistas in all of the poetry. The beauty of the loved woman is described as the stuff of which all legend is made: "There is no other body in all myth . . ."

But since beauty is a magnet for evil as well as for good, myth does not confine itself to the annals of happiness. When Yeats warns "there's a light in Troy" he is not referring to the glory of Helen's hair. Something of the same feeling is in our poet's praise of his love:

> . . . The raiders' ships
> All sailed to your one port . . .

In these poems, the electric charge is not in the love, which is unclouded, but in the lover, sometimes torn between the spiritual and the sensuous:

> Bravo and monk (the heads and tails of love)
> I stand, a spinning coin of wish and dread

Or it is in reality itself. In the most moving poems, there is a realization of the

conflict between timeless and legendary beauty and the contingency, the chanci-
ness, of an existence made up of whatever is begotten, born, and dies. This is
the thought of the love poem whose first line is its title:

> The deaths about you when you stir in sleep
> hasten me toward you. Out of the bitter mouth
> that sours that dark, I sigh for what we are . . .

The chill of apprehension is felt also in "To Judith Asleep":

> . . . my fear and miser's panic
> That time shall have you last and legendry
> Undress to old bones from its moon brocade.

Yet the realization that love is imperiled, that time must have a stop, teaches us
to cherish what we cannot long possess. That realization sparks a defiance that
is, at least for the moment, a protection against the conturbations of *timor
mortis*. In "Men Marry What They Need. I Marry You," this defiance is explicit:

> I marry you from time and a great door
> is shut and stays shut against wind, sea, stone . . .
>
> I marry you by all dark and all dawn
>
> and have my laugh at death . . .

After the marriage poems we have poems to the children. Ciardi has written
about as many books for children as for us overgrowns—but I think not many
poems about them. Is it because it is as hard to write children poems as to write
love poems? Are the tots too cute and adorable—at least in the verse about
them? Swinburne saw them that way, as in the poem he had the nerve to call
"Etude Realiste," which begins:

> A baby's feet, like sea-shells pink,
>     Might tempt, should heaven see meet,
> An angel's lips to kiss, we think,
>     A baby's feet . . .

Gerard Manley Hopkins, poet and holy man, admitted that such "rot about
babies" made him see things King Herod's way.

But as the children grow older and more refractory, dramatic tensions begin and the interest picks up. The poet finds himself, in regard to them, in the position his mother was in toward him. But, perhaps because of his own early experience, he has more understanding and tolerance than her traditions permitted her to have. The father-son polarity is felt first in "Boy":

> He is in his room sulked shut. The small
> pouts of his face clenched. His tears
> as close to holy water as I recall
> any first font shining. A boy, and fierce
> in his sacrament, father-forced this two-
> faced way love has . . .

Racked by the need for extending sympathy and for enforcing discipline, the father concludes:

> . . . I confess
> I don't know my own reasons or own way.
> May sons forgive the fathers they obey.

Later poems are about forgiving, but with an amused tolerance he had not quite learned when he wrote "Boy."

The decibel levels of the younger generation come in for comment in "Craft":

> A cherry red chrome dazzle
> with white racing stripes
> screams into my drive spilling
> hard-rock enough to storm Heaven,
> and young insolence sits there
> honking for Benn, who's not in.

When he finds that Benn is in Boston, the young insolence says, "Well, tell him I was here."

> "He knows," I say. "It's only
> two hundred and fifty miles.
> That's within earshot." . . .

Meanwhile the father has been pressing his "crafty buttons," imaginary magic buttons that spray-paint the car black, puncture its tires, blow the radio circuits, crack the axles. The last magic button would have sprung a trap door and pitched the youngster into boiling oil. The boy speeds off in a spray of gravel, but without wrecking anything. The poet's last sad comment on magic buttons is only

> . . . It takes none
> to know he'll work it out himself
> some loud night on the Interstate.

"A Poem for Benn's Graduation from High School" is galvanized by the same polarities: the casually funny against the profoundly earnest. The late-sleeping father has been called in to see an assistant principal "at 9:00 impossible o'clock A.M." about his son's misconduct. That evening, hours later, awakening in the den after some TV supercinema, he finds the son drowsing in a chair near him.

> "Well?" I say. "Hello, you old bastard,"
>
> he says. . . .

From those words, it might be hard to guess the depth of the affection here. But a few lines later the poem concludes with:

> . . . It does not, finally,
> take much saying. There has even been time
> to imagine we have said "Goddamn it, I love you,"
> and to hear ourselves saying it, and to pause
> to be terrified by *that* thought and its possibilities.

What gives these poems, like those to his mother, their credibility is their upsetting candor. In all of the family poems we are in the presence of a spirit warm, tolerant, sympathetic, forgiving. But never blindly so; it sees, but makes allowance for, the imperfections in all of us. In "My Father Died Imperfect as a Man" is the sentence, "Love must intend realities." Ten years later, in *The Little That Is All*, it became the substance of the one-liner called "Exit Line."

> Love should intend realities. Goodbye.

Ten more years, and the poet returns to the insistent "must" in *Selected Poems*. But with the people he loved, though he saw the realities almost too vividly, it was never "Goodbye." A truer summary of his feelings is to be found just a few lines from the end of the "Epilogue" to *Lives of X:*

> Let what I love outlive me and all's well.

102

There is one life he is closer to than to any of these: his own. "Closer," he says, "than mother and son." He regards himself with not only the same unsparing honesty as he regards others, but with a frankness that is ironic, if not openly sarcastic. Looking at a photo of the soldier he was, he can say

> The sgt. stands so fluently in leather,
> So poster-holstered and so newsreel-jawed . . .
> My civil memory is overawed.

The "fine bravura look of calm," he confesses, is a deception. The poet allows himself no heroics in his own regard. There are several poems of self-criticism, or even of self-derision. In "Coming Home on the 5:22" he can mock the "prosperous well-tailored plump / middle-aged man" he has become, showing off by leaping from the train it comes to a stop. That incident leads to further self-analysis:

> —How did this fat and foolish man
> come over me? He is not I.
> Yet I am he, though I began
> as something else. When did I die?
> Well, tell the truth: not I but they.
> All those I tried in prayer or play,
>
> Like trying on a self . . .
>
> —I used to say this sort of thing to God.
> He didn't like an idiot for a son.
> I wasn't pleased himself, so I changed style . . .

A poet, in writing about himself, becomes a divided personality: observer and observed. "No mind can engender till divided into two," said Yeats, who also observed that "we make out of the quarrel with others, rhetoric, but of the quarrel with ourselves, poetry." A dramatic example of the poet quarreling with himself is Ciardi's "Tenzone." The title is literary, one of only two or three such in *Selected Poems*. As such, it permits a pedantic romp into fields of genre, source, influence, parallels. "Tenzone" is a two-part poem: in the first part Soul accuses Body of abandoning the higher reality that it, the Soul, aspires to, and of corrupting its talent, if any, to devote itself to such earthy pleasures as big cars, bourbon, good clothes, "cash, free-loading, and the more expensive bitches." "He actually likes it here!" Soul concludes in disgust. In the second

103

part, Body, in matching stanzas, answers the "eternalist of boneyards" by saying that Soul by itself is ineffective,

> . . . a glowworm. A spook. A half-strung zither
> with a warped sounding box . . .

At any rate no poet, because "the poem is belly and bone." In defiance of Soul, Body admits that it does want the physicality of the here and now:

> . . . And, *yes,* I want it all—
> grab, gaggle, and rut—as sure as death's no breather.

The poem will remind us of Yeats' "A Dialogue of Self and Soul," which, though in imagery and diction very different, is a similar debate. It also has two parts. In the first, in alternating stanzas, "My Soul" exhorts "My Self" to sublimation and transcendence. But My Self clings to such emblems of earth as an ancient Japanese sword and royal embroidery. In the second, My Self passionately defends its earthiness, sometimes in lines which parallel those of Ciardi's poem.

> A living man is blind and drinks his drop.
> What matter if the ditches are impure?
> What matter if I live it all once more?
> Endure that toil of growing up;
> The ignominy of boyhood; the distress
> Of boyhood changing into man;
> The unfinished man and his pain
> Brought face to face with his own clumsiness . . .

We could annotate each of these lines with references to *Lives of X*. And as Yeats has My Self say,

> I am content to live it all again
> And yet again, if it be life to pitch
> Into the frog-spawn of a blind man's ditch . . .

so Ciardi has Body say to Soul:

> Yes, I like it here. Make it twenty times worse
> and I'd still do it over again, even with you
> like a monkey on my back . . .

(An earlier amoebaean poem of Yeats is a dialogue between two aspects of his personality, there called *Hic* and *Ille*—or, as Pound is supposed to have joked, *Hic* and *Willie*. The two are like Soul and Self, but there Soul seems to win on points.)

Although Ciardi handles his theme in his own twentieth-century way, he is sturdily in an ancient tradition, that of *conflictus* or *débat*. We can easily think of earlier examples: the fifteenth-century dialogue between Natura Hominis and Bonitas Dei, Samuel Daniel's debate between honor and pleasure in "Ulysses and the Siren," Marvell's "A Dialogue Between the Soul and the Body." Outside of our own literature there is Villon's ballade in the form of a *débat* in which his heart rebukes his body for its indulgences.

But Ciardi's poem is called "Tenzone"—and that word takes us into Italian literature. It still means *dispute* or *fight*. If our poet is indebted to any one author for his title, that author is Dante, whose "Tenzone" with Forese Donati is, for many admirers of Dante, a stain on that great reputation. "Deplorable" is about the mildest word that has been applied to the exchange of six sonnets, three by Dante, three by Forese. It is thought they were written when Dante was having some kind of breakdown after the death of Beatrice, and before he started on his way to Paradise in the *Divine Comedy*. The two writers exchange somewhat obscure objurgations, but it is clear that Dante accuses Forese of leaving a wife coughing in her chilly bed, not only because of his sexual inadequacy, but because he is out mugging people to support his habit of gluttony. Forese retaliates by saying that Dante is a coward just like his father, the crooked usurer, and that Dante himself will be lucky if he makes it to the poorhouse. What about your mother? Dante counters; she knows you're a bastard, and maybe she could supply the details. Hardly edifying; perhaps we should be grateful that all it gave Ciardi is his title. His poem "Birthday" is more of a *tenzone*; in it his soul is awakened by his body, and the poem begins with:

> A fat sixty-year-old man woke me. "Hello,
> Ugly," he said. I nodded. Ugly's easy.
> "Why don't you punch yourself in the nose?" I said.
> "You look like someone who would look better bloody."

But in the most recent of his dual poems, in which the poet wakes up "inanely happy," there is a joyful reconciliation between the mind and its "animal." The poem is called "Happiness"; it is appropriately the first poem in his most recent book. The two poems that follow it, equally exultant, are "The Glory" and "Praise."

As a gunner in a B-29 in the South Pacific, Ciardi had another kind of life, close to death. The poems that deal with these experiences remind us more of the starkness of Wilfred Owen than of the romanticism of Rupert Brooke: grim accounts of bomber missions and their casualties, of what goes on in the mind of a downed pilot in an isolated jungle, or, of one who, without provisions on his rubber raft, drifts in mid-ocean toward his lonely death. These accounts are not preserved in the *Selected Poems*. The only poem there that copes with the reality of modern war is "The Graph," from *Lives of X*. In this he can confess, "I studied dying all that year," and can tell us graphically what some of the lessons were like:

> I practiced thinking I had died last week
> and could relax with nothing more to lose.
> Still in the night sweat before every mission
> a wet rag whispered: "By this time tomorrow
> you may have burned to death." . . .

Another time he found himself in a cave facing a concretion of corpses that had been charred to mummies by the flamethrowers. In the open mouth of one was a living rat, working there so grim a glance at the horrors of war. Ciardi plays down the heroics, and his own part in them. His epigraph for the group of war poems in *As If* is a line from Melville's "The March into Virginia":

> All wars are boyish, and are fought by boys . . .

He saw integrity and heroism in those campaigns, and gave them the honor they deserve. If the spirit of irony seems to prevail, it is because he saw so clearly the difference between the heroic and the heroics. His attitude was no less ironic about himself, as we see in his best known war poems, "Elegy Just in Case" and "On a Photo of Sgt. Ciardi a Year Later." Long after the war he wrote a poem with the title, "Ten Years Ago When I Played at Being Brave." His final comment on that period of his life would seem to be the title he gave the section of war poems in his *Selected Poems:* he called it "Bang Bang."

A life the poet lived after the war is referred to in the title of a poem in *From Time to Time:* "Image of Man as a Gardener After Two World Wars." It begins:

> In the dead hour of the afternoon,
> When the sun has overshot the sky
>       . . . I stand
> Hosing, householding my lawn.

106

In poem after poem we see the poet as householder. In *Selected Poems*, a group subtitled "On the Patio" has twice as many poems as the "Bang Bang" section. It is there that he can say

> . . . Now I sit
> Happy to look at what I look at.

In these poems the ironies are quieted. Much of what he looks at is in the landscaping around the patio. No mere chaise-longue gardener, he knows and lets us know the sometimes painful pleasure of working with soil, compost, burlap, wax, a grafting knife.

One of the poems in *From Time to Time* is called "The Cartographer of Meadows." Looking at nature first from near the house, he begins to be a naturalist in the wider world, scanning with scientific exactness what is to be seen there. Everything is specific: "I have never seen," one poem insists, "a generalized blue jay." When he looks at bees he sees them not merely as a buzzy blur, but as

> hunchback bees in pirate pants and with peg-leg
> hooks . . .

When he sees a deer, neck deep in mist, he does not see just a moving head. He sees

> A brown swan with a mythic twist
> of antlers . . .

Ciardi's nature poems are rare, like Frost's, in that they are based on the realities of nature. The writers of sentimental verse like to fancy that birds are talking to *us*, really piping sweet somethings in our ear. Frost—and Ciardi—know better. As Frost writes in "The Hill Wife,"

> One ought not to have to care
>   So much as you and I
> Care when the birds come round the houses
>   Or seem to say good-by;
>
> Or care so much when they come back
>   With whatever it is they sing . . .

Whatever it is! Ciardi knows too that whatever there is between man and the rest of nature, it is not rational communication. He "intends realities" when he looks at the world, just as when he looks at the people in it. He is unsentimental in recognizing that nature is by no means always endearing. We are surrounded by oddities, mysteries, horrors. One section of *Selected Poems* is called "Thickets"—looking at nature, we are always looking into a thicket of the inscrutable. "Thoughts on Looking into a Thicket" has to do with a spider who resorts to one of the strangest and unseemliest of camouflages—it can make itself look like bird droppings, to attract butterflies and such who regard that as their gourmet fare. Planning to eat, they light there and are eaten.

Frost is reported to have said that he had never written a nature poem. He too took what he needed from wild nature to tell us something about our human nature, often no less wild.

We might be surprised to find that in *I Marry You*, which is subtitled "A Sheaf of Love Poems," the first poem ("Snowy Heron") after the dedicatory one is about a bird. It begins:

> What lifts the heron leaning on the air
> I praise without a name . . .

St. Francis, seeing "the heron on his two soft kissing kites," might have praised God for it. "Cry anything you please," says the poem,

> But praise. By any name or none . . .
>        . . . And doubt all else. But praise.

In the same "Sheaf of Love Poems" is "Two Egrets," birds that are

> like two white hands
> washing one another
> in the prime of light.

What the two, there in their "lit heaven," remind the poet of is "a prayer / and the idea of prayer."

These nature poems, then, are really love poems, poems of the praise which is prayer. Even in the poem about the spider dabbling in its mucky *trompe l'oeil*, the poet professes

> I believe in the world to praise it. I believe
> the act in its own occurrence.

If the birds of the world could get together (as in Chaucer's "The Parlement of Foules") to pick a laureate for their nation, they might well pick John Ciardi, among his other lives a knowledgeable ornithologist. He mentions many kinds of birds, as we might expect from one who in his "Bird Watching" tells how he thumbs through a field guide to identify one that is a

> . . . miracle while it
> is happening, and then instantly incredible for-
> ever . . .

Gulls seem to have been an early favorite,

> . . . ultimate bird
> everywhere and everything pure wing and wind
> are . . .

But later on there are mentions of birds more likely to be seen from the patio or in the neighborhood, birds of at least a dozen different species. These are by no means all of the birds on his life list; there are also birds imagined or read about: the dodo, the Rhino-bird. The sight of even a dead bird "pasted to muck" inspires his "Small Elegy"—seventy lines and more, not one of them mawkish, leading to deeper considerations:

> Have I lost most by wanting less?
> I have not happened anywhere
> on more regret than I could lose,
> nor on more love than I could bear,
> nor on more pity than I could give
> the small sad days to which we live.

In "Back Home in Pompeii" birds stand for the animation that was buried under ash and lava:

> Back home in Pompeii
> birds crunched underfoot,
> stones flew away,
> statues began to bow . . .

Twenty-five years later, the lines gave a title to his 1985 volume, *The Birds of Pompeii.*

A reference to birds can take us into yet another of his lives. About the warbler of "In Some Doubt but Willingly" he writes:

> What an engine this dawn
> has going for it on
> that limb I cannot find . . .

Very well: the bird is an admirable little engine. But for engines in general—
and in his work generalities turn to particulars—he has a limited admiration.
There are exceptions. Possibly remembering his father's death in a traffic accident, he does like the safety of big cars. When he mentions a brand name, it is
likely to be Cadillac. In his "Memo: Preliminary Draft of a Prayer to God the
Father" he can say

> Thank you for the expensive car, its weight and sure tread
> that make it reasonable to go reasonably fast.

In spite of his war experiences, he seems comfortable with the planes that take
him so many places:

> There is no cloud I cannot mount
> and sip good bourbon as I ride . . .

The power mower that helps civilize the environs of the patio comes in for several mentions; it is the subject of his "On the Orthodoxy and Creed of My Power
Mower"—a title that illustrates his tendency to ascend from particulars to a
more reflective and imaginative level. In the poem, the power mower is a dangerous beast, needing to be wheedled and placated by its priest from the service
department. Though fascinated by its might, the poet is not wholly at ease with
this frenzied thing. Twenty-five years before, he had similar misgivings about
farm machinery at harvest:

> Look: there are monsters in the wheat
> . . . all an enormous mouth . . .
> Contraptions of intestines, a surreal sex,
> A planned miscarriage, a hybrid, spit-and-gum
> Lopsided, cockeyed, mad, impossible theorem
>
> That works. Or almost works . . .

Machines are most savagely execrated in the poem bluntly called "Machine,"
the lead-off poem in *For Instance*.

> It goes, all inside itself. It keeps touching
> itself and stinks of it. The stink
> moves a wheel that moves an arm that moves everything.
>
> Or it hunches like a fetus and spins
> its own umbilicus till it sparks.
> Hands off, or it sizzles your hair straight!

> . . . When it dies, we melt it
> and make another that looks different
> no better but does more of the same faster.
>
> . . . There is always that look
> of being inside itself, always that stink.

Confronted by many products of the modern world, Ciardi is contentedly behind the times. In "Obsolescence" he expresses his discomfort with "an Omni-Function Digital Synchro-Mesh / Alarm-Chime wrist watch that beeps *Caro nome,* / (also available with *Vissi d'arte*)." He prefers the old ways of telling time:

> I know time only as a circle. Star time.
> Rotation and orbit time. Dark and lit as tides. . . .
>
> Because I am obsolete, I cannot read it.

As obsolete, he is in many ways Horace's "laudator timporis acti se puero"—a praiser of the good old days, when he was a boy. Most satirists are. Ciardi not only distrusts some of the products of the modern age; he also has a shrewd eye for its follies. When one is as sharp an observer of humanity as he is, one cannot fail to be indignant; indignation can inspire verses, said Juvenal, if all else fails—not that anything else has failed our poet. We have seen a good deal of irony at his own expense: satiric views of himself as soldier, himself as prosperous citizen. The vein of satire grows stronger in the late books. It is directed at Washington, D.C. and its leaders in such jabberwocky-like poems as the "Ballad of the Icondic" (Ike and Dick), at the Internal Revenue Service, at people who build air-raid shelters in their back yards (he once said he was going to build a platform out there, take up a bottle of bourbon, and settle down to watch the spectacular finale). He has poems against officialdom and bureaucracy, against red tape and blue movies, against those who administer cultural programs. As a poet who watches the language and believes in

> . . . his own profession, which is in praise
> of the enlarging word. . .

he is especially sensitive to mishandlings of the language that turn it into cant and jargon. "Elegy Just in Case" burlesques the officialese with which next of kin are informed:

> "Missing as of inst. oblige,
> Deepest sorrow and remain—"

A recent example of this kind of satire takes a line from Dante as its title, "Donne ch'avete intellètto d'amore," in order to parody, by reducing to an absurdity, the trivialization of emotion by our psychosocial jargon. The title contrasts modern interfacing with the romantic but idealistic love that Dante is exalting in *La Vita Nuova;* it is the first line of the famous canzone whose opening might be translated as

> Ladies, who have understanding of what love is,
>> I wish to speak to you about my lady,
>> Not that I can ever praise her enough . . .

It goes on to say such things as

> An angel in heaven offers a prayer, in the mind of God,
>> Saying, "Lord, down on earth is to be seen
>> A creature so marvelous in the effulgence
>> Of her soul that splendor is felt even up here.
>> Heaven, in which nothing is lacking except that
>> She be here with us, implores you, Lord,
>> To convey her hither, and so prays every saint . . .

The modern couple talk like this:

> Mary and I were having an emotion.
> "Thank you for having this emotion with me,"
> Mary said, "I needed a reinforcement
> of my identity through an interaction.
> Have you accomplished a viable realization?"
>
> "I know it was a formative experience,"
> I said to Mary, "and yet, as I critique it
> at my own level, I still feel under-achieved . . ."
>
> "Is that susceptible of remediation?"
>> . . . May I suggest
> a release-therapy impromptu now,
> and a more fully structured enactment later?"

They go on to talk about how "an optimal interpersonal encounter should emphasize mutuality" and how "approval is to be strongly indicated as tendency re-inforcement in trait development . . . relating fully to . . . raised consciousness . . ." Our poet concludes with a prayer:

O intellect of love, may I prove worthy!

There are other lives of Ciardi I wish I could consider: his life as fantasist or fabulist, for instance, as expressed in such poems as "In the Hole." Or the lives he has imagined himself into: those of Ulysses, Launcelot, Hamlet, Leonardo— many others. Or his life as guardian of the language, as shown in his talks on public broadcasting and in the volumes of *A Browser's Dictionary.* Or his life as translator of one of the noblest of poets. Or his life as observer of the process of writing, as revealed in such poems as "An Apology for Not Invoking the Muse," in which he and Erato, Muse of lyric and love poetry, have a discussion about talent, in which he is much too modest, or as revealed in "An Interruption," in which he and Aphrodite have a talk. She is not one of the nine licensed Muses, though she does like to horn in on their function; Ciardi probably liked to hobnob with a Muse who was not establishment.

The life that united all of these other lives, that made them livable and makes them live, was of course his life as poet. Though I have not dwelt specifically on this life, I hope that this little anthology of quotation has given some notion of its richness. I do not believe I know of another poet of the time who more unsparingly translated the events and interests of his several lives into poetry, or another of whom it might more accurately be said, as a great predecessor said of his own life work,

Camerado, this is no book,
Who touches this touches a man.

# *Ciardi at* The Saturday Review

## Norman Cousins

John Ciardi came to *The Saturday Review* as poetry editor in 1956, several years after the death of William Rose Benét, Pulitzer Prize winning poet and one of the founding editors of the magazine. The contrast between the two couldn't have been more striking. Bill Benét sometimes allowed his personal qualities of kindness and supportiveness to affect his choice of poetry for the pages of the magazine. Bill encouraged new poets, not all of whom justified his kindness or his hopes. After his death, Amy Loveman, one of the noblest and kindliest of humans on this earth, selected the poetry—much in the style of Bill Benét.

John Ciardi, on the other hand, was unambiguous, unequivocal, uncompromising. He was the stern sentry at the gate, permitting no one, however needy, poignant, or appealing, to cross the threshold to the pages of *SR* who didn't meet his standards. John Ciardi encouraged no incompetents. The tradition he inherited at *SR* did not prevent him from finding his own voice. And what a voice it was, audible to distant reaches, startling to some, respected by most, understood by all. Sometimes his message seemed to be more the product of a howitzer than of a vox humana. One such occasion found us on opposite sides. John reviewed a new book of poems by Anne Morrow Lindbergh.

> Mrs. Lindbergh's great personal distinction, together with the popularity of her six earlier volumes, some of poetry and some of prose, may be taken as evidence enough that the present volume will sell widely. Poetry, nevertheless, is no reliable consort of either personal distinction or of bookstore success. Everyone is in trouble when he looks at the stars, and under the stars I am as humanly eager to grant Mrs. Lindbergh the dignity of her troubles as I am to enjoin my own. One of my present troubles is that as a reviewer not of Mrs. Lindbergh but of her poems, I have, in duty, nothing but contempt to offer. I am compelled to believe that Mrs. Lindbergh has written an offensively bad book—inept, jin-

gling, slovenly, illiterate even, and puffed up with the foolish afflatus of a stereotyped high-seriousness, that species of esthetic and human failure that will accept any shriek as a true high-C. If there is a judgment, it must go by standards. I cannot apologize for this judgment. I believe that I can and must specify the particular badness of this sort of stuff.

After the review appeared, the roof fell in. Never before or since in the history of *The Saturday Review* had anything in its pages produced a response of such dimensions. Thousands of letters flooded our mailroom. It was no surprise that Anne Morrow Lindbergh had so many admirers. What was surprising was that so many of them were prepared to do violent battle in her behalf. The first wave of the attack on Ciardi produced a counter-wave. Somehow an impression was created that the only way one's letter could be taken seriously, pro or con, was if it was accompanied by a cancellation of subscription.

I was awed by John's courage in taking on one of the most admired individuals in the country, an admiration vastly augmented by deserved sympathy over the tragedy of the kidnapping and death of her son. At the same time, I felt the need to keep the controversy from exploding all over the place. I wrote an editorial in which I tried to bring the contending factions together. I wanted to make known our continued confidence in John. At the same time, I thought we were justified in stating our disagreement with some of the personal references in the review. Some excerpts from the editorial:

> In fairness to Mr. Ciardi, before he is gobbled up alive by our readers, some points ought to be made clear. First, he did inform the editor, before the latter went abroad (there being no connection between the two events), of his intention to write a highly critical review of Mrs. Lindbergh's book. Mr. Ciardi was told that so long as he was Poetry Editor he would continue to enjoy the same authority over his department possessed by other members of the staff. He would have direct access to the columns of the magazine. We would stand behind his right to unobstructed critical opinion; but this did not mean he could count on our automatic support for his views. . . .
>
> It is impossible to edit an independent journal of criticism if the contributors feel free only to mirror the pet ideas of the editor. Our job is to build up a roster of critics with integrity, authority, vigor, and a point of view. The magazine belongs to them and the readers to no less an extent than to the editorial board and the stockholders. The quickest way to devitalize a magazine, we feel, is to claim a monopoly in these pages for tastes of the man who is lucky enough to be editor. . . .
>
> Nor can we accept the adjective "illiterate" when applied to Mrs. Lindbergh or her books. There are few living authors who are using the English language more sensitively or with more genuine appeal. There

is in her books a respect for human responses to beauty and for the great connections between humankind and nature that gives her work rare distinction and that earns her the gratitude and loyalty of her readers, as the present episode makes clear.

This editorial is not intended to chastise Mr. Ciardi. From the moment he joined *The Saturday Review* staff he added real salt to our stew. We have never caught him in an ambiguous moment. He lives as he thinks and writes, with vast energy, freedom, conviction. He has won the very real affection and respect of the entire staff. We believe that in the months and years ahead his relationship with our readers will be no less rewarding to them and to him.

Thirty years later, in retrospect, I wish I had it to do all over again. I'm not sure it was a good idea to indicate any difference with John because of the severity of his review. Whatever my personal feelings, I think I should have given him my unqualified support. In any case, I like to think that that particular episode did not affect our relationship.

Few men have been more consistent in their values or have been more uncompromising in applying their values than John Ciardi. I have cherished his friendship. I have no hesitation in saying that, when I opened a book he published some years ago and saw that he had dedicated it to me, I could think of few honors I prized more highly.

In any event, I am delighted that John is the subject of a Festschrift, and I am especially pleased at the privilege of joining the party. John Ciardi gave contemporary American poetry and criticism a surge and sweep it badly needed. We are all in his debt and it is important that we say so.

# John Ciardi: National Treasure

## Lucien Stryk

John Ciardi's death has diminished our lives. It is just a little comfort to know that in recent years he was made aware of our admiration for him. In times when artists are hardly considered earthshakers it is also a comfort to know that there are still corners where they are made much of in their later years, in other lands more than in our own. In England, for example, posters over gateways and fa-çades of museums proclaim thirty, forty, fifty years of life, on canvas or in stone or in music scores; concert halls, airwaves, resound with fiddlers, and trumpeters rejoice for a too-little-known composer in his golden season. How rarely such generous gestures are made in our harsh country. It is a joy, therefore, to say just a few words about John Ciardi, maker of poems, singer of Dante, crafter of children's tales.

I got to know him a quarter of a century ago, while he was poetry editor and a lively—how often provocative—columnist for *The Saturday Review,* in those days a special place for poetry. His sure taste made the reading of that magazine an adventure, made its pages a living poet's corner, and made it an honor for the chosen to be there. In those days he was active, much in demand, on the circuits, and on occasion he would visit our campus. His poems were bold and stimulating, humorous and wise; his lectures often electrifying, delivered in a measured yet powerful manner. His frequent potshots were well aimed—always at the stupid, cruel, dangerous. His was a classical mind—how clear that was to become when he turned, with such success, to etymology. Yet no one was more sensual in the pleasure he took in the words of poetry, whether original or in translation. His was a mind both civilized and wild, a potent combination, and always with a clean, sharp wit. And in that mind what mattered was poetry.

Who knows by what he will be most fully remembered? All who love Dante will continue to honor Ciardi for the gigantic labor he put into his translation of *The Divine Comedy.* Those who care most for his deeply refined sensibilities will continue to turn to his essays. He wore more than one hat, but all with style and with a keen sense of appropriateness. But I have a strong feeling that he will be best remembered for his poems. I thumb through his *Selected Poems*, stop at one of my favorites, "October 18: Boston." In the next room my wife reads softly to our grandson from *I Met a Man*. John Ciardi made an important difference. I am happy I met him a quarter of a century ago, for the years—as much filled with pain as all others—were made more bearable because of him.

# *Seeing Ciardi Plain*

## Stanley Burnshaw

What to write for the Festschrift on John Ciardi? First question: Which Ciardi? The poet? Naturally, but—the author of the insufficiently lauded *Lives of X* or the writer of—lost for an accurate term—the "lyrical" poems? Neither, of course. In our Age of Literature-Critics others will surely "explain" his verse by one or more of the currently favored "strategies" and, besides, I have already had my say on the basic subject in *The Seamless Web*.

Which John Ciardi, then? The poet-translator of Dante? Out of the question, for lack of requisite scholarship. Why not the writer of children's books? Same answer: incompetence. The anthologist, then, or the lexicographer, or the public speaker, or the man whose *How Does a Poem Mean?* I've all but thumbed to pieces over the years. The jacket of his latest book distinguishes nine John Ciardis, none of whom I am foolish enough to brave. Which leaves me with little choice but to reach beyond—write of a tenth, and in shamelessly personal ways; for at least I should know whereof I speak, grounded in matters recalled, as vivid today as when they occurred twenty-six years ago.

"Your luncheon date has arrived. Mr. Ciardi's behind me—here!" my Holt secretary, Frances Keegan, announced, certain we'd known each other for years. She was wrong. He had been alive in my thoughts for a decade or more, through *The Saturday Review,* his poems, some friends in common; and once, from a hidden spot at an MLA meeting, I had watched while he sparkled before a group of adorers. It was silly, I came to realize, to allow the distance between New York and Metuchen to keep us apart. I suggested a date "to discuss a number of things including verse translation." Having spent much time comparing his recent *Inferno* with a number of other versions, I had questions to ask—and something to show him. What might he think of my new translation project which was not translation at all?

Over lunch we talked of so many people—from Robert Frost to Dudley

Fitts—that the time we'd allotted threatened to end before I could show him the double-page experiment I had carried along. Without explanation, I broke in with, "My daughter's entering college next fall and I want to make sure that she gets to *know* the modernist poets of France, and to judge from my knowledge of what goes on, she'll never really *hear* what their poems are saying. I decided to try my hand at one of the difficult poets—Mallarmé—with a literal rendering, though she's rather familiar with French. But my literal, much more faithful than any translation, wasn't nearly enough to enable a reader to get *into* the poem: very much more was needed—explanations, the same word's multiple meanings, and so on. I did what I thought might work and had it set into type: Mallarmé's 'Don du Poème' on the lefthand page and underneath I wrote a discussion which took up the rest of the space and went on till the foot of the facing page—interweaving the literal line-by-line with all that I thought would bring out the poem as a whole. I mailed it to Henri Peyre and Harry Levin. I want you to see it. Here!"

He started to read at once. He read every word, his eyes swinging back and forth from the French to my English. The instant he'd finished, he turned with a confident "This is *it*! Exactly what has to be done!" I was overwhelmed. "But you can't do this only for French," he went on. "Do you know the Italian poets?" . . . But I'll spare the reader the rest of our conversation, since he may be familiar with John's comment which appears on all the paperback editions of *The Poem Itself*. John had seen in a flash why I'd had to break out of the limits of verse to enable a person with or without any knowledge of French to experience "Don du Poème."

"If I go ahead, I'll be needing helpers. Fitts may be willing to work with me on the Spanish and Calvin Brown on the German. What about *you* for Italian?"

"John Nims is the man. If you've read my anthology, you know that he's also a poet."

"Nims is a friend of Dudley's, too. Oh, if anything comes of this almost-now-too-much-for-me—*pace* Frost's 'Directive'—what in the world should I call it?"

"*The Poem Itself*, of course."

He had not only blessed the idea and offered the perfect title; he also printed my "model" in *The Saturday Review* in the spring of 1960, helping to launch the soon-to-be-published volume.

Thereafter we were able to see each other and talk when his lecture-touring allowed him time to spare in New York. We would usually lunch together, speak about friends—Bill Sloane who had come to the Rutgers Press, for instance, we had both been fond of for years. Often our conservation turned upon Frost. John had seen him from so many vantage points at Bread Loaf and elsewhere as to make whatever he had to say of especial interest to me—the same Robert Frost with whom I'd been spending numberless hours, who could sometimes leave us both equally baffled or at least surprised.

After a lapse of many years, when I found myself trying to write on the long-dead poet, John and I talked about Frost again, but now with a different purpose—with an earnestness to know what we really knew. For the most part, we talked by letters, which opened for me some windows on the Ciardi mind—one complexity pondering a different complexity, in the course of which, by putting words down on paper, he seemed to learn the fill of his thoughts as they clashed to rest. Our correspondence taught me to see the uniqueness of one facet of this multifaceted poet-translator-anthologist-orator-critic-*et al.* which had gone, so far as I knew, unmarked by his fellows. Myself included, despite the fact that at least two decades before it was there for me to behold: an almost fatal capacity for piercing into the core of a personality which had made an art of its self-revealing concealment.

I had seen it plain in his Frost memorial issue of *The Saturday Review* of February 23, 1963. "Robert Frost: To Earthward," John had called his editorial, after the well-known poem: the centerpiece of a tribute made of thoughtfully chosen essays by John F. Nims, Charles Anderson, and others. I quote only parts of the whole, but each sentence has a truth of its own that takes its place in a large, encompassing whole. I might even call it a documentary poem in prose: documentary of a person known by name in a public time and place; a poem interweaving figures, metaphor, statements, ideas under the pressures of feeling—of wonder—of quiet awe, if you will:

> Robert Frost was a primal energy. There were serenities in the man as time brought them to him, but there was in him a volcano of passion that burned to his last day. . . .
>
> To be greatly of the earth earthy demands the bitter sweat and scald of first passions. That heat could erupt into cantankerousness at times, and even into the occasional meanness of which violent temper is capable. But the splutters of cantankerousness and the violences of temper were only surface bubbles on the magmatic passions of the man, part of the least traits that accompany intensity.
>
> It is just that passionate intensity that must be realized before the man can be loved, mourned—and read—in his own nature. . . . His genius, wild and ardent, remains to us in his poems. It is the man we lose, a man salty and rough with the earth trace, and though towering above it, never removed from it, a man above all who could tower precisely because he was rooted in real earth. . . .

"Documentary poem in prose" falls short of a faithful description, and it cannot, of course, serve in discussing certain kinds of shorter Ciardi poems which have made a special place in my mind. Yet for reasons past my trying to state in a Festschrift contribution, "Robert Frost: To Earthward" and the something in it that makes it unique bear unmistakable kinship with certain other Ciardi poems that for me have especial significance. One of them is the first in the "Conversations" part of his book of *Selected Poems*. It comes forth—to borrow the jacket-writer's phrase—"in a voice no reader of poetry would mistake for any other," and continues to speak in that voice till the end. It is called "Memo: Preliminary Draft of a Prayer to God the Father"—

> Sir, it is raining tonight in Towson, Maryland.
> It rained all the way from Atlanta, the road steaming
> slicks and blindnesses, almost enough to slow for.
> Thank you for the expensive car, its weight and sure tread
> that make it reasonable to go reasonably fast.

I have no way of knowing when this "Memo" was written, but whatever its date, the author set it free to live on its own at least a year before releasing "Mutterings," in *The Birds of Pompeii*—

> I may have no more to say to my left arm.
> We used to be friends till it took to hanging out
> with a cervical pinch. Now it sleeps all day
> or wakens to needle me. When I try to sleep
>
> it raises foolish questions. I do not care
> to be interrogated by my components.

It goes on for almost 28 lines till we hear it saying

> I'm bone-weary
> of being nagged to death from inside. And still
> the questions come, and one of them is the answer.

It is tempting to mark out aspects of these poems, compare them, point to "curious" ways in which each one of them faces the world. Or how these poems both differ and relate to Part II of "Three Views of a Mother" and, again, to "In the Hole," both in *Selected Poems*. By now, however, I've come to consider it wiser not to attempt such a disquisition; to read and reread such poems as these instead, never forgetting that others also call from this poet's pages with quietly compelling voices of their own.

# *For John Ciardi: In Praise of Humor*

## William White

I have been leery of a Festschrift since reading one produced for a professor I once knew whose entire bibliography consisted of one book and a handful of articles that filled a page and a half and who was honored because he was an affable fellow and played a good hand of bridge.

Now, John Ciardi was also an affable fellow, and I don't know how his bridge was; but in 1959, when Wayne State University Press published my *John Ciardi: A Bibliography*, his list of books, poems, anthologies, articles and book reviews filled 65 pages. As the bibliography was published in connection with an exhibition of Ciardi's manuscripts and books (from the Charles E. Feinberg collection) and a lecture by Ciardi at the Detroit Public Library, Ciardi began his amusing prefatory note to the *Bibliography* by saying:

> When a friend of mine heard that Charles Feinberg was arranging for a bibliography of my writing, he said: "But you're not even dead yet!"
> "Knowing Charles Feinberg," I told him, "is better than being dead."

Continuing in this funereal tone, John said: "A good friend is not only better than being dead; he is the best thing to be alive for. . . . A bibliography does seem like a portentous thing to carry around the neck. Or is it more like incipient rigor mortis? . . . [And] a bibliography is a bit more like a bronze casket." Finally, in my own copy of the book, the subject of the bibliography wrote: "For Bill White, / the Friendly undertaker / from John Ciardi, / the happy corpse, / with lively thanks / for good burial / service."

I have quoted this at length not because it's an unpublished John Ciardi inscription, but because it shows how his sense of humor made a dull chore lively and prevented him from taking himself too seriously. For, though he took the writing of poetry with all the dedication and seriousness the craft demands, he used a light touch on other matters. This enabled him, over the years, to combine writing serious poetry with a wide variety of interests, some of great seriousness, some otherwise.

Award-winning poet (Avery Hopwood, Oscar Blumenthal, Eunice Tiejens, Levinson, and Prix de Rome prizes), English professor (Harvard, Kansas City, Rutgers, Florida), columnist (*The Saturday Review*), translator (Dante's *Divine Comedy*), and anthology editor (*How Does a Poem Mean?*), John Ciardi not only was heard and seen on radio and TV, he lectured to thousands from coast to coast. In doing all this he became one of the best-known figures in current American letters.

In *Odyssey: A Journal of the Humanities*, published by Oakland University in November 1979, which introduced six new poems from Ciardi's then new volume of poetry, *For Instance*, my wife, Gertrude M. White, summed up this multifaceted aspect of his career:

> On the face of the record, Ciardi has thus lived a remarkably active and public life, not to mention earning a great deal more money than most poets ever see on the club, college, and university lecture circuit. There would seem to have been little time in such a career for meditation, introspection, and for waiting upon a notoriously unreliable Muse. No one knew this better than Ciardi himself or has said it so well. "An Apology for Not Invoking the Muse" puts the case crisply:
>
> > "Beloved," I said, "I didn't want to bother you.
> > I thought I could say this little on my own,
> > the way it happens to us in our smallness."
>
> But Erato, Muse of lyric and amatory poetry, will accept no such plea. "See for yourself what comes of that!" she snaps and "was gone wherever she goes. . . ." In silence the poet reads what he has written and despairs:
>
> > How had I dared imagine I might dare
> > be only what I am?
> > > and yet . . .
> > > > and yet . . .
>
> Ciardi has dared to imagine that he might, as a poet, be only what he was. And what that is he sees as clearly and puts far more forthrightly than would most observers.

I knew John Ciardi for about thirty years: yes, he was always affable: more than that, much more, he usually had something to say, something worthwhile, and when he said it he used his deep, rich voice that, once you heard, you

124

recognized. It was the same thing when you read his poetry or his prose: it always sounded like John Ciardi.

In 1956, just after I had been asked to take over the editorship of the *Walt Whitman Newsletter*—which shortly after that became the *Walt Whitman Review* and is now the *Walt Whitman Quarterly Review*—I needed articles for the very first issue. For nobody knew we were alive, having just been given birth by Wayne State University Press, with a big assist by Charles E. Feinberg. I asked Ciardi, busy as he was with teaching, *The Saturday Review,* poetry, and a dozen other enterprises, for a contribution. Looking over my file of back issues of the *Walt Whitman Newsletter* recently, there on pages 10 and 11 of my issue No. 1, I discovered Ciardi's interesting—everything he wrote is interesting—piece "Whitman's Principle of Selection." And looking over another file, I find a new small publication, the Walt Whitman Birthplace Association's *Starting from Paumanok,* Vol. 1, No. 1, Fall 1984; and there on page 3 is "Ciardi: On Whitman." Just as interesting as in 1956, as sensitive, as readable, as stimulating.

Speaking of Charles Feinberg, it was usually at his home in Detroit, among his wonderful collection of books by and about Whitman and by and about modern American poets that I met and talked to and had a drink or two with John Ciardi. When you're here, the owner of these beautiful first editions and hundreds of rare manuscripts is so enthusiastic about his literary treasures and has so much to show you, no one else can do or say much, but when Ciardi was there he was a lot of pleasant competition for Charlie Feinberg. Naturally, both had a great love for great and fine books. Both also loved Jack Daniels. Those were wonderful nights.

Looking at the photo in *John Ciardi: A Bibliography,* taken at the Bread Loaf Writers' Conference, where the poet was director, I find it hard to think of John as almost seventy. Even so, he was still full of energy, still full of poetry, full of pleasant talk—he always was on the occasions when I saw him. Both for what he was and especially for what he did for poetry and for spreading the love of poetry among those who came into professional and personal contact with him, he deserves to be honored. And I am flattered and also honored to make a small contribution to that end for a fine fellow and a friend.

# Looking for John Ciardi at Bread Loaf

## John Williams

Bread Loaf lies in a cluster of mountains in central Vermont, some ten or fifteen miles from Middlebury, the nearest town of any consequence. It is a landlocked island of a wilderness so soft that it seems almost contrived. A dozen or so buildings—from tiny cottages to spacious three-story houses—are scattered randomly upon many acres of gently rolling fields, and in the near distance Bread Loaf Mountain lies squat upon the horizon. The quietness is palpable, and the remoteness sudden.

I first came to Bread Loaf in the summer of 1966 at the invitation of William Sloane, who had been a longtime staff member at the Bread Loaf Writers' Conference. Sloane had apparently read a novel of mine published the year before, had liked it, and on that basis had issued the invitation. The novel had, I thought, fallen into that abyss that seems to await so many novels, and I was pleased that someone other than a friend or acquaintance had read it. I knew that John Ciardi had been director of the Conference for a number of years, and I believe I thought at the time that it was odd that Ciardi had not written me himself, and that my correspondent remained Bill Sloane. But that was the way it was, and I came to Bread Loaf knowing only Ciardi's work and reputation; I did not know the man, even through a letter. And I wanted to know him; I had admired his work, from which I knew that we both had been poor boys during our growing up in the Depression and that we both had fought as enlisted men in the Air Force in World War II.

But I did not get to know him until much later, later than I would have thought.

I was driven up to Vermont by a friend whom I had been visiting in Massachusetts, and I arrived on the Bread Loaf grounds the day before the Conference

126

was to begin. The place was nearly deserted, though it was mid-afternoon. I settled myself in the room to which I had been assigned, accustomed myself to the high ceilings and a closet as large as many a bedroom, and at last walked outside into the amber softness of the late Vermont afternoon.

The literature that Bill Sloane had sent me suggested that one might find a drink at a cottage named Treman, a tiny three-room house set apart for the use of staff and fellows. So I found Treman, met a few members of the staff, and had a few drinks. I began to think that there was no John Ciardi, for he was nowhere to be seen. In my nervousness and dislocation, I got into a senseless argument with Dan Wakefield (who, like me, was there for the first time as a staff member). I went to bed early, wondering not for the first nor the last time in my life why I was where I was. Thus, unpromisingly, began the first six consecutive summers that I was to be on the Bread Loaf staff.

The ruffled feelings caused by the argument with Dan Wakefield were soothed by both of us in a few days, we became friends, and we have remained friends for more than twenty years. But there was no such unlikely beginning of friendship with John Ciardi. I saw him first the next night, when he gave his opening welcome to the students and fellows of Bread Loaf; I was to learn that it changed very little from year to year. The welcome was warm and assured; without it being said, it was clear that Ciardi assumed that we all were engaged in an enterprise that was serious, though not necessarily earnest, and that good writing mattered. It was a civilized welcome, and Ciardi seemed wholly at ease, almost intimate, with the two hundred odd people who were his listeners. It was not the last time that I was to see this extraordinary rapport that Ciardi managed to establish, almost immediately, with an audience of strangers. We all had the feeling that Ciardi was speaking to us individually, rather than to a group.

This was not the way that those of us who did not know him felt the first few times we talked to him alone, or in a small group. There was an awkwardness that was almost brusque, a manner almost impatient; one felt held off, excluded—from what, one did not quite know. Once or twice during the two weeks of Bread Loaf, he would slip unobtrusively into one of the classes we taught, sitting always at the back, listening intently and without expression; he would come in a few minutes after the class began and leave a few minutes before the class was over. We never knew what he thought, which might have been disconcerting had we had time to consider it. But we did not. Within a very few days we were caught up in the intensity of Bread Loaf, an intensity that few of us had known before, at other conferences or in our classrooms, wherever they were. Time was unlike ordinary time, and we began to think of that vast area that stretched in all directions below the mountain as the Other World.

By the end of the two weeks at Bread Loaf, I had established friendships with several members of the staff that have lasted over the many years since, and I had managed a civil, if distant, acquaintanceship with John Ciardi. I left Bread Loaf that summer of 1966, glad that I had gone, faintly disappointed that I had not got to know Ciardi better, and assuming that I would not return. I had looked for John Ciardi, and I had not found him.

But I was asked to return the next summer (this time by John Ciardi himself), and I went back every summer thereafter until 1972. And if in those six years I did not find John Ciardi, at least I discovered the territory he lived in, and we became friends.

Looking back, I begin to realize how difficult those years were, the middle and late sixties; anyone who could afford a ballpoint pen or a typewriter was allowed to think of himself as a poet or a novelist; talent and craft were suspect, more often than not described as "elitist," a curse-word of the period; and literacy was thought by many to be a species of corruption, a loss of innocence or a kind of damnation. It was, alas, a hysteria to which a few staff members, who should have known better, surrendered. And yet in those difficult years, somehow Bread Loaf managed to survive, even to thrive, against the pressures of mediocrity. I'm afraid that it took me some time to realize that, at Bread Loaf, at least, the mainstay against the encroachment of that old enemy was John Ciardi himself.

To all appearances, he was an unlikely mainstay. He was always around, but he seemed to be not intimately connected with the running of the Conference itself. I saw him (and I see him now) sitting, night after night, at the large table in the living room at Treman, playing cribbage, first with Doc Klompus and later with Miller Williams, drinking his bourbon steadily and almost soberly; in the late afternoons, throwing a Frisbee to his German Shepherd, Dippy, a dog that seemed almost as much a loner as John himself; or perfecting his stroke by swinging a golf club against the undriveable meadows of the Bread Loaf fields. He seemed to me almost indifferent to what went on around him.

He was not, of course.

Somehow, without being told, he knew everything that went on. That seemingly indifferent eye was always the first to see when a student (or for that matter a staff member) might begin to crack under the incremental intensity of the Conference; and the voice that could be brusque and impatient in casual encounters seemed always to know exactly what to say to calm the raw nerve or to steady the teetering psyche. With an irascibility that was almost sentimental, he protected the privacy of the staff and the dignity of the students; and if there were privileges accorded to any, they were the privileges of talent rather than rank. The essential kindness of the man was not displayed casually, as a social grace; thus it sometimes went unperceived. But it was there always, in an extremity of need.

Appearances do not always deceive, but often enough they do; for appearances are what we make of things that sometimes we do not understand. I think I first began to allow my friendship with John Ciardi when I realized that his occasional brusqueness with acquaintances, and even friends, was the mask that tries to disguise affection and an innate shyness; and when I realized that the salient quality of the man's character was loyalty.

He was loyal to his own past, to the circumstances in which he was born and from which he emerged, perhaps more determined by them than he wished to be; he was loyal to his friends, to their strengths as well as their weaknesses, knowing that the one is always necessary to the other; and perhaps above all, he was loyal to the art he practiced, the principles of that art, and to the integrity of his work. However posterity may judge the ultimate worth of his own work (if, indeed, posterity has any business making such a judgment), it cannot but admit him into the select company of those who are essential to the stubborn and somehow miraculous persistence of civilization.

I shall let others in this volume speak of John Ciardi as poet, translator, literary journalist, lexicographer, lecturer, teacher; few Americans have been such men of letters, and it seems evident that even fewer will be in the immediate future. But for some of us who were there during the Ciardi years, it must seem that Bread Loaf was the circumstance in which Ciardi could best and most truly be seen, the circumstance in which the strengths of the writer were most clearly manifest in the world outside his own work, the world we all live in. He was deeply loyal to Bread Loaf, to the idea and the actuality. It was a dream, perhaps, but a dream that now and then touched upon what we sometimes think of as reality. It was a community of writers that Ciardi imagined, a community that worked toward something other than the preening of pretty feathers, the promotion of self, or the display of sensitivity. For many of us the days we spent together there those summers were a time of magic, in the older sense of that word. Though we had been to other conferences before, and would be at others afterwards, to all of us Bread Loaf was in another country, a better country. After we had been there for a while, we knew that we would never be quite the same again, nor did we wish to be.

For we began to see more clearly than we had done before what Ciardi knew and what Bread Loaf was all about: that there were others like us, alive and dead, that there was a community of writers, alive and dead, and that what we did was ultimately important—important beyond our imperfections, our weaknesses, our vanities. That most anticlerical of men, beyond himself and beyond us, showed us the pride of work, and the sacramental nature of work. And the joy.

Those are the Bread Loaf years, the Ciardi years, those late New England summer days, that I remember—and John Ciardi, who seemed to do nothing and who did everything, who sat at his table in Treman, drank his bourbon, played his cribbage, growled, and made it all possible.

# *John Ciardi and the "Witch of Fungi"*

## Maxine Kumin

Long before I actually met John Ciardi, he had attained a mythic stature in my eyes. My mentor in the late fifties, Professor John Holmes of Tufts, who arranged for me to teach freshman composition part-time at his university, had befriended Ciardi, a student there, twenty years earlier. Holmes delighted in describing the young John, a lanky undergraduate, slouching half-diffidently, half-belligerently into his office to toss a sheaf of new poems on the desk.

"See what you make of these," I imagine him saying, as offhandedly as if he were delivering laundry lists instead of lifeblood. And Holmes, taking a long time over his pipe, scraping the bowl, sucking the stem, striking three or four matches, while young John (as I imagine it) wanders around the room, pulling books of poetry off the shelves, poking them back in, probably deranging Holmes' careful alphabetizing.

All of us poets have shared the desperate ardor of the new poem and many of us have been lucky enough to attach ourselves as disciples to a master. Eventually the balance shifts and we are then mentors ourselves—not nearly so comfortable a situation. Ciardi then stood with a foot in both camps for me. He had studied with the eminent teacher of poets, he had gone on to fame as a poet himself, he was listed on the masthead of *The Saturday Review* as Poetry Editor.

Moreover, he was a charismatic reader of his own poems, filling the hall with acolytes and admirers, holding them spellbound with his easy articulation. My favorites were his tribal poems: "Three Views of a Mother" in which he describes his mother foraging for wild mushrooms and himself sitting across the table from her, helping to clean them, is surely a classic. Then there was "Elegy," which begins: "My father was born with a spade in his hand. . . ." Best of all, I remember Ciardi reciting, from the cycle dedicated to Judith, "Men marry what they need. I marry you . . ." to a hushed gathering, and how I went away in a kind of trance, thinking that poems could say so much in such gorgeously

131

constraining ways. John Ciardi was the first poet who alerted me to the oral-aural possibilities of the public performance. He did not dramatize, he did not embarrass; he simply spoke the lines and they lodged themselves in my head so that I may always have them, in his tone of voice.

Years passed, as they say in storybooks. In the summer of 1969, at Ciardi's invitation, I joined the staff of the Bread Loaf Writers' Conference, which he directed. It was the first of seven seasons for me there, all stamped with Ciardi's sometimes formidable presence. Sometimes, on drizzly afternoons, a group of us would stump out to forage for mushrooms, which abound in late August in Vermont. I can still hear John, who punctuated most lunches with a call for silence in the dining hall in order to make his announcement: "The Witch of Fungi will lead a mushroom walk at three o'clock." It became our custom to fry these comestibles in the staff kitchen to accompany the cocktail hour. I can't remember whether John was an eater or avoider of our exotica. But, judging from his poem and from his general zest, I think he partook.

# *Dionysian Memories*

## Diane Wakoski

I am part of the generation which was in high school and college in the 50s and remembers *The Saturday Review of Literature* as a force in American culture. Our teachers all read it, and I think I read *at* it in the library, and I remember that I was always intrigued with the wit in John Ciardi's "Trade Winds" column when I read it, but in fact I really only knew him as a name until I went to Bread Loaf as a fellow in 1964, after my first (trade) book of poems, *Discrepancies and Apparitions*, had been published by Doubleday. As I am now, I was then a maverick, but like all mavericks I especially enjoy the recognition of "the establishment" and John was certainly as much a part of it then as anyone. What I remember most from that first year of being there was that I brought the new order with me, the interest in writing "workshops" as opposed to "clinics": both the more Dionysian and the more democratic vision to poetry. And that John, contrary to some people's beliefs, was in fact the first to endorse this new order and one of the first to be generous to me about my poetics. In fact, it was he who labeled me (I suppose at first just punning on my name) "Dionysian" Wakoski. The following year I was invited back to Bread Loaf as a faculty member, and the succeeding year; then John was deposed, and I've never been back to Bread Loaf. And I seldom had the opportunity to see John in succeeding years, but I often teach or recommend some of his poems to my students who represent quite another generation of American poetry. In so many ways, John always seemed to be the epitome of what the Whitman tradition honors: he valued his roots in common people, he embraced the "crudeness" of American culture as its vitality, and demonstrated this by his love of gambling, of sexuality, of the physical nature of the world, and he did have a vision of how big our language really is, how its European stream is only a trickle into the wider American mainstream of language. I say these things because I think many people see only

133

another side of the man, one that because of its erudition seems to exclude the vitality of the New American Poetry. But, as he was misunderstood at Bread Loaf, he continues to be mis-viewed in the light of current fashions. But then this country has a history of not honoring its real poets as it should. Thus, in this way I see John Ciardi as another important poet participating in the truest of American traditions.

# *Ciardi Remembered*

## Judson Jerome

The name *Ciardi* and how to pronounce it were introduced to me when I was a Ph.D. candidate at Ohio State, about 1951. We used as a textbook in modern poetry John Ciardi's *Mid-Century American Poets*, a seminal anthology in which all of the fifteen major poets who had emerged since WWII made a personal selection of the poems by which they wished to be represented, accompanied (except in the case of Robert Lowell) by the poet's own statement of poetic principles (an essay on Lowell's poetry by Randall Jarrell accompanied Lowell's work). Ciardi proclaimed in his introduction that American poetry had outgrown the "barbaric yawp" of Whitman and that a new "sanity" was emerging. That sanity seemed for a while to be a castle in the sand, all but obliterated by the orgiastic waves of "Howl" and its imitators, but nonetheless it is one of the few anthologies I have gone back to again and again and recommend often to others in my books and articles.

In the mid-fifties I was a professor of literature at Antioch and poetry editor of *The Antioch Review*, for which I wrote an annual roundup review of recent books of poetry. That's how I came upon *As If: Poems New and Selected*, published in 1955. There, among other remarkable poems which have become some of the lasting furnishings of my mind (such as "Men Marry What They Need. I Marry You"), I found one of the least likely titles for a poem in our literature: "Thoughts on Looking into a Thicket." I still advise poets not to use titles like that. But the poem shook me to the roots with its brawny, magnificent celebration of life. "If I ever let myself become miserable," I thought, "if I ever fail to make use of the material life dumps upon me, I am a fool."

I don't want to discuss it again at length here (I devoted a column to the poem in *Writer's Digest*, later incorporated in *The Poet and the Poem*) but I will mention a couple of things that made it especially powerful for the shavetail professor and budding poet who happened upon it thirty years ago. It seemed to me

135

to open up whole ranges of new ground for poetry, doing things with the language which I, at least, had never seen done. The poem starts off talking about a particular species of spider, *phrynarachne d.* Who had used such terms in poetry? That spider was one "to whom a million or a billion years / in the humorless long gut of all the wood / have taught the art of mimicking a bird turd." That blunt term, too, staked out acres of new ground. The next stanza quotes an entymological text, apparently verbatim, though the language falls gracefully into pentameter as Ciardi arranged it—suggesting still more possibilities for poetry that I had never dreamed of—explaining how the spider weaves an imitation of "the more liquid portion" then squats in the center to imitate the "more solid central portion of the excreta."

*Who writes poems about such matters,* I wondered; *who incorporates such material, and why?* And how often had I read a poem that kept me on the edge of my chair as this one was doing? The justification of the poem is contained in some of its most memorable lines: "If you / will be more proper than real, that is your / death. I think life will do anything for a living." I can only describe that statement as profoundly liberating. Liberating, too, were the poem's brilliant techniques, the lifting of such unpromising information as the opening stanzas contained to an iridescent art. The poem concludes:

> if there are kisses, flies will lay their eggs
> in the spent sleep of lovers; if there is time,
> it will be long enough. And through all time,
> the hand that strokes my darling slips to bone
> like peeling off a glove; my body eats me
> under the nose of God and Father and Mother.
> I speak from thickets and from nebulae:
> till their damnation feed them, all men starve.

He was teaching us the oracular manner, the stance of eloquence, in the age of Eisenhower! Here was passion, vision, profundity and poignancy all combined. How does a poem earn the right to make any statement about all men? How does it rise to such majesty from the perspective of a bird turd and the dry language of a scientific text? This was a poem a young poet (well, ten years younger than Ciardi; I was nearly thirty, with a wife and three daughters) could learn from.

Among other things, I was learning to feed on my damnation, to find at least some way to bet on the imagination, whatever hand was dealt. In 1956 Ciardi came out of academic seclusion into popular prominence by assuming the post of poetry editor of *The Saturday Review* with a manifesto announcing his commitment to publish good modern poetry instead of the very conventional verse

136

that magazine had customarily printed. He also wrote a column for the magazine, bringing to it what the magazine most needed—"controversy."

One of Ciardi's first articles as poetry editor was a strong and serious attack on the popular verse of Anne Morrow Lindbergh. This set off a spate of enraged letters to the editor, a brouhaha such as the magazine had not known since the controversy over Ezra Pound's winning of the Bollingen Award in 1949.

Among other things in his manifesto, Ciardi had said that another sonnet would appear in *SR*, if I remember correctly, "over my dead body." Until that point I had had no personal contact or correspondence with Ciardi, but he was my hero, which meant my natural antagonist. I began sending sonnets, sonnets, nothing but sonnets, to *The Saturday Review*.

And he took one, but only after insisting that I work on it more—not making specific suggestions, but pointing out a weak line; I revised the line and the poem improved immensely. I have known only one other poetry editor, Robert Wallace, who would do that—comment very specifically on a rejected poem to help me see the problem in such a way that I could get back inside the poem and discover it freshly, and then invite resubmission of the poem.

One poem ("Love, the First Decade," written on the occasion of my tenth wedding anniversary in 1958) went back to him at least three times. It was the ending which was wrong. I was trying to make the point that I accepted and celebrated the steady but less exciting love that sustains a marriage after the romance has passed. But it came out as sounding as though my love for my wife had become routine and dull. "That's a hell of a thing to tell a woman," he wrote me. I tried again and again—and finally hit upon a pair of lines I still like: ". . . how stodginess conquers love. Love, love me fast / and witlessly: the serious years fall fast." The poem finally appeared in *The Saturday Review* on the same page as a new poem by Robert Frost.

Meanwhile we had developed a somewhat substantial correspondence, and I was using his textbook, *How Does a Poem Mean?* in my classes. (Incidentally, I have never found a better explanation anywhere of the inner dynamics of a poem, of the way to know when a poem is *over*, than the discussion of "countermotion" in that book.) Eventually I arranged for an invitation for him to speak at Antioch. That was 1957, shortly after the first City Lights publication of "Howl." I had a review copy of the pamphlet, which was already being banned by the Post Office for its language, thus bringing Allen Ginsberg to national prominence. Robert Lowell, on the basis of this poem and other early "beatnik" poetry, had hailed a "West Coast Renaissance" in *The New York Times*—and had renounced pentameter in his own work. "Academic poetry," as it was labeled, the poetry following the tradition of those poets (including myself) that Ciardi had collected in *Mid-Century American Poets* was broadly perceived to have gone stale.

137

And what a speaker John proved to be on our assembly stage! His powerful voice and frame would become familiar to millions who heard him on radio or saw him on television or in the lecture hall, but it was all new to me then, and though I could never attain his physical stature and dramatic baritone, I was learning the importance to a poet of presence, of delivery. I wanted to mount a production of *Antony and Cleopatra* with John playing Antony to Eartha Kitt's Cleopatra, a notion I shared once with him, but he laughed it off. Imagine it: "I am dying, Egypt, dying," gasped out in a rumble like a barrel rolling down stairs.

In 1960 John recommended me for the Amy Lowell Traveling Poetry Scholarship, which, coinciding with my first sabbatical, enabled me and my family to spend the 1960–61 academic year in England and Spain. I had started writing my poetry column for *Writer's Digest;* my poetry was appearing regularly in magazines, and my first collection appeared in 1963. I was, one might say, launched; it was John Ciardi who, in large part, had launched me.

In 1967 John invited me to join the staff of Bread Loaf, and again in 1968. The experience completely changed my attitudes about writers' conferences. The few appearances I had made at such gatherings had convinced me that they were no more than occasions for the untalented to gather autographs of the dubiously glamorous; but the quality of both the student and staff writers at Bread Loaf was impressive and the social contacts were at the least worthwhile personally and sometimes of genuine benefit to young careers. I attended every workshop and found myself learning as much as I taught from such regulars as John Frederick Nims, Miller Williams, Hollis Summers, Robert Pack, and, of course, Ciardi.

But they were heady times—and the times had gone to my head. In addition to their serious purposes, the Bread Loaf sessions were for some the occasion for partying and philandering, activities I participated in as eagerly as I did the workshops and lectures. I earned enough of a reputation in that regard to receive a warning along with my invitation to return, but my indulgences in 1968 turned out to be even more extensive than they had been the year before. The walls of the buildings at Bread Loaf are paper thin, and though John and the management had no desire to regulate morals, they demanded a discretion I failed to muster.

I can think of a lot of excuses, but they won't stand up in court. 1968 was one of the watershed years of our century. The assassination of Martin Luther King had brought the nation close to revolution. Then the assassination of Robert Kennedy at the crest of a brawling, bitter, multisided contention for the Democratic nomination. Then, while we were at Bread Loaf, Russia's invasion of Czechoslovakia. We went home from Bread Loaf to the news of the Democratic

Convention in Chicago and all the violence which surrounded it. Black power. The counterculture. Drugs. Communes. I was wearing my hair shoulder length and making inflammatory speeches on campuses around the country. I had an article accepted by *Life*, "The System Really Isn't Working," which was launching me on a new career as a social and educational reformer—and I was a little crazy with it all. And in my mind, licentious behavior was somehow mixed up with political radicalism, part of the agenda for the emerging counterculture.

Each of the staff members was given the opportunity to present an evening lecture or reading, and never before or since have I felt so challenged to perform well for my peers and superiors. Though I had given many public lectures (beyond the classroom, that is), I had never done so without a written script, as I had to do that evening at Bread Loaf—one of the last sessions—because I simply didn't have the time (given my heavy social schedule in addition to my duties giving workshops and holding private meetings with individual poets) to prepare one. So I winged it, talking about how I felt my own poetry was shifting to meet the emergency demands of the age, interspersing the talk with readings from my poems. To my astonishment the audience responded with such enthusiasm that I have never since written out a speech. I looked through the audience for John, but I could not find him and assumed he had skipped it. But afterward, back at Treman, he came over to congratulate me. "I didn't think you were there," I said, and he explained that he sat in an overstuffed chair back in the wings, out of sight.

"Well, I'm glad you liked it, John. That gives me courage to say something I have been wanting to say all summer. I realized that I have promoted you in my mind—from father to brother."

"Thank you, Jud," he said. I think that he was pleased, and so was I; one who has a brother is a brother.

Still, I knew that I would never be invited back to Bread Loaf. I didn't mind *that* so much, but I was sorry to have wrecked, I thought, my friendship with John. He didn't answer my letters. I saw him once as our paths crossed in the Newark airport, and he was cordial enough. But as my books appeared and I sent them to him, once with a letter reviewing and apologizing for my behavior at Bread Loaf, there was still no response.

When to my surprise he supplied my publisher with favorable, quotable comments on a couple of my books, I didn't know what to make of it. I would write him my thanks and get no answer. A dozen years of communal life wearing hard on our middle ages, Mary and I moved back to Yellow Springs, Ohio, where Antioch is located, and, considerably mellowed, settled comfortably back into a more conventional life. Then, after seeing John interviewed on the CBS *Sunday Morning* show, I tried another letter—and this time he answered warmly. I was suggesting that he do another anthology which might sum up the age as well as *Mid-Century American Poets* had done, that he issue another call for "sanity," collecting those poets who, like himself, have never abandoned form, abandoned art, in pursuit of indulgent self-expression and trendy experimentation. John suggested I do it myself after canvassing the poets listed in the *Directory of American Poets and Fiction Writers* published by Poets and Writers to see if there was any consensus at all in the literary community as to who were the major poets writing today. Whether that project will ever come off, I don't know, but meanwhile I felt back in touch with my major mentor.

I know now, because he was kind and honest enough to tell me so, why he didn't respond to my letters. I asked him directly and he answered directly. I pass it along here only for what it says about John Ciardi. Why didn't he write?

"I simply did not know how," he wrote me finally. "You seemed to be full of big pronouncements and hot positive assertions. I'd find myself saying, 'What the hell do I say to that?' . . . Those letters troubled me in ways I couldn't deal with."

I know of no other modern writer who has been as generous of spirit and outreaching in recognizing talents (often—in fact, usually—quite different from his own) and finding ways to support and assist newly emerging writers. Again and again he "discovered" both novelists and poets early in their careers and gave them boosts as he gave me one. He was as eloquent and convincing in the language of praise as in that of condemnation.

I remember him at Bread Loaf sailing a Frisbee for his great German shepherd, Dippy (for Serendipity, he reminded me—"which was to please the kids. His kennel registry pedigree name was Bejomy's Neo, which was for (Be)nn, (Jo)nnel, and (My)ra, plus Neo because that's what he was when we got him"). Dippy was a great bounding beast tearing across a wide swath of lawn to leap, twist, and snatch the Frisbee unfailingly from the air. John would take it from the—rump-waggling, slobbering dog—and would swing his arm back to hurl it like a discus, his lithe body like a tightening and unwinding spring. *Achieve! Achieve!* he demanded. And the dog, like so many of us, went after it. It was a romp.

# *John Ciardi: His Wit and Witness*

## John Stone

*wit* n. [ME fr. OE; akin to OHG
*wizzi* knowledge, OE *witan* to
know]

At the age of fifty, I've known many people who lived by their *wits*, but none
have done so more successfully and more completely, in all etymologic senses of
the word, than John Ciardi.

From what I can tell, this living by his wits came very early—certainly it was
present during his military service in WWII. During those horrific years when
so many of his comrades failed to come back (and of which he writes so com-
pellingly in *Lives of X*), John's resourcefulness equipped him, his wit saved him,
and luck brought him back alive—to teach us all, both in and out of academia.
The clear turning point seems to have come while he was at Rutgers, his last
formal teaching post. He was fond of telling—and writing—about the two
stacks of papers needing attention on his desk: his own writing and the papers of
his students. There came, inexorably, the day when (John liked to chuckle here)
"my own papers seemed more interesting to me than those of my students." At
this point he'd been in academia many years (Kansas City, Tufts, Harvard, and
Rutgers) and, as he phrased it to me a few months ago, "was in mortal danger of
becoming Chairman of the Rutgers English Department." Resigning from Rutgers, John decided to trust his wit completely and it seems never to have failed
him during the remaining decades of his life.

I knew John's wits well before I met the man. His wits and his wit I met first in
the pages of *The Saturday Review*. The man, I met at the Bread Loaf Writers'
Conference, in 1969. I'd been asked, at the suggestion of my friend and fellow
poet, Miller Williams, to be the Conference Physician. John Ciardi's wits, I
learned, fit the man—both were writ large, both were full of ambiguities and of
grace, and both were in indelible ink. John was on center stage at Bread Loaf: it

was *his* conference and I was privileged to sit in on the endless evening and early morning conversations that took place in Treman Cottage, where the faculty gathered to drink and talk. I learned quickly that alcohol was the prime social lubricant and that its application began early in the day: just before noon, Bloody Mary's were available to the faculty (and the physician); drinks also were served before dinner and after the evening lecture (about 9 P.M.), all in Treman and all in the best company. It was only half-facetiously that, as I got to know John, I made him an offer: we'd work out a research protocol which would consist of drawing "liver function tests" from the blood of those attending Bread Loaf, doing this before and after the conference—our findings might need corroboration by liver biopsies, again done before and after the bouts at Treman had taken place. I was turned down, with grace and good humor, and another promising research paper went by the boards. Ah, the writers that were there during the three summers I served as physician: Miller Williams, John Frederick Nims, William Meredith, Maxine Kumin, Isaac Asimov, Diane Wakoski, William Sloane, Robert Pack, Barry Hannah, James Whitehead, and many others. It was a privilege to hear these writers and others in daily workshop sessions as well as evening readings from their work. In the Theater, I heard John hold the rapt attention of us all as he discussed "Valediction Forbidding Mourning" by John Donne and "The Eve of St. Agnes" by John Keats. The discussion was all the more remarkable for John's never using notes and quoting huge stretches of the poems from memory. And the readings from his own work were likewise incomparable. I was also privileged to be at Bread Loaf at John's last lecture, the year he left Bread Loaf: it was a time of sadness because John had devoted so many years of his life to the Conference. Late August, to this day, brings with it a certain nostalgia for the fireplace and camaraderie of Treman—and the words, words, words of the place.

I remember one evening in particular: everyone had gone to bed except John, Harry Crews and me. John was holding forth on any subject offered up by the Muse of Treman. Often the Muse offered up limericks, but etymology was beginning to seize John's imagination and we were introduced to the sweep of linguistics as we threw logs on the fire and toasted whomever seemed appropriate. Harry had noted that the pulse in one of the arteries around his ankle was intermittently irregular. I did a brief physical exam and gave a brief lecture on the physiology of ventricular premature contractions (which can be a normal variant or can be exacerbated by sleep deprivation and alcohol). About four A.M., the three of us decided we were hungry, so we lit out for the Director's house next door, made for the kitchen, and John concocted something out of eggs and a variety of leftovers and canned goods: I remember only that it tasted wonderful. And that I slept hard.

In October 1974, I received an always-welcome letter from John. It read, in part,

> Things go as things go. Norman Cousins just wrote to say that the cost squeeze (price of paper is up 115% in 20 months) means a slimmer mag and all columns must be once a month only. I seem to be becoming unemployed faster than any man in town. Ah, well. My mind to me a (dwindling) kingdom is.
>
> Joys,<br>John

John's mind was *always* a kingdom to him—and never a "dwindling" one. In later years, when he visited our house in Atlanta for days at a time (often on his way down to, or back from, Key West or for a periodic medical checkup), I watched in awe as he sat at the kitchen table, doing *The New York Times* crossword puzzle, not only with dazzling speed, but *in ink,* as if to say this had better be right the first time *or else.* He also took to the parlor game *Trivial Pursuit* with his limitless appetite for competition (it showed itself in poker and cribbage as well as in verbal badinage). He never slept well and, always, to my knowledge, stayed up late. As a result of this chronic insomnia, he was often fatigued—a condition which showed itself in sometimes humorous ways: not long ago, at our house after dinner, John and my wife Lu and I were relaxing in the family room. We noticed that a new episode of "Wild Kingdom" was about to be shown. John said gleefully of this program, which depicts the goings-on of the animal world, "Great. I love this kind of show." But within 3–4 minutes of its starting, Lu and I heard a deep satisfied snoring from John's end of the couch. After a thirty-minute nap, John was, as usual, ready to take on the evening until the early morning hours.

Somewhere along his 69-year way, John became complete master of the epigrammatic phrase. I remember encountering that mastery in the pages of *The Saturday Review.* One of the most memorable of these phrases seems also to characterize John's approach to life. The epigram appeared in one of the essays in *Dialogue with an Audience* and spoke to the major contribution that a university could make to a writer's life: it could give him *time,* the most valuable commodity of all. John went on to say, in his compelling way, ". . . finally, a man is defined by what he does with his human attention." That phrase has stuck with me through the years and I have marveled at John's application of it to his own life. He went at life uncompromisingly, always in search of excellence, always certain that he was giving his "human attention" to that which would, over the years, define him as he wanted to be defined.

This fascination with the epigram is, of course, a central concern of the poet—a way to say major things in a small space. One of his books, from which I'll quote later, is called *The Little That Is All.* John was thoroughly prepared, by the time he got wrapped up in etymology, to take on the world a word (or a phrase) at a time. That is why, in 1985, he was able to hold the Atlanta Bar Association's undivided attention as he conjured up the origins of such words as "hornswoggled," such phrases as "the whole nine yards." Two of his short poems come immediately to my mind in terms of his use of the epigram: one appeared in his last book, *The Birds of Pompeii:* the poem is called "True or False":

## True or False

Real emeralds are worth more than synthetics
but the only way to tell one from the other
is to heat them to a stated temperature,
then tap. When it's done properly
the real one shatters.

             I have no emeralds.
I was told this about them by a woman
who said someone had told her. True or false,
I have held my own palmful of bright breakage
from a truth too late. I know the principle.

And then there is "The Gift," to my mind one of John's most eminently successful poems. It tells of Josef Stein, a poet who survived Dachau, coming out "like half a resurrection, his other / eighty pounds still in their invisible grave." "In the spent of one night," Josef Stein wrote down "three propositions," which close the poem and which seem to me a very good writer's credo—the propositions are these:

That Hell is the denial of the ordinary. That nothing lasts.
That clean white paper waiting under a pen

is the gift beyond history and hurt and heaven.

I believe that John felt that way about writing, that he lived by the propositions of the poem, and that he achieved, in its epigrammatic closure, one of the great poems of our time. But John's epigrams were not confined to his writing. His everyday speech was full of them. I remember once, in my office at Emory, asking him whether he'd ever written fiction—to which he replied, "Fiction is like drinking beer when what you really want is bourbon." Speaking of which, over the years John put away his share of alcohol. But several years ago, after an examination at Emory (at John's request), I was able to prevail on him to give up alcohol for his health. John gave the matter some thought, assented to the plan, and stopped alcohol *cold turkey*, with only occasional asides to let me know that he missed the stuff. He refused my other suggestion to him—that he stop smoking cigarettes: he'd be damned, he said, if he'd give up *both* cigarettes and alcohol. So he continued smoking—heavily (he astonished some of the Emory physicians by once manifesting completely normal pulmonary function—a finding I can explain only by suggesting that his pulmonary function was supranormal to begin with). John's more colorful way of refusing to stop smoking was captured in yet another epigrammatic response to me: "I refuse to die of a constricted halo." Another of my favorites, said with variation to me over the years was "One should not abandon any vice one has strength enough to continue."

Counseling John with respect to his health was filled with humor: once he came into the office and the first thing he said to me was, "Doctuh! I need to have my sex drive lowered. From *here* (pointing to his head) to *here* (pointing to his pelvis)." He was never at a loss for a ribald comment, often a limerick, at a second's notice.

Once John and I collaborated on a limerick about a prominent neurologist who'd seen him in the hospital (John wrote the first part, I the latter), teasing the neurologist just a bit:

> A certain physician named Karp
> Whose reflexes weren't very sharp
> > Staggered out of a bar
> > And encountered a car
> Which is why he's now playing a harp.

Dr. Herbert Karp brought forth his inimitable broad smile on hearing our effort.

John frequently wrote short poems for those around him. One that he wrote out in script for our son, Jim, hangs proudly on his wall at home. It exhibits John's refusal to "talk down" to children, a characteristic of his children's poetry:

> I really don't know about Jim.
> When he comes to our house for a swim,
> > The fish as a rule
> > Jump out of the pool.
> Is there something the matter with him?

Once, in Fayetteville, Arkansas, John and I were guests in the home of Miller and Jordan Williams. Miller had had recurrent problems with an in-grown toenail, which needed removal. As Miller was helping Jordan in the preparation of a meal, I noticed that John was scribbling away. Within a few minutes, he read aloud the following, an ode on Miller's toe:

> Miller's toe
> (At least the nail)
> Has got to go.
> All hail! All hail!
> The Grand Exciser!
> Teach him preciser
> Means of excision.
> Thyself, physician,
> Remains to heal.
> Feel! Feel!
> Be not a heel
> (And calloused to boot)
> To Miller's toe.
> Take in hand his foot
> And cut and sew
> And do it well
> Or go to hell.

Not, perhaps, a great poem, but one that means more to me for having seen him write it. The inscription also was personally meaningful: "for John, the healed physician, to keep him on his toes / John / Fayetteville. Oct. 18, 1974. In the 41st year of the 1000-year Reich." The latter part of the inscription reflects John's great pleasure in his having survived the early years of Hitler's reign and in being able to sit in Fayetteville and mock the Nazi madmen after so many decades.

John was always most gracious in his responses to my own poetry. When my second book came out, I got a most enthusiastic note from him. One poem, "He Makes a House Call," ends with a line concerning a patient, "seven years ago / when you bled in my hands like a saint." In his note to me, John pronounced that line "an instant epiphany." In a review of the book for *The Chicago Tribune*, he ends the review with reference to that line: "Few poems in our time have either achieved, or earned, so powerful a resolution." I mention this review not to aggrandize the merits of the poem, but to underscore John's generosity of spirit toward younger writers.

Finally, I recall hearing at Bread Loaf a "one-liner" which John was working on during the early 70's. Called "Exit Line" when it appeared in print, there were several variants of the poem, with differences in punctuation and the verb form used. When he wrote it down for me several years ago (as we waited for his plane at the Atlanta airport), it read:

Love must intend realities. Goodbye.

When it appeared in print in John Nims' anthology *Western Wind*, it read:

Love should intend realities: goodbye!

And, finally, when it appeared in his book *The Little That Is All*, it read:

Love should intend realities. —Goodbye.

Such preoccupation with "the little that is all" of poetry is what I'd expect from a major poet and translator, a superb etymologist, a compelling lecturer. Because of John's work in this place we have a better idea of the realities that love should (or must) intend. Goodbye, John. We will miss your wisdom, your witness and presence, your love.

# A Trenta-sei for John Ciardi (1916–1986)

## John Stone

In the beginning was the word, as noted
(in the end, too, if truth be known)—
Mercy next, then Love, and, gravel-throated,
a distinctive Grace enduring as the stone.
From these were made a better man than most.
We say goodbye today, old crow, gruff ghost.

In the end, too, if truth be known,
was clean white paper waiting under a pen—
a gift of hand, eye, ear, and knuckle-bone
from Boston to Vermont and back again
to Jersey, Georgia, Key West—in every state
he came to talk and stayed to celebrate

Mercy next, then Love. And, gravel-throated,
the man became the word on which he fed
until he fed us all—and what he quoted
was from the major kingdom in his head
comprised not.least of children's poems—crows,
pythons, sharks with teeth in rows.

A distinctive Grace enduring as the stone
or bronze or steel sculptors bring to life
he brought to his—and ours—though not alone,

for one enduring grace became his wife:
To her he'd bow and gratefully concede
that men have always married what they need.

From these were made a better man than most
who moved the word from mind to pen to writing
and made the books from wisdom and a host
of wars he never seemed to tire of fighting
especially those he thought he'd surely win
(as well as some he revelled in like sin).

We say goodbye today, old crow, gruff ghost.
That's never worked before—and will not now.
No good comes of goodbye. Instead, a toast
(in whatever form the authorities will allow)
to you—to us—in minor fifths and thirds.
Along the way you found we'll find the words.

# Light Years Near:
## John Ciardi's Poems for Children

### Joann P. Krieg

Fifty times fifty years go by.
Corn keeps best when it's cool and dry.

Fifty times fifty one by one
Night begins when day is done.
— "There Once Was an Owl"

Critics have not concerned themselves very much with Ciardi's poems for children, perhaps because of feeling inadequate; once having passed the age of those for whom these works are written one hesitates, quite naturally, to attempt judgment. Furthermore, the field of criticism of such writings for children is strewn with schoolmarm and children's librarian condemnations of such things as L. Frank Baum's *The Wonderful Wizard of Oz*. One becomes wary. Better to let the young folk comment in the privacy of the nursery, or, in the modern home, of the TV room where it is hoped that on occasion the din of the endless reams of video tapes which for many children have replaced the human presence, is temporarily hushed in favor of *The Man Who Sang the Sillies* or *You Read to Me, I'll Read to You*.

It is through the mechanisms of this world of electronic communication that in "Interstellar," (published in *The Birds of Pompeii*) Ciardi reveals the depth of emotions and the sense of reverence for the universe which have given rise not just to an occasional poem intended for children, but to a sustained effort on their behalf throughout his poetic career. What one understands from the poem is that this effort stems from something other than the educator's commitment, or even from the humanist's devotion to the unseen future. The relationship that exists between Ciardi's poems for children and his total *oeuvre* is that which connects subatomic particles to the universe at large, the primal and ongoing stuff of creation from which the greater is derived.

Subtitled "FM Wireless Intercom. REALISTIC [an electronics company's brand name] / U.S. Tested. PLUG'N TALK," "Interstellar" connects the now childless home of the poet to the source of all creativity, "the word that began the world. . . ." The word in this case is "In-GA! In-GA!"—not some strange tribal chant from outer space, but "a baby's primary wail" that mysteriously emanates at two in the morning from the intercom system through which the poet in his attic study maintains touch with his wife in the regions of the house below. The infant's cry (it cries in Norwegian, Ciardi claims, hence "In-GA") is followed by lulling parental attempts to soothe, "voices without words," the poet calls them, adding, "Had I tuned in Bethlehem without its beasts?" With this reversal of both the Christ-centered Bethlehem and the Yeatsian anticipation of the slouching anti-Christ, we are thrust outward, away from this world's images of creative cycles, toward the galactic realms of past and future to which our present seems hastening, outward toward that point of origination which in the poem is signified by the cry "In-GA!"

Inquiries put to neighbors and to the mailman bring no help in identifying the source of the electronically transmitted wailing, and the poet finds himself in constant expectation "for that defined baby and its vague parents." He becomes a kind of "voyeur" at the exchange of love and finds he could, had he faith enough, build a church around it, remembering how once he did so but his *paternoster* was reduced to patter "for lacking of the solving words."

On a night when the baby's cry brings no response from its parents, the poet, listening in his attic study, loses patience and thunders into the talk box, "This is God. My baby is crying and where are you?" Imagining his explosion as the basis for a new religion if it has been overheard by some easy believer, he waits, but there is only silence, indicating childish sleep. Three succeeding nights bring no further sound; then, just before daylight on the fourth, there comes "echoing from a star, / the word that began the world: *In-GA! In-GA!*" The interstellar distance traveled by the sound fills the poet's study with the glow of light years until a flicked switch disrupts the connection on the electronic monitoring device in the infant's crib, and child and poet are thrust back at "two ends of a broken ray / that almost promised there might be something to say."

The "almost" promise of the poem is of course realized in the "something to say" that Ciardi has continued communicating to children over the years, for in fact his relationship to the young has not been that of a broken ray of light years. Responding to children as to a message beamed from distant star-flung reaches of the universe, the poet has kept alive a form of communication which for most of us has long since shut down or, at best, has trailed off into static. When moved to some expression of faith in the world we know, as well as in those we know not but only sense through intermittent beeps of sound and rays of light years, we would do well to whisper back into the universe, "In-GA! In-GA!"

# Energy and Gusto: A Note on John Ciardi

## William Jay Smith

For almost half a century John Ciardi did the work of several men—as poet, translator, editor, essayist, writer for children. Not content with having put one of the world's great poems—Dante's *Divine Comedy*—into clear and readable English, he turned his attention to English itself and as poet-lexicographer guided his reader with wit and wisdom through the thorny thickets of our language and showed him where words come from and where they are going. More than a man of letters, he was an encyclopedist. And everything that he undertook bears the mark of a quality singularly lacking in much that is written today—energy.

John and I both began to publish in the forties and we have followed many of the same paths. When I first met him in Rome some thirty years ago, I sent him a copy of *Laughing Time*, my first collection of children's poems, which I had written for my four-year-old son David. With his characteristic generosity, John wrote to tell me how much he admired the book, especially since he felt that he could never do anything of the sort himself. He could, of course, and did. He took his cue, I am sure, not from me but from his own children. Naturally I am envious of the results, but then who wouldn't be of verses like these:

> As I was picking a bobble-bud
> > Out in the bangle-thicket,
> A Crow with a voice the color of mud
> > Lit on a croquet wicket.

or:

> There once was a Hunter from Littletown.
> > He made his bullets of sugar cane.

And every duck that he shot down
    Got up and flew away again.

He shot a Lobster out of a tree
    And up it rose again and said:
"Sorry. Which way is the sea?"
    Said the Hunter: "Aren't you dead?"

These are from *The Man Who Sang the Sillies* (1961), admirably illustrated by Edward Gorey. It is a book filled with oysters and lobsters and kangaroos and parents who ask at bedtime if they have screwed their children's heads on tight, everything made sparkling and fresh with memorable verbal play, and children love it. The writing of good nonsense verse is not, needless to say, as easy as it looks: anthologies are filled with the dead weight of many unimaginative attempts. The twentieth century has made few additions to the lasting body of children's poetry that are worthy of attention, and many of those that are worthy are the work of John Ciardi.

The energy and gusto that characterize the best of the nonsense poems are particularly evident in my favorite of all his adult books, *In the Stoneworks*, also published in 1961. The book presents, alongside poems on a wide variety of subjects skillfully couched in the vernacular, finely drawn portraits of his own family and of the whole human family. The poems are straightforward and funny, tender and affecting, and all have a bold strength, quarried and cleanly cut, as if from stone, meant to endure.

# A Note on "Ciardi's Dialogue with Children"

## Vince Clemente

I recall a 1983 Metuchen visit. John and I were in the living room drinking the espresso he had just made. At day's end, he was lounging in his favorite chair, the room a rosy glow. I'm sure it was his red suspenders. It was a good visit. I hated to leave the man, dreading the drive back to Long Island.

"But before you leave, Vince, I want you to see this." He coaxed down from a glass cabinet above him a mahogany award plaque. "I'm proud of this," he beamed. I read:

For John Ciardi
Award for Excellence in Poetry for Children
National Council of Teachers of English
1982

"An award well earned and a long time coming, John," I said. I shared his pleasure, remembering how I had raised my daughters on books like *The Man Who Sang the Sillies, You Read to Me, I'll Read to You,* and *Scrappy the Pup.* And I spoke as a friend, who would one day receive in the mail a copy of *Doodle Soup,* inscribed "For Wee Vinnie and Lil Annie, with doodles of love from Johnny Ciardi, Age 69½." The book includes a holograph poem that begins, "How old am I? I really don't know." Only a man who doesn't "know" his age can continue to write poems for children, even into his seventh decade.

This "dialogue with children" began in 1959 with *The Reason for the Pelican* and continued to his last days. Shortly before his death, Annie and I were guests at the Ciardis' home in Key West. I slept in John's study and discovered, among his works in progress, a batch of new children's poems.

This American man of letters took seriously this facet of his writing life. In a recent letter, he reminds me, "I glow when a handsome lady tells me she grew up on my doodles and is reading them to her tadpoles." And in a most revealing sentence he adds, "The critics, I think, have screwed up our view of poetry, but the kids have a fresh eye. I would rather grab them than Helen Vendler."

Just what is it, then, in his children's poetry that "grabs" kids? I put this question to Terri Arrigon, an English teacher at Rocky Point High School. Rocky Point is not a typical Long Island school district. It is a blue-collar community and its children, as a rule, will be first in their families to attend college. Yet it is a district where, for years, Ciardi poems have been a staple in curriculums for grades two to seven. I suggested she sound out the young readers.

Terri, wanting a more representative sampling, a truly variegated readership, invited students and teachers of Half Hollow Hills and Three Village districts to take part, as both are predominantly white-collar communities with many college-educated parents.

Terri met with classes, talked about Ciardi's poems, swapped favorite lines, and encouraged journal responses. Some students even wrote "love letters" to the poet. Her piece, "Ciardi's Dialogue with Children" is their testimony.

# Ciardi's Dialogue with Children

## Terri Arrigon

In 1972 the National Council of Teachers of English conducted a nationwide survey of preferences in poetry among 422 upper elementary grade-school children. John Ciardi's "Mummy Slept Late and Daddy Fixed Breakfast" was chosen the most popular poem in a field of 113.[1] This, I'm sure, pleased Ciardi, the man who insisted, "Children are a jury that can't be rigged,"[2] for they respond to poetry as they respond to life, ingenuously, unabashedly. In the study, the NCTE warned, however, "Children are the best judges of their preferences," surely an audience to be reckoned with.

More than a decade later, a new "jury" made up of second to seventh graders in three Long Island school districts, Rocky Point, Half Hollow Hills, and Three Villages, was asked to state its "preferences." They speak with the same fervor and candor that characterized the responses of those who delighted in "Mummy Slept Late" in a time before many of them were born. (It should be noted that Ciardi suspected that "the kids liked 'Mummy Slept Late' because it gave them a chance to upstage Daddy without being actually naughty or sassy."[3])

The question arises, then, just why do children react with such relish not only to "Mummy Slept Late" but also to the fourteen or so volumes of children's poetry that Ciardi has faithfully logged in during a period of over twenty-five years?

Kelly, in Grade 2, for example, in a letter to Ciardi quipped, "You're a good rhymer. How did you learn rhymes? Did you go to a special school?" Angela, in Grade 7, enjoying "Speed Adjustments," wrote in her journal, "One thing I like is that it is 'racy.' It has a fast pace. I also like the way it rhymes."

What prompts such pleasure? A clue may be found in Ciardi himself, in what he calls "the play impulse in poetry . . . the child clapping its hands in response to a Mother Goose rhyme," reacting "in an immediate muscular way," wanting "to act with" the poem, swept up with its music—the delight in pure sound, the tingle in the spine.

The child's ear is finely tuned, receptive to this dance of words, and the child is prepared for language that is "surprising and surprisingly right," as Ciardi writes in *How Does a Poem Mean?* The child stands ready for such "surprises." Mark, in Grade 4, notes in his journal, "'How To Tell the Top of a Hill' was good because it isn't like any poem I've ever read. I like the way he wrote, 'For there is no more up to go.' I like it because of the way its words are used."

Often, as is the case of Ethen, Grade 4, the child singles out individual words and enjoys them sluicing down the tongue. Ethen likes "Rain Sizes" because "the vocabulary is terrific like the words *sparkle, twinkle, tingles, sprinkle, rattles, roars,* and *splash.* There is some alliteration. Some with the *S.*"

At times such "terrific vocabulary" prompts similar diction in the journal response. Inspired by a Ciardi poem—even children have their Muse—they speak like poets. "I liked 'Rain Sizes' because it had words that painted a beautiful picture in my mind like our chandelier when the sun catches the crystals and makes a rainbow for each crystal on the wall." Kristen in Grade 4 said that—stunning metaphor for a fourth-grader! Her classmate Eric added, "'Rain Sizes' paints a picture in your head. For instance, when you think of rain sparkling, you think of water catching the sun."

And kids love to catch the "sillies," to frolic with the poem, snared in its humor, but in a humor they insist be close to life, in situations they perceive as "real." The Ciardi dictum, "Nothing is really hard but to be real," a truth that has served him well as a man of letters, informs his poetry for children. Advocates of realism, children will laugh if the poem's performance is close to life, an *honest* portrayal of life.

Janice, in Grade 7, noted, "I think that 'Speed Adjustments' is a lot better than other poems I read because it was funny, but still it had truth in it." Aaron in Grade 4, after reading a number of Ciardi poems, concluded, "John Ciardi teaches things in a funny and truthful way."

When Ciardi observes that children reading a poem want "*to act with it,*" he could have had in mind Heather in Grade 7: "'Speed Adjustments' was funny and realistic. When John was talking to his dad, it seemed like I was there."

Experiencing the poem, children not only "*act with it,*" they act *in* it, breaking, smashing the barriers of the poem as illusory world. As Nancy in Grade 7 put it, "You're in the inside looking out rather than the outside looking in." Leslie, Grade 3, spoke of a similar experience: "John Ciardi's writing makes me feel, see and actually sort of hear the autumn leaves that the purple-polka-dotted bear turned into beautiful colors. He made me feel like jumping into the poem, into the action."

Over thirty-five years ago, introducing his own poems in *Mid-Century American Poets*, Ciardi recorded the simple precept—Number Three—that "Poetry should be about the lives of people." His poems for children began as poems for his own, Myra, Jonnel, and Benn. He wrote poems that first "grabbed" them. Simply put, then, children see *themselves* in a Ciardi poem, poems "about the lives of people."

Our old friend, Ethen of Grade 4, liked "Someone" because "it is telling you about time and age. You can't stop the clock. It keeps on ticking. You have to grow up. You can't stay a kid." And about "The Top of the Hill," he added, "The goal is like when you get educated. You go to higher and higher levels. When you're at the highest level, you're at the top of the hill. When you reach your goal, you stop and go on to a different one."

No, this is a "jury" that can't be "rigged," nor will it accept unequivocally what the poet has to say. It is prepared to challenge many basic assumptions. Some readers questioned the father's disciplinary tactics in "Speed Adjustments." Heather, Grade 7, admonished Ciardi: "I don't think the father's method is the best one because it really doesn't solve anything. It just teaches the kid that anytime he or she does something bad, they are going to be smacked." Cathy in Grade 7 wondered, "Maybe the father thinks if he hits the boy, he will get the point across directly. But in other cases, I think you should talk *first*— it's true that kids who were hit as children are more likely to take their grief out on their children by hitting." She goes on to add, however, "But if you don't get the point across after two or three times, an occasional smack will do."

Even fourth graders have an axe to grind. Joanne took Ciardi to task for his stance in "The Top of the Hill": "I don't agree with this poem. I think you can always go further. You just make your goals higher. I don't agree when he says, 'There's no more up to go.'" There is always something in a Ciardi poem worth their time, something earning their "attention." "A man is what he does with his attention." How often has Ciardi been heard to say that!

John Ciardi, writer of "tribal" poems, the poet as father, as husband, son. The family is his milieu as it is the ideal habitat for his young readers. Kids are at home in such a world, a world where Mummy sleeps late and daddies make the most awful breakfasts; where parents dread to suffer practice sessions of their blossoming child-musicians; a world where children sometimes dream of running away from "manners, baths, and bed." Yet it is a world, as Janice in Grade 7 remembers, in which "the father double-checked to make sure nothing was wrong." And she went on to add, about "Speed Adjustments": "This showed John's father cared about his son."

Ciardi contends, "Poetry—any of the arts—is for those with a willing attention and must not be diluted for those who haven't found an attention."[4] This principle carries over to his world for children. His poetry for them has a richness, a craft that invites the child to form this "willing attention." One child may delight in the sheer pleasure of the poem's music, another in the original turn of phrase that is "surprisingly right," while another will apply a theme to his or her own life—and suddenly grow up! The result, though, is the same: a young reader is introduced to the joy of interacting with a well-crafted work of art. The child is learning to develop an "attention." This, then, is John Ciardi's gift to his many children.

I'd like to give the poet the last word. Here are some lines we—the children, their teachers, and I—enjoyed reading together. I think you would have liked them too:

> The stranger in the pumpkin said:
> "It's all dark inside your head.
> What a dullard you must be!
> Without light how can you see?
> Don't you know that heads should shine
> From deep inside themselves—like mine?
> Well, don't stand there in a pout
> With that dark dome sticking out—
> It makes me sick to look at it!
> Go and get your candle lit!"
>
> —*"The Stranger in the Pumpkin"*

> I meet few bears and few meet me.
> But still it's my belief
> That, meeting bears, the thing to be
> Is—brief.
>
> —*"Last Word about Bears"*

> I met a man with a triple-chin.
> Whenever he smiled, his chins would grin.
> The strangest sight that ever I saw
> Was a smile with three grins in its jaw.
>
> —*from "The Man Who Sang the Sillies"*

> When you are at the table
>    And you need to kick your brother,
> Be as sweet as you are able
>    To your Dad and Mother.
>
> —*from "The Lesson for Tonight"*

I have one head that wants to be good,
   And one that wants to be bad.
And always, as soon as I get up,
   One of my heads is sad.

*—from "Sometimes I Feel This Way"*

1. Ann Terry, *Children's Poetry Preferences: A National Survey of Upper Elementary Grades*, National Council of Teachers of English, Urbana, Illinois, 1972.

2. Letter to Vince Clemente, October 8, 1985.

3. Letter to Vince Clemente, December 17, 1985.

4. Vince Clemente, "'A Man Is What He Does with His Attention': A Conversation with John Ciardi," *Poesis: A Journal of Criticism*, Bryn Mawr College, Vol. VII, No. 2.

# John Ciardi:
## "Nothing Is Really Hard but to Be Real"

### Miller Williams

The poems of John Ciardi are introspective, iconoclastic, humanistic, and world-affirming, as straightforward as poetry is likely to be. To a remarkable degree the poems are directly about the experience and knowledge of the man who wrote them. It is especially remarkable, therefore, that the poems are rich and varied, that they ought to have been written and ought to be read. Not every poet can appear as himself in his works and interest us in what he is saying about experiences that in a special autobiographical sense are still his. A superlative craftsmanship, a ruthless objectivity, and an unfailing sense of what all people have in common are even more necessary for such a poet than for the writer who wants to step outside himself, to extrapolate from his own experience the story of all people and to tell Everyman's tale with the "detachment" of fiction.

Ciardi's poems belong to that tradition most clearly exemplified by *The Divine Comedy*, in which the *I* is clearly, literally the poet. We may, perhaps, call this the Dante tradition, as opposed to, say, the Shakespeare tradition, in which the writer is at once nowhere and everywhere in his work.

The self-conscious presence of the poet in John Ciardi's poems is the condition from which all their other qualities arise. Ciardi follows Dante into the poem, and he goes in for much the same reason: to find himself and whatever heaven there is. That they do not find the same heaven—that Dante found it supernal while Ciardi finds it emphatically terrestrial—is a fact that shows us the way through almost all of Ciardi's poems.

What kind of self-consciousness is this that makes the writer his own protagonist? Almost always it is the self-consciousness of the exile, one who lives

162

removed from Everyman's world, the prodigal son who returns to find his family moved away and a parking lot where his house was, a grouchy and yellow-toothed attendant guarding the entrance to his bedroom. He is disoriented and lost. He wants to rebuild the house, but the lot is covered with asphalt; he wants to find his parents, but he doesn't know where to look for them. What he wants most is to find what the house held, what the parents knew, to find the man in the boy he came from, the boy in the seed, the seed in the parents and in the house. Ciardi was a man searching, hunting for his face in a mirror that never looked back as clearly as he looked into it:

> One day I went to look at the Mediterranean
> and I found myself on an infected hill.
>
> > —*"Fragments from Italy"*
>
> > > We are damned for accepting as
> the sound a man makes, the sound of something else,
> thereby losing the truth of our own sound.
>
> > > > How do we
> learn our own sound?
>
> > —*"Nothing Is Really Hard but to Be Real—"*
>
> I move through darkness memorized
> feeling for doors.
>
> > —*"Christmas Eve"*

What, then, did it mean to be John Ciardi? Ciardi came to the question honestly. A man generally begins to understand his own being as the son of his father. Of course, he may feel himself the son of a region or of a nation with cultural roots running down to invisible and ancient rivers, or he may feel himself a child of God, one of the ninety-and-nine secure in the fold of the Church, but usually and more importantly, he is the son of his father. However, in Ciardi's case, all these ways to and understanding of the self were closed. When he was three years old, his father died. In his poems, that man is an absence, a created memory the poet tries continually to bring into focus. He is stories told by the poet's mother; sometimes he is a photograph.

> A ceremonial rose in the lapel,
> a horseshoe wreath of pearls in the tie-knot,
> a stone-starched collar bolted at the throat,

a tooth on a gold chain across the vest—
this is the man. . . .

> —*"Bridal Photo"*

To the old-world Italian, the family is important. More than most people, the Italian is identified in terms of the family. What Ciardi lost at the age of three was the center of that family, the father around whom, for better or worse, all personality is polarized.

> . . . By all flowers and all fall
> I am the son of this man and this woman.
>> —*"Bridal Photo"*

> In a great plain, the ticking grass above
>> my head and reach, I waited with my ear
>
> to the thudding ground. What passed me out of sight?
>> My father was one. When I had died enough
> I made a perfect pink boy of my fright
>> and used him to forgive time and myself. . . .
>
> . . . all men are their fathers and their sons
>> in a haunted house of mirrors to the end.
>>> —*"Poem for My Thirty-Ninth Birthday"*

> My father died imperfect as a man.
> My mother lied him to perfections. I
> knew nothing, and had to guess we all mean
> our lives in honor of the most possible lie.
>> —*"My Father Died Imperfect as a Man"*

But whether from that loss or for other reasons, the old world of Italy lost John Ciardi. And somewhere along the line the Father who was God also died.

The religious fold Ciardi left was the Roman Catholic Church, the most secure, the most comfortable of all religions. Father, Italy, Rome—all died. So Ciardi was left to himself, and in that wood, he took the only path available—into himself and out to the world. He looked in both places at once for the meaning of the world that was—or was believed in, the world he came from—and he believed in the world of the present. Thus, in half his poems he says, "But oh,

164

children, what eyes our father had!" and in the other he says, as surely, "This is, I am, we are."

Ciardi, therefore, looked for the perspective that gives dimension and meaning to the self and celebrated the world-as-it-is because it is—because it is earth, inferno, and heaven, such as they are. It is all we have, and for that reason, if for no other, is to be loved.

We meet the man as he met himself in the honestly titled "Autobiography of a Comedian":

> Years long in the insanities of adolescence—
> because my father had died but still
> spoke to me, because my mother was mad,
> because the cross was bloody on the One Hill—
>
> I wrestled God gaunt on my knees and wet
> in the sizzle of nightmare wakings till
> there was nothing to do but die or embrace
> a more comic spirit. Which, being hard to kill,
>
> I did. I told jokes my family fled from.
> My friends knew me through cracks in the door.
> Father Ryan black-sheeped me from the pulpit.
> —God knows he had more than enough to deplore.
>
> Then suddenly my jokes became lucrative.
> My wallet acquired a vocabulary. My four
> thumbs and twelve toes turned jugglers.
> I learned to dance loose. And the more
>
> I shuffled the more money, cars, houses
> I got for it. I grew rich grinning.
> Bankers learned to pronounce my name.
> I even won at Harold's Club. I'm still winning
>
> what I have no real use for but
> might as well take. In my beginning
> was no end of a wry humor. I am my broker's
> keeper. Not even my hair is thinning.
>
> I tell you this world's as crazy as I was once.
> Even scholars take me seriously. And why

complain, you say? Friend, I am trying
as simple and as marvelous a thing as honesty.

As I might say I love my wife, enjoy
playing with my children, expect to die
and not to profit by the experience—
I think we are of some Stone Age, you and I.

How do we make sense of ourselves?
I do not understand presidents, popes, kings,
ministers, marshals, or policemen
except as I see the ritual featherings

of the tribes in their hair. What do I know
of the invisible people I killed for wings
when I was a gunner for our tribe?
I remember the fires we started, not the things

we burned in them. I think Harold,
crazy as he is for God now, has our real
mystery in his spinning department store.
What we all pray to is the dice, the wheel,

and the holy jackpot. Have you *seen*
the grandmothers praying at those steel
altars where the heaven-eyes blink and wink
fruit, bells, and dominion? It's God they feel

coming at the next click. But Harold
keeps the books for his three per cent. Another
comic spirit, except that he believes it
and works at it. As once my grandmother

in *her* tribe's dark, kept herbs and spells
and studied signs and dreams. Why bother
to believe what there is a sure three per cent of?
Somehow we must keep our brother

by what will not be kept. Between
our slapstick successes and our wry
confessions, there is the day the sun starts.
The low sea to the west of Reno and the high

desert to the east. This world. And in it
the mercy that sees and knows why
we must not love ourselves too much—
though, having no other, we must, somehow, try.

This was John Ciardi speaking. It is irrelevant to ask whether it was mostly the man or mostly the poet speaking. The poet and the man lived busily together in a mind in which the lights were on in every room:

Were I to dramatize myself,
I'd say I am a theologian who keeps meeting
the devil as a master of make-up, and that
among his favorite impersonations he appears,
often as not, as the avuncular old ham who winks,
tugs his ear, and utters such gnomic garbage
as: "Nothing is really hard but to be real."

—"*Nothing Is Really Hard but to Be Real*—"

The sense of loss and alienation, the need to identify with what has gone before, what has made us, become explicit in what is surely one of Ciardi's finest poems, which also contains the climax and perhaps the resolution of his endeavor to understand the struggle itself, "Tree Trimming":

. . . I know him. But he is
more than I can teach my children. They
have no first life. *That* is their loss.
I wish we were Jews and could say
the names of what made us.
I could weep by slow waters for my son
who has no history, no name
he knows long, no ritual from which he came,
and no fathers but the forgotten.

While the Church itself meant nothing, was hardly ever referred to, did not trail after Ciardi like the yellow smoke of guilt that trails many of our contemporary writers, the poems are imbued with a sense of religion, a consciousness of that part in man which builds myths and needs relation, form, and direction— what we call ritual. Ciardi wrote a lot about ritual, saw the world in terms of ritual to such a degree that he replaced the forms of the Church with those patterns of living that are most timeless and universal among us, that have been so long and so indispensably a part of us that they now have a level of meaning all their own. These patterns are important for their own sakes, for they are in fact the rituals of the faith that is fully human. Perhaps Ciardi was saying that no one can, in fact, cast off the past, that it is always there, that when we believe we are replacing it, we are only reshaping it.

> When saints praise heaven lit by doves and rays,
> I sit by pond scums till the air recites
> Its heron back. And doubt all else. But praise.
>
> —*"Snowy Heron"*

> Ritual wars have climbed your shadowed flank
> where bravos dreaming of fair women tore
> rock out of rock to have your cities down
> in loot of hearths and trophies of desire.
> And desert monks have fought your image back
> in a hysteria of mad skeletons.
> Bravo and monk (the heads and tails of love)
> I stand, a spinning coin of wish and dread, . . .
>
> Yet sleep and keep our prime of time alive
> before that death of legend. My dear of all
>
> saga and century, sleep in familiar-far.
> Time still must tick *this is, I am, we are."*
>
> —*"To Judith Asleep"*

> . . . I think
> what feeds is food. And dream it in mosaic
> for a Church of the First Passion: an ocher sea
> and a life-line of blue fishes, the tail of each
> chained into the mouth behind it. Thus, an emblem
> of our indivisible three natures in one:
> the food, the feeder, and the condition of being
> in the perpetual waver of the sea.
>
> I believe the world to praise it.
>
> —*"Thoughts on Looking into a Thicket"*

                                . . . just as the waiter
                          in his priesthood laid before me
                          a silver-capped ritual steam. . . .

                                        —*"Coq au Vin"*

It doesn't matter that there is nothing supernal behind the ritual; from the start,
the play is what matters.

    And then, not wholly apart from ritual, Italy matters—the family, the lan-
guage, the land. These are to found in the poems in countless ways; they are
named, examined, picked up, and put down again, as if the poet hoped to find
in them some shape of himself. Take, for example, these lines from "Fragments
from Italy":

                                     The child
                    . . . stares at me. I am part of what he knows.
                    I am the traffic forever in his eyes
                    and damnation, the way all worlds go
                    leaving him neither admission nor understanding,
                    as, somewhere in a thicket like the mind,
                    a gargoyle might stare down at running water.

                    What the Roman sun says to the Romans . . .

                    I have said to you in all the tongues of sleep.

    But God and father and country were gone from him, and they were not to be
had again. The search for meaning, for identity, brought the poet—perhaps it
had to bring him—to the self, its consciousness and meaning, and finally to a
celebration of the self as the reality which has replaced—or reshaped—the col-
lapsed forms of the Church, the fallen bridge of the father, the home of the unseen country.

    Nothing else symbolizes the self, the persistent yet changing self, as much as
the name. This perhaps is why Ciardi was so concerned that he be true to himself, to the name that means only what his faithfulness can give it. I know of no
poet who has considered his own name more than Ciardi has. He said it all the
ways there are, in all his voices, as if he felt that if he said it right, heard it echo
off the right wall, he might understand.

                                        . . . *John! John!*
                    I cry in the fossil present. My breath, my name. . . .

                                        —*"Landscapes of My Name"*

                    . . . Light shared
By half the world before it made
This last turn through the window shade,
And, after half a world, involved
John Ciardi in the thing revolved.
                    —"*Goodmorning with Light*"

Here lies Ciardi's pearly bones
In their ripe organic mess.
Jungle blown, his chromosomes
Breed to a new address. . . .

                    . . . .

Fractured meat and open bone—
Nothing single or surprised.
Fragments of a written stone,
Undeciphered but surmised.
                    —"*Elegy Just in Case*"

. . . they ducked me and called me John.

. . . when I

Was not yet ready for evil or my own name,
Though I had one already and the other came.
                    —"*The Evil Eye*"

The first thing people want to do, when the world gives them something they don't understand, is to name it. We are all taxonomists. If we do not deceive ourselves into thinking that having named a thing we therefore know it, we are at least committed to the belief that the naming must come first, and that somehow in the incantation of the name may be the magic of revelation.

This is not to imply that Ciardi alone of his generation followed Dante into the poem. Among his contemporaries, several poets wrote primarily about themselves: Robert Lowell, Theodore Roethke, Dylan Thomas, for example. Of these three, Ciardi was closest by far to the mind of Roethke. Lowell also was searching for himself, but he did not celebrate the present so gladly as Ciardi did. Thomas sang the world but generally took himself for what he was and sang that freely and simply. Roethke, like Hamlet—or like Ciardi—was haunted by the ghost of his father. He never, I think, found the balance that Ciardi came to, that full celebration of the world and man that is sanity for the haunted, possibly because he could not be angry enough in his love of that world. In contrast, Ciardi's anger became an important part of his voice.

And there is another difference. Ciardi was haunted only part of the time by his own father and by his Father; all of the time, he was haunted by John Ciardi. As we see Ciardi moving from loss to discovery, to a ringing celebration of the self that is conscious of that celebration and therefore real, through all the lines of all the poems of affirmation, through all the voices in which Ciardi says, "This is, I am, we are," there is the inescapable feeling that he was not always as sure as he seemed to be that even the self, love, and logic are what they appear to be, or that they will work to carry us through. While there is a reasoning, a rationalism, in his poems that is clean and consoling, and a mercy that tempers them well, on the shoulder of the self, is a shapeless incubus, whispering confusions that are almost audible in the poems.

The introspective search is not so much a part of Ciardi's earlier work, where the most distinctive characteristic is rather an iconoclasm set forth with a matter-of-factness that has persisted and grown stronger. It is Ciardi's voice at its best. This iconoclasm comes to us as a quiet sort of "knock it off" attitude, a poetic expression of anger, the voice of the social critic. It is seen first, as we might expect, in the war poetry.

> The bomb whose metal carcass, dressed and bled,
> Is our day's gift to populate the dead.
>
> —*"Poem for My Twenty-Ninth Birthday"*

> The health of captains is the sex of war:
> the pump of sperm built in their polished thighs
> powers all their blood; the dead, like paid-off whores,
> sleep through the mornings where the captains rise.
>
> —*"The Health of Captains"*

> . . . it was no goddamn good,
>      and not bad either. It
>      was war (they called it) and it lit
>      a sort of skyline somehow in the blood,
>      and I typed the dead out a bit
>      faster than they came—just keeping ahead—
>
> and the gulls blew high on their brinks,
>      and the ships slid, and the surf threw,
>      and the Army initialed, and you

were variously, vicariously, and straight and with kinks,
raped, fondled, and apologized to—
which is called (as noted) war. And it stinks.

>                               —*"To Lucasta, about That War"*

The poems of Ciardi that are not intensely introspective—and some that are—fall loosely under the heading of social criticism, a disapproving, often angry comment on the world man has made. The poet points his finger and calls by name the gods and demigods we have raised.

I remember the United States of America
As a flag-draped box with Arthur in it. . . .

>                               —*"A Box Comes Home"*

Everyone in my tribe hates
everyone in your tribe. . . .

>                    . . . we

shall all finally kick all of your
heads. We are united.

>                    —*"My Tribe"*

The day I can tear up my pass-
port and take out citizenship in
the human race—which I would
gladly the cries of Treason face—
that day I will buy ice-cream
for all the kids . . .
and gladly as many shares
of Consolidated Everything as I
can get margin for and even and
beyond treason gladly bourbon
for those same Senators crying
whose flags I will gladly waive.

>                    —*"Oration"*

. . . winged and wired against The Fall,
And a paper halo overall—
A nineteen hundred year old doll

In a drying tree. What does it see?
The house is sleeping; there's only me. . . .

*—"Christmas Eve"*

Idol-breaking is a natural function of the humanism in Ciardi's poetry. It comes with the rejection of metaphysics and the refusal to relegate anything that matters to another, later world. This is the humanism that forms when a man gives his whole attention to the moment he is living—whether he does it by nature, or because he senses that no other moment exists, or because he believes that that is the only way to make the next moment be anything but another sentence to be served while waiting for the next. Whatever the reason, the affirmation of the eternal present demands an honest eye for things as they are, a refusal to settle for pretense, for mere superficiality. It demands that the face behind the face be seen. And Ciardi's social criticism stemmed, I think, from this honesty.

His refusal to accept the pomp of the world as reality, and his great rage, which seems to tear like an underground river just beneath the words of the poem, were caused to a great extent by an inner turmoil that had nothing to do with society as such. I suspect that a zoo of angers—against all that was lost for having been lost, against the absence, the past which is no past—that had nowhere else to go fired the furnaces of the poet's impatience with our social ways.

It is possible for the poems of Ciardi to bring Alexander Pope to mind, not only—or primarily—because both men channeled the energies of inner turmoil into social criticism but also because of the tone and the directness of their criticism, and of the rational terms in which it is usually couched. It is as if in Ciardi, as in Pope, the raging furnaces were banked by an objectivity that was all but classical.

The same objectivity that keeps the fires of passion under control keeps Ciardi from falling prey, even as social critic, to the pandemic twentieth-century sickness of intellectual pride. His kind of paganism—this humanism which is what we have when all our gods, heavens, hells, and purgatories are nowhere but in every man's moment—was completed with a humility that must surprise, not only the believer, but also the utopian atheist, who is simply the believer's Mr. Hyde. The utopian atheist, as well as the believer, trades the present for the future and scorns the world-as-it-is for the world as he dreams it will be.

Ciardi was in love simply with this day. He knew it was full of folly and said so, knew the folly was his and said so. It is as if he took the day as his bride, for better or for worse, celebrated and scolded, was true to her until the sun set and rose; then he took another, was as true to her as to the last, knowing that, if she were imperfect, he was no great shakes as a groom to begin with, and settled for it, never anticipating the next death, the bride to come.

Notwithstanding his search for self and his need to be both inside and outside his poems, Ciardi as a man was notably whole. The struggle within him was a struggle, not of the man against himself, but of the man against a void he sought to fill. Which is to say that if his psyche was hunting for the father and the family, so was his mind; if the mind had rejected God, so had the spirit. Ciardi, unlike Prufrock, looked not now from the head, now from the heart, while each existed as a mortal threat to the other; he looked from both at once, and we sense that, for all his rationalism, he was moved in his head's direction by his heart, that he thought what he felt and felt what he thought. He was the annalist at the scene, the man in the street. Or let it be that his view of the world was touched enough by modern physics so that every place is the center and every place sat as near the edge as any other. Thus he was resolved in a humility the effect of which was real but not centrifugal. As here:

> I'm wrong as a man is. But right as love,
> and father of the man whose tears I bless
> in this bud boy. May he have cried enough
> when he has cried this little. I confess
> I don't know my own reasons or own way.
> May sons forgive the fathers they obey.
>
> —*"Boy"*

and here:

> I am dark, hungry, blind, absurd
> At every opening motion of a rose.
> I am the cartridge that admires the bird
> By metal sights until my triggers close.
>
> —*"I Meet the Motion of Summer Thinking Guns"*

In "Fast as You Can Count to Ten" he speaks with an unembarrassed honesty as a person among people and in the need that is the need of men:

> Fast as you can count to ten
> commandments, I would count to
> twenty forgivenesses, could I
> think which twenty, and till I

can, let me offer all and without number and beg for myself,
if you please, your used mercies.

Probably the poem that best tells of the man, important and nothing, a little
higher than the animals and yet also dust, at the center and yet seen from the
center, is one of Ciardi's most read and best remembered, "On a Photo of Sgt.
Ciardi a Year Later." Here is the man who in every sense is both subject and
object. Here the humanism, the humility, the social criticism, the quiet anger,
and the plain agony of introspection all come together.

The sgt. stands so fluently in leather,
So poster-holstered and so newsreel-jawed
As death's costumed and fashionable brother,
My civil memory is overawed.

Behind him see the circuses of doom
Dance a finale chorus on the sun.
He leans on gun sights, doesn't give a damn
For dice or stripes, and waits to see the fun.

The cameraman whose ornate public eye
Invented that fine bravura look of calm
At murderous clocks hung ticking in the sky
Palmed the deception off without a qualm.

Even the camera, focused and exact
To a two dimensional conclusion,
Uttered its formula of physical fact
Only to lend data to illusion.

The camera always lies. By a law of perception
The obvious surface is always an optical ruse.
The leather was living tissue in its own dimension,
The holsters held benzedrine tablets, the guns were no use.

The careful slouch and dangling cigarette
Were always superstitious as Amen.
The shadow under the shadow is never caught:
The camera photographs the cameraman.

There are two qualities beyond humility which save Ciardi's poems from intellectual pride, and so set them apart from many that look with a hard eye at society. One is his ability to accept, even to love, the world. Few wrote with more open and unembarrassed compassion for the things of this world than did Ciardi. He cared for everything that honestly is:

> . . . mechanics with wrenches,
> taxi drivers' photos on licenses,
> Drunks lighting cigarettes. . . .

because, he says,

> . . . What the hell else is there to like
> After you've kissed your wife and gone to sleep?
> —*"Philosophical Poem"*

because, he says,

> A man can survive anything except not caring. . . .
> —*"Joshua on Eighth Avenue"*

The other redeeming grace is a sense of the comic, which with love is the only antidote to madness for the humanist who is a critic of a world he is committed to. We may think of Pope again, and of Swift. There is almost nothing in which Ciardi did not see the ridiculous, almost no pose—especially his own—in which he did not see the fool. Thus his story is the "Autobiography of a Comedian": he was left by his father "a comedian without the price of a jokebook," and, as he tells us, in "Coming Home on the 5:22":

> —The rest I've been. That ape up in the tree.
> The botanist below it. The moon boy
> at every bodice. The missionary bee
> sucking for souls. The gunner with his toy.
> The stink of small ambitions. Party clown.
> Professor Poop, pride of the noumenon.

He saw the comic even in that which matters most, which is closest to the bones and most serious. In "Tenzone," a dialogue between his soul and his body, his body says, going straight for whatever jugular the soul has:

176

I've watched you: a scratcher of scabs that are not
    there. An ectoplasmic jitter. Who was it spent
those twenty years and more in the polyglot
    of nightmares talking to Pa?

All of this, the honesty, the insistence on fact, the impatience with hypocrisy, is of course part of the poet's search for himself. A man whose concern is with his own identity, with recognizing who he is, is bound to be concerned with the face behind the face. This was Ciardi's total concern, what he looked for and wrote toward.

He wants to relate all the things of this world to himself, and to understand those relationships. Without an absolute, without a Father, he wants confirmation of the family of things.

What Ciardi was related to finally was the place he found here and us, the readers of his poems for whom that place is a real one. In the strange ecology of the world we call art, his search for a name has named him; his hunger is our bread.

# Some Clerihews for John

## Richard Wilbur

*These verses for fun,*
*obviously composed*
*before John Ciardi died,*
*capture the man too well*
*not to be included here*
*for the joy in remembering.*
*V. C.*

John Ciardi
Mopped his brow and said, "Guardi!
I am done with the *Paradiso*.
It's a blessèd relief to be so."

For John Ciardi
All gods are falsi e bugiardi.
Each time he takes up his pen
He sees right through them again.

Said John Ciardi,
"I agree with old Vince Lombardi.
It's a positive pleasure to win.
Gin."

When John Ciardi
Is relaxing out in his yard, he
Enlightens the flowers and birds
Regarding the roots of words.

John Ciardi
Disapproves of Chef Boy-ar-dee.
But his *own* spaghetti sauce
Strikes him as boss.

John Ciardi
Is not the author of *Mardi*,
And most certainly not of *Typee*.
No South Seas escapist he.

John Ciardi
Writes limericks with no holds barred. He
Has thus somewhat blotted his scutcheon,
Say the purer folk of Metuchen.

When John Ciardi
Wrote the tragical poem "Kiss Me, Hardy,"
One could no longer quarrel
With his being awarded the Laurel.

# *John Ciardi, Science Fiction Writer*

## Elly Welt

John Ciardi, Peter Welt and I are settled on the back patio of the Ciardi house in Key West, catching the last of the day's December sun, John and Peter with diet Pepsis and cigarettes, I with a cigar and scotch. A marinara sauce simmers on the range in the kitchen.

I, a novelist, ask John Ciardi if he has ever written fiction. He answers that he had taken a "science fiction journey" at one time. I express doubt and accuse him of finally having "flipped." But he insists that he has, indeed, written science fiction. I tape the following interview:

ELLY: I am recording this in Key West on what Peter calls a unique day in this year, December 29, the only December 29 in 1984. All right, John.

JOHN: Fletcher Pratt was a very dear friend of mine. He was a historian as a matter of passionate interest, primarily a military and especially a naval historian and wrote huge amounts of science fiction as a way of making a living. He also had a bats' roost house on the Shrewsbery River. It is now burned down. Weekends at what he called the Ipsy Wipsy Institute were a marvelous part of our lives in the late forties and early fifties when I was still teaching at Harvard. I took the family down for a weekend once and Fletcher had gathered science fiction writers. As I recall, Willy Lei was there, Fred Pohl, Lester Del Rey, some others, and Fletcher himself.

They began talking about science fiction as if they were discussing literature, and I began to kid them. I said, "Let's face it, you've invented a form"—I was quoting Benny DeVoto at this point, though I had edited some science fiction for a small house called Twayne Publishers—"You've invented a form in which characterization is irrelevant, motivation is up for grabs, and the narrative may stop at any time for the intrusion of any amount of technical material which stops the flow of the reading. Sometimes a very interesting exercise. I've enjoyed some of it. But don't use the vocabulary in which you would discuss *Moby Dick* or *War and Peace* or *The Magic Mountain* for this hoke stuff. Because anybody who picked out the formula could write this stuff, and if he happens to be literate that's an unfair advantage."

"Oh, yeah, well, I'd like to see you write it."

ELLY: Who said that?

JOHN: That was the consensus of the group—that I was talking through my hat. I ended up with a bet. I faded fifty dollars around the table. Five people put up ten. Fletcher Pratt held the stakes. The conditions of the bet were that it would take me Sunday to get the family back home, and Monday I had classes to teach at Harvard, that Monday night I would start writing, and by midnight of the next Monday, I would have in the mail to Fletcher a science fiction short story. The agreement was that he would send it to *Fantasy and Science Fiction* as number one; to *Galaxy*, I think that was the name of the magazine, as number two; and to *Thrilling Wonder* as number three, if I have the names right.

ELLY: Thrilling wonder!

JOHN: And one of the three had to buy it or I would lose my bet, but if any one of them accepted it, I would collect. So I drove back to Cambridge thinking, what on earth do I know about science that I haven't seen in other science fiction stories? And I hit upon tropism, the condition in general whereby organisms are attracted by certain things and repelled by others. Cats would rather be warm than wet. That's a tropism. Fish would rather be wet than dry. That's a tropism. It's a tendency in their nature.

I began to pull the long bow in every direction. I picked out the star Deneb Kaitos and decided that its third planet was inhabited but had a very, very cloudy atmosphere. Very little ultraviolet could penetrate the atmosphere, which made it important that all of it be absorbed, so that obesity with very fine skin got to be a survival characteristic. The women of Deneb Kaitos III used to lounge around on terraces soaking up what little ultraviolet came through the mist, and they developed such marvelous control of their skin surfaces that having sex with one of them was like riding a roller coaster.

(LAUGHTER.)

JOHN: I pulled out all stops. Moreover, as a survival characteristic, none of the animals on the planet had any fur. Fur would block out the ultraviolet. So they all had very sensitive hairless skins. As it happened, the men had bred down into scrawny sorts of runts but were rather strong, and used to run naked through the woods setting traps.

The traps consisted of feely sculptures like Japanese netsukes or Greek worry beads. And once one of these animals with its supersensitive skin, as part of its tropism, rubbed against these feely sculptures, it couldn't stop stroking. It was hypnotically there until the men came along with the club and whanged it and took it back and the women cooked it.

This was in the twenty-sixth or -seventh century—that gave me a chance for an excursion into tactile sculpture and the wonders that follow from it when the great master of tactile sculpture developed his motifs. He even succeeded in curing constipation forever by sculpting a toilet seat that was so perfect to the touch that it loosened all.

(LAUGHTER.)

JOHN: I pulled out no stops. I was doing this very tongue in cheek. The basic story is about a young man—a boy—who is figuring on going out into space, who calls to interview an old space traveler. The old space traveler had been up in a huge spaceship, and had found the remnants of a high carbon planet that had suffered a collision and had been made into an asteroid belt orbiting a sun, and, of course, since it was high carbon and a planet, the core was all diamonds, the result of heat and pressure. So he loaded his spaceship full of diamonds and carved some of them into his furniture and the decorations of his house, and the others were just in bins around there. And he had collected all sorts of space stuff.

The boy was avidly interested in this loot. The man talked on in a seductive and affable voice, and the boy became more and more glassy-eyed as he looked about. Finally, inhaling the smoke of a Martian cheroot as he drank some Venution brandy, the man leaned over and blew the smoke into the boy's eyes. The boy gave no response. He was hypnotized. And at that point the man went to a dark enclosure off to one side and pulled the curtain and there was a white blob inside. "He is ready, darling," the man said.

For it had been found that earth men could mate with Deneb Kaitos women and refresh and renew the genetic pool. That made them very welcome and the people of Deneb Kaitos gave them all sorts of benefits and grants and franchises. This, along with his diamonds, was the basis of the old man's enormous wealth and power.

I did it all tongue in cheek, piling on everything I possibly could.

ELLY: Did you put your own name on it?

JOHN: I wouldn't use my own name. I left Ciardi off. John Anthony.

ELLY: John Anthony.

JOHN: And I called it "The Hypnoglyph." The hypnotic carving.

Well, I sent it to Fletcher. He sent it to the editor of *Fantasy and Science*

182

*Fiction,* Tony Boucher, and Tony made one suggestion. The boy was looking around with greed as the man said, "There are, as you can see, certain advantages, to a successful space voyage."

"And how," said the boy.

Tony Boucher wanted a little touch of characterization. So I altered it to "'And how,' said the boy with an avid leer."

That did for characterization.

The story was published. I got one hundred dollars for it at the time. I collected fifty on my bet. I thought it was a pretty good joke. But then a number of things started to happen. A man named Dichty (this was 1950, I may be wrong) did an anthology called *Best Science Fiction of the Year.* He included this story, and I got a check for that. Then August Durleth did the same thing—*Best Science Fiction of the Year*—included my story, and I got a check for that. Then I began to get a small rain of "rights." Seventeen dollars for the Norwegian translation. Eleven for the Arabic translation. So many dollars for the French. British rights. German rights. These science fiction stories go into every damn language in the world. I've never had anything that was so often translated. Small checks—but they added up.

In the course of the next two years, I had nearly a thousand dollars as driblet income from this. Then some time went by and Judith Merrill, former wife of Fred Pohl, did an anthology of the best science fiction of the past fifty years and included my story. So I got another check.

Time went by, and I'd just about forgotten it when I got a last check for seventy-five dollars from *The New York Post.* They reran the story in their Saturday magazine.

I ended up making something under fifteen hundred dollars on that joke. And I think I proved my point.

ELLY: Did you talk to any of the science fiction writers after you won the bet?

JOHN: Oh I met them here and there.

ELLY: Do you recall any comments from them?

JOHN: I kept on kidding them in the same way. A few people who are pundits in these things said I wasn't really a science fiction writer, I was just a flash in the pan, and they'd have to see some more from me. But I only did one more story.

I was reviewing some books by Archibald MacLeish. One poem was about a letter to be left in the earth. As I reviewed the book, there came to me a notion. Very rapidly, I knocked off a story I've lost track of, but it appeared in *Fantasy and Science Fiction.*

ELLY: Under John Anthony.

JOHN: Yes. It was about a robot, number three in the series. It goes way, way back—for centuries. These were early self-repairing robots. The later robots were technically programmed. This one was programmed for the humanities as well. Later robots had the humanities left out of them. But now, centuries later, even though it's capable of repairing itself, it's beginning to think, "My entity is tired."

It's sitting under a tree transposing Bach variations into color patterns and doing these other things to pass the time. But it thinks, finally, "My entity is tired," and it switches itself off. Back to oblivion.

Tony Boucher bought that. So those are the two science fiction stories I did.

ELLY: Did you ever write any other fiction?

JOHN: No, that was all of it. Fiction can be wonderful stuff, but I've always suffered from the illusion that it was like drinking beer when what I really wanted was bourbon. Poetry is more concentrated. And I simply discovered that I don't have the skills for maintaining the flow in the dilution of prose. I need the tightness of poetic—what shall I say—essence?

ELLY: Why does it sound so condescending when you speak of prose? Why don't you compare fiction to, at least, wine, rather than beer? Bourbon and wine I could accept, John.

JOHN: If that pleases you. I'm just talking about relative alcoholic content.

(LAUGHTER.)

JOHN: And in all defense of your drinking habits, there are those who think beer is good stuff. I don't mean it to be condescending because I don't have the skills to manage the long pull of fiction.

ELLY: Do you think poets are better gin rummy players than fiction writers?

JOHN: It's obvious to me.

(LAUGHTER.)

# *John Ciardi and the White Line under the Snow*

## Isaac Asimov

I met John Ciardi for the first time in 1951, when he was 36. He was slim in those days and he had a craggy face, with a magnificent mane of black hair, and an operatic bass voice that could recite television commercials and hold you enthralled with the poetry of it. What else?—Oh, yes, he had a noble nose that any two Roman Emperors would have been proud of.

Since opposites attract, he also had Judith, who was blonde and beautiful.

In the following years, he slowly gained avoirdupois and embonpoint. (You see the advantage of French. In English one must say "gained weight and grew fat," which would be coarse and graceless. The *meaning* is the same, though, if you're interested in meaning.) His face was even more craggy and his voice even more de profundis. As for his nose, you will be relieved to know, it held its own.

And he still had Judith, still blonde and beautiful.

I have two favorite stories about John that he told me himself. He couldn't, however, tell them as well as I can because, unlike me, he wasn't a talented writer. Of course, he was a poet, but that's not the same as a *writer*. (That reminds me that once, when I was taking leave of him, I held out my hand and said, "Farewell, O minor poet!" Without missing a beat, he said, "Farewell, O major pain in the ass!")

The first story is set on a gray and dismal December morning, when the ground was covered with a thin, fresh layer of snow and John was steering his car into a deserted Central Park. He was suddenly stopped by a young policeman, who had apparently not handed out his quota of tickets and was filled with ambition to correct that blot on his escutcheon.

"What's the matter, officer?" said John.

"You crossed the white line, mister. Let me have your registration card and driver's license."

John looked down at the solid layer of white on which his car rested and said, "What white line, officer?"

"Underneath the snow is a white line and you've crossed it," said the policeman.

"But there's not another car on the drive or in the entire park. What's the difference?"

"Your registration card and driver's license," said the admirably dutiful policeman.

John, with gathering fury, handed them over.

The policeman copied the information on the documents and then said, "What is your occupation?"

And John, who had had all he could take, put his head out the window (did I tell you he looked like a Godfather of the whole eastern seaboard who has just heard that a pipsqueak messenger boy has failed to show him respect) and growled, in bass, "I'm a poet, damn it!"

A less likely poet never did in this world exist, but the policeman looked at him calmly and said, "Does that mean you're self-employed?"

That broke John's spirit, and he took his ticket and drove off, carefully remaining on the right side of the white line thereafter.

Personally, I think John missed a beat there. He should have replied. "No, I am *not* self-employed, damn it. I'm a research poet for Union Carbide."

The second story involves John's penchant for collecting little terra-cotta images produced by the ancient Etruscans. An Etruscan woman, you see, might fail to become pregnant after she had had a few chances at that interesting condition handed her by the assiduous attentions of her husband, or of some desirable substitute. This would frighten her, for pregnancy was the only acceptable reason for retaining a wife. To avoid being kicked out she would make an offer of a terra-cotta image to a local god who was in charge of pregnancies. In order to please the god, or to remind him what it was he was supposed to do, the image was usually in the form of a male generative organ.

For whatever reason, John loved to collect these and line them up prominently, in a glass-enclosed bookcase, where he could freely gaze at them and absorb their beauties.

Judith viewed the images with less pride. While appreciative (I am sure) of their artistry and of the thoughts to which they might give rise, she did, on occasion, entertain the cream of local society in her home. On those occasions, she was not entirely comfortable at the thought of having the well-brought-up ladies of the parish assaulted by these sensuous objects. She would therefore gather them up and bestow them elsewhere temporarily.

Of course, Judith had a great deal to do, and when the gathering was over why, as like as not, she'd forget that she had meant to return the terra-cotta representatives of the genital organs to their accustomed place and, after a few days, she also forgot where it was that she had bestowed them temporarily. They would then remain missing for an indefinite period till John came upon them accidentally.

And then, one day, when John was allowed to obtrude his presence on the genteel company that Judith had carefully gathered, he became aware of the gaping hole on the shelf where the terra-cotta images ought to have reposed gracefully. The tide of his exasperation rose till he looked like a Godfather of the entire eastern seaboard with a pipsqueak messenger boy not only failing to show him respect, but coming over and kicking him in the shins.

"God damn it, Judith," he roared in a rumbling thunder, "what have you done with my genitals?"

There is no record that Judith had a coherent answer for that question, though I imagine the rest of the company waited for one with the greatest conceivable interest.

# Una Festa con John Ciardi:
## *Random Thoughts*

## John Tagliabue

It does me good to be in on a gathering of thoughts concerning John Ciardi. I didn't want to be formal and write a review (when do I ever do that?); I wanted to *enjoy re*reading his poems and some of his prose; and while doing that, between lectures (in which I often quote him), I've written down a few notes; so be it, Festschrift.

Surveyor and moderator that he was, his work stands us in good stead, helps steady the soul. In a time of much breakdown and chaos, it helps make things clear. He reminds us of the mystery and complexity of good sanity—a sanity *rare enough* these years. Free of murky *weltschmerz*, free of self-indulgence. Slowly and thoughtfully he gives us a poetry free of the frenetic and crabbed convolution; a poetry rich with references and relatives; a poetry which maintains a control of *tempo;* and it *does* cohere. Thanks also to Nona Domenica Garnaro.

And so I think of him as a guardian of the faith—the faith in the tribe/family . . . dignity-and-dictionary. Finding the right words, respecting the roots of words and their flowering, translating, transplanting with care—that's benevolently revealing. Many relatives-and-words; immigration and making a go of it, book after book of poetry, of remembering-and-declaring; making a stanza, taking a stance. This earth craftsman has a steady hand and a certain moderation that reveals strength. This reminds me of something my great teacher Mark Van Doren wrote about a writer that the three of us admire: "The way of Robert Frost consists in occupying or touching both extremes at once, and inhabiting the space between. It consists in being capable of excess while actually achieving more than excess achieves. It consists in finding that golden mean which, far from signifying that the extremes have been avoided, signifies that they have been enclosed and contained."

I just finished reading "Driving across the American Desert and Thinking of the Sahara"; Ciardi is resourceful in making road maps that don't get us lost, that help us remember. (Didn't that other Italian, Boethius, say somewhere, "We are sick because we forget *how* to *remember*"?) His poems take us to all sorts of places—New Jersey, Rome, Napoli, Missouri, Dante's Paradiso, Bates College, Tufts, etc.—to make us more thoughtful. They keep their sense of perspective, of humor; and they never lose the power of the personal touch. I think of Chekhov too now because of family scenes and revealing details and because of Ciardi's ability to tell a *story* in a poem. Frost and Robinson and a few others can do that well but not many others in this century of fragmentation where "things fall apart, the center cannot hold." Ciardi sustains, maintains. It's obvious that just to quote first stanza from a long story-telling poem can't do justice to it; but I want to remind you of its virtues of vividness and affection.

> At first light in the shadow, over the roach
> like topaz on the sill, over the roofs,
> the Old North Church spire took its time to heaven
> where God took His to answer.
> > I took my drink
> at clammy soapstone round a drain of stinks
> and slid back into bed, my toes still curled
> from the cold lick of linoleum. Ma was first,
> shaking the dead stove up. Then Pa,
> a rumble hocking phlegm. When the cups clattered
> I could get up and climb him and beg *biscotti*
> while Ma sipped cups of steam and scolded love.

(That's from "The Shaft.") I can't help but understand and like these humorous and sometimes sad poems—about John Follo and Uncle Alec and Frank Fiore. Poems that certainly *keep democracy, keep open house* (the way my father kept an open restaurant in New Jersey where old Italians played *bocce*).

Ciardi's poems *want* to be clear and enjoy and find unity, are personal and primary that way. Somewhere he wrote: "Do not ask the poem to be more rational than you are. The way to read a poem is with pleasure: with the child's pleasure in tasting the syllables on his tongue, with the marvel of the child's eyes . . . to read a poem come prepared for delight."

The *Selected Poems* makes a collected *character*—and one that has variety. There are the "Bang Bang" poems, for instance, that know the ordeal of war, the wasted lives in war. Poems that are aware of sorrow and difficulties and yet fortunately keep their/our *equilibrium*. And poems that show the definite pleasure that Ciardi takes in coming to knowledge, in words, in rhyme, in marriage, the good game as to his *definite choices* (in *I Marry You*, for instance); many poems that have internal harmony and create the strength of a good character within them. I agree with Ciardi, who wrote: "What the universities and the new criticism they have bred seem to have lost sight of in the course of achieving other and admirable insights is the simple fact that once the poet has achieved technical competence the badness of the bad poem is always a failure of character."

I was glad to be on the campus and not traveling as I often do when he was here in 1970 to receive an Honorary Degree from Bates. He had started his college studies here; I came here as a teacher in 1953, many years later. Maybe it would have pleased him to know that he had been helping me and my students out since then—when I was talking about Dante (and using his translation) and when I was talking about other poets. I just a few minutes ago copied out of his book *Manner of Speaking* some comments he made about Richard Eberhart and that I'll be quoting in my New England poetry course that starts soon. Here's one of his thoughts that I've been passing on for years: "The one great school of poetry is the poets *in* their poems, and there is no other. Any writer who really wants his work criticized need only turn to the masters to ask of their pages in despair—if he is capable of reading them and capable of an honest despair— what is wrong with his own."

Now much of this sounds in certain Emersonian ways open and generous and with that gift outright that Whitman finds supreme in his 1855 Preface—the virtue of candor. And sometimes the manner (as in much of the best modern poetry) seems matter of fact, prosaic; the poems are fortunately aware of the mundane (and its miracles). Again I am reminded of that sturdy down-to-earth, down-to-Calabria, poem—"Nona Domenica Garnaro"; I imagine many of his writings as blessed by that grandmother's nature. Somewhere he said that a person is finally defined by what he gives his attention to. Relations, how people are related, one of his major ways of getting the act together. But expansive as he naturally is, he makes many connections; and so we are related to saints and bees and crocuses. Specific and objective; in "Saturday, March 6th" this descendent of Columbus goes out in his pajamas to pick up the newspaper, the *Times*, and he discovers "the first three crocuses half open . . . And that's what day it is."

O what a *relief!* poems *without* an "identity crisis"! There are many poems that I want to go back to—"Two Saints" . . . "Bees and Morning Glories" . . .

190

"A Five-Year Step" . . . "A Conversation with Leonardo" . . . "Naples" . . . and
the "Poems from Italy"; sometimes they are sort of prayers; anyway they *increase
our respect;* this one for instance—"Thoughts on Looking into a Thicket"; here's
the third stanza.

> Must I defend my prayers? I dream the world
> at ease in its long miracle. I ponder the egg,
> like a pin head in silk spit, invisibly stored
> with the billion years of its learning. Have angels
> more art than this? I read the rooty palm
> of God for the great scarred Life Line. If you
> will be more proper than real, that is your
> death. I think life will do anything for a living.

Readers, find your own favorites, become familiar with them. Many of their
thoughts can help give us strength, good feelings.

# Ciardi's Winter Words:
## Some Oblique Notes on a Southern Education

### Edward Krickel

If a reader of (some) general culture approached John Ciardi's poems for the first time by way of reviews of recent books, *For Instance* (1979) and *Selected Poems* (1984), he would probably not go on to the poems. It might serve him right, but it would serve many other things wrong. Forty years ago, Ciardi thought such a reader might in the long run be more important to poetry than Eliot and Pound.

As any good reviewer should do, the one in *Poetry* cut both ways, but the negative slashes are deeper. (The *Virginia Quarterly Review* was ambivalent on the *Selected Poems*; see the Spring 1985 issue.) Not only is it "fashionable to consider John Ciardi a poet long past his prime," but even to defend his recent work is to risk "being labelled hopelessly out-of-touch." The reason given is that "for years he has published no new volume in which the bad poems do not greatly outnumber the good." To be sure, "a few times in each book Ciardi has struck exactly the right notes, creating poems that are strong, memorable, and unmistakably personal." When details are given, they seem personal to the reviewer, as much individual preference as judgment, and not better than another taste. The values are those of the young, progressive, and *au courant*, and, it follows, pose the possibility that the old fellow may be "on the verge of an important new phase" (*Poetry*, May 1982, 112–14). Reviewers said much the same thing of *Homeward to America* in 1940. It is a nice way to end a review.

However innocently the points are made, the assumptions back of them provoke me to comment. As a reconstructed but unregenerate Southerner, may I speak up for values other than the progressive? I propose in the rest of this essay to give some kind of answer to the question, "Why read Ciardi?" His mastery of his idiom is real and admirable and not in question. Careful rereading will solve most of the problems any of the poems pose. Since I have elsewhere submitted what I found in the other books of poems, let me here keep in mind the recent ones, or at least the aspects that interest me of the late poems of the poet allegedly "long past his prime." They are the concept of the "unimportant" poem (Ciardi's word) and what the winter view of life offers a reader.

Ciardi said of his own long and fruitful reading of Dante, "I do not read him because he is of the fourteenth century but because I am of the twentieth." (Dante gives me too many reasons why I should be in Hell.) If I cannot claim quite the same thing for my reading of the modern poet, something like it may pertain.

It is not personal. Ciardi in the flesh I met only once, long enough to shake his hand, a decade before I ever thought to write on him. He talked on the silences of poetry, without notes, reciting whole poems and analyzing them. He spoke quietly, yet held the attention of a large audience. As a new teacher, I was impressed.

The only work of his I knew then was *Mid-Century American Poets*, which included himself. I did not especially like his poems, though his prose made plenty of sense even in my new-doctoral arrogance. "Elegy Just in Case" was clever, damned clever, but not one of my favorites—I learned later it was one of his and much revised. To me it lacked dignity, substance, the kind of tension I was schooled to value. The tone was brash, hardly polite, not sober or somber, not at all like Tate's "Ode to the Confederate Dead" or the elegant Pyrrhonism of Ransom's poems. I was replete with the ignorance and vulnerability of my arrogance. Didn't I know how to analyze poems? Hadn't I read poetry textbooks and the English and American standard authors? I knew *Understanding Poetry* and *The Well Wrought Urn*. I could tear up Joyce Kilmer's "Trees," which I had been told students liked, and could even add a clever point of my own. The education I got from Ciardi's work began at these low lumens of enlightenment. Before I got through reading his poems, I knew a great deal less than I did on beginning, and by knowing less, I knew a great deal more.

There were many other obstacles. I was Southern; conservative (whatever that meant); innocent of large segments of life and the world; rural and small town orientation; middle class; Protestant (more inherited than practiced, but certainly not Catholic). The only Italians I had seen were fruit vendors, first making their rounds in a horse-drawn cart, but later ensconced in a thriving shop in a far-away part of thriving Nashville. They had dark skins and dark oily hair. The children went to Catholic schools. The parents spoke with a funny accent which we knew was Italian.

When I read Ciardi's Missouri poems, I was annoyed. He insufficiently understood his in-laws (who reminded me of my Arkansas relatives); he was the city boy afield, and the discomfiture of such was a traditional country pleasure. And for a veteran of WWII to worry about boys with .22 rifles as a cause of wars seemed more liberal doctrinaire than real. Forty years later in "Censorship" more of the story comes out, told with grim humor. The squeaky bed springs kept the new husband from his bride; her disapproving parents were a thin wall away. To hell with the rural and its puritanical ways! Any sympathizer with young manhood would agree.

The only actual student of Ciardi's I ever met was a lady whose poems he had read at Bread Loaf. She had suffered a nervous breakdown from his harsh criticisms of her work. As best I could make out, they were to the effect that she should not write Elizabethan poems in the second half of the twentieth century. (Readers may remember the furors he provoked by his negative responses to the poems of two other ladies, Edna Millay and Anne Morrow Lindbergh.) The lady did not know that as bad a shock had happened to youthful Ciardi when John Holmes penciled beside one of his poems, "All right; you're haunted. When does it haunt me?" The mature poet recalled, "I was never pretty again in any mirror." The lady of my example, sufficiently attractive in person, never again, I will bet, admired her countenance in an "enchanted glass"; whoever looked from her twentieth-century mirror, made in Taiwan, it was not an Elizabethan lady. And whoever wrote her post-Ciardi poems was starkly of our time. A note on another southern education!

Dante did much to educate Ciardi. The medieval poet spoke to him about the craft and art of poetry, about things worth doing; these are endlessly plumable. Surely, too, the older spoke to the younger as a human being, the differences between the two probably more important than any similarities. If I cannot claim all of this, I do claim some of it. And so, whether or not it follows, I read Ciardi *because* I am Southern, WASP, the descendent of slave owners. (In my childhood, I actually saw a black man, older than the hills, who had been a slave of my great-grandfather.) Nevertheless, there was the family tradition that back a few years we had been fugitives from Prussian military conscription. Reading Ciardi with every difference acknowledged, I am thrown back upon myself. His idea expressed at the time of *I Marry You* that any man's depths uttered truly speak to any other man's is undoubtedly sound. Even if it were not true, any man's experiences of life however extrapolated and imaginatively twisted for the sake of a poem will appeal to another man's interest in the lives of his fellow men. Southerners have a well-known relish for such tales, as both hearers and tellers—however extrapolated and imaginatively twisted. But I also read Ciardi for what he tells me about the life I inadequately lead. I feel better about my failures, better about the modest successes, the complacencies, aware that this is far from "high aesthetic" experience and based upon self-proclaimed "unimportant" poems.

Ciardi got excellent poetic use out of the idea of the "unimportant" poem, the poem done his way, in "An Apology for Not Invoking the Muse." His fullest statement is a prose essay in the *Michigan Quarterly Review* (Winter 1982), entitled "On the Importance of Unimportant Poems." As a young man in the red thirties at Michigan, he, like his young compatriots, wrote important poems on the social issues of the day by the requirements of the prevailing dogmas. The mature man, survivor of many conflicts and disillusionments, sees a warped reflection of his earlier days in "young, socially-activated poets" with their evident "assumption that the one prerequisite for poetry is the excitation of one's own ignorance." Instead of poetry being an assertion or act of will, he now understands it as "a being, a hearkening to being, and a way of being." He can say with the authority of many books behind him:

> I write unimportant poems because I am human and gross and have nothing to say. I am, however, a language suppliant. The language is wiser, deeper, more sentient, and more haunted than anyone who uses it. I mean only to woo the language, to submit myself to it as best I can, and to hope that when I have hearkened to it humbly and gratefully, it will now and then empower me to do what I could never have done when I was important and came to the poem with a half-prepared speech, intending only to raid the language for flourishes.

An artist may, like James and John Crowe Ransom, redo earlier works, ruining them for some readers, or he may refuse revision, like Jeffers and Dylan Thomas, on the ground that he would be kept from new work. Or like Ciardi put out a winnowed selection that includes less than a fifth of the published work, but one that presumably meets his mature standards. Why is it not as good as, or even better than, an "important new phase" for a poet to give us what fruits his maturity will bear? (Auden called it "dry farming.") Ciardi has done this, if the poems of *For Instance*, written in his sixth decade, qualify. Should we not want our poets to write all the way to the grave and to leave a volume for posthumous publication? Anything else is absurd. Think of Lawrence's "Bavarian Gentians" and "Ship of Death."

What is an "unimportant" poem? Presumably, one that is personal, in that it conforms to as much of truth as the interaction between poet and subject will allow and words will vouchsafe. Frost's statement would seem to be related when he said he wanted to lodge a few pebbles where they could not become unlodged. A distant cousin at least is Yeats's pronouncement, "the Romanticist deceives himself, the Rhetorician deceives his neighbors, while Art is but a vision of Reality."

The forty-two poems in *For Instance* continue the poet's longtime themes and attitudes, chiefly coming to terms with the contemporary world as its bits and chips scatter about the patio of the self-made rich man who writes when something provokes him to write. I think he must have taken a lot of pleasure writing such poems as "Suburban," "Knowing Bitches," and others out of daily, mundane life. If some of the poems seem thin, could suburban life be thin? As Ciardi had said in "Tree Trimming" twenty years earlier, it lacks the dimension of the past. My rural students can recall anecdotes of their forebears in the Revolutionary War, rarely heroic and probably not literally true, but a long family tradition is part of their identity. Ciardi's tones, still recognizable as his own, appear in *For Instance*, and ironies are as pervasive and necessary to his poems as breath to life. The Italian peasant heritage is now only a brush stroke in the picture of suburban affluence—like a Verga novel, with the final chapters still to be written. Education is spoofed or mocked one more time for the inexactness of its jargon. Best of all is the acceptance, making the best of a good but not flawless existence. What better could a flawed human creature do? His work is made out of everyday experiences that his responses lift to the level of poetry because of his intelligence which sees meaning, parallels, analogues, and relations with the world—the circles widening. Ciardi has a metaphysical mind, in every sense of the term, as Donne's was, only in a different world.

I will not try to illustrate the depths in any Ciardi poem—which I might not be able to do—but we know his commitment to the accurate use of words all the way back to their origins; see his brief disquisition on the right use of "arrive" in *How Does a Poem Mean?* or see Eliot's use in "Prufrock" of the word "overwhelm," as called to our attention in the *Second Browser's Dictionary*. Much of the effect of the poem "Stations" depends upon the play from one meaning of the word to another, often more than one at the same time. This kind of thing offers both poet and reader a sufficiency of aesthetic pleasure. And of course the awareness of the depths of words corresponds to living life with an awareness of its deep places. Thus, more than the aesthetic results, again for poet and reader, so that poetry, whether solemn or not, becomes a moral experience.

Surely, a significant poem is one that echoes through our experiences and explains the meaning of our lives, our actions, and gives us hope, consolation, at the very least something to measure by, so that understanding results. Here a reader may take his choice of poems. The possibilities are several. If enough readers over a period of time make the same choices, perhaps the poems are major.

But why do minor poems and lines stick in my mind? An avid bird-watching friend of mine reads Ciardi because of one of his gull poems. Who knows what else may stick, even if it starts in sentimentality? Could some of the small poems I like be true poems, or do I like them because of my manifold inadequacies? Pebbles are as real as boulders. Perhaps I do have a disinclination for the imposing, the major so tagged in our PR-inundated age. When I was in graduate work at a southern university, I announced the same dissertation topic at the same time as a young Yaleman. My graduate dean, himself a Yaleman, accepted without hesitation the primacy of the other boy's claim and the priority of his announcement. His director, a grand scholar of the old school, had earlier been my dean's director. My rival was said to be "the brightest young man of his generation." It had to follow that his work would be definitive. Encouraged by my director's sage remark that he had never known a Yaleman who was not "the brightest goddamn young man of his generation," I entered the race. Perhaps because of not bearing the burden of his superlatives, I beat him through by some months, with a dissertation I long ago realized the faults of. It was acceptable. Fifteen or so years later, his book came out, adapted from the dissertation. It was a nice book. I had it reviewed in a journal I edited. Thus—I like the modest disclaimer that Ciardi makes about the "unimportant" poems he writes. He may not be a modest man, but he is an honest poet.

Basil Bunting characterized Pound's *Cantos* as the Alps. I will continue my cautious climb, acknowledging the grandeur and possible profundity, but I respond increasingly—a man grows older—to Ciardi's "Washing Your Feet." It is as moving in its quiet presentation of what a life comes to as is Pound in Pisa admitting the connection between his ego and his plight. If it is wrong to find help in poetry for one's daily realities—if only the help of better understanding by means of recognition and on to perspective—then I admit my crime, my guilt, my lack of sophistication, my need. But since I am not an inexperienced reader, still a long way from dotage, still the enemy of too-easy sentiments, and since I continue to expect poets to work for the responses they get from me, I suggest such poems are true ones, small or not.

Ciardi's "unimportant" poems—I like "In the Hole"—do not aspire to shake the world or swerve things in their course. Leave those ambitions for youths writing important poems. To those of us who are shocked at the years we have accumulated, watching our diets, sunk not altogether happily into our relative complacencies, many of them speak poignantly. We might have been different, we set out to be, we might be yet!—no, not that. We do understand better that life is always as it is, not as it might have been. And, as Ciardi said:

> It's good enough. At least not bad.
> Better than dog bones and lamb stew.
> It does. Or it will have to do.

I must not pretend that I do not value Pound's Pisan admission that an adult thirty years of thought was in ruins forever. It is almost like Lear on the Heath.

But I also respond to the old Hardy, the telephone lines humming with no message for him ("Nobody Comes") or taking in a stray cat in winter ("Snow in the Suburbs"). Hardy wanted it said that he noticed little things ("Afterwards"), in which case why is the fallow deer looking warily into the lighted window at night so unforgettable? Ciardi could have gotten a poem out of any of the above. The tone and manner would of course be his own. The same with William Carlos Williams' "Turkey in the Straw," "The Artist," "The Sparrow," "To a Dog Injured in the Street." Is part of their quality that they are old men's poems? Whatever, I would not want to have missed Ciardi's "Firsts," "Tuesday: Four Hundred Miles," "Birthday," "No White Bird Sings," "Jackstraws," "On Passion as a Literary Tradition" from *For Instance*, these barely noticed or not at all by reviewers. The truth is, as Kenneth Rexroth pointed out, major poets are always writing about everything—he cited Pound's "Les Millwin." In all the cases, including John Ciardi's, I am grateful.

# The Good Influence of John Ciardi

## George Garrett

*"Not everything that happens*
*is a learning experience. Maybe nothing is."*
*—John Ciardi: "For Instance"*

I am thinking here of influence not in the complex, gnarled and often crabbed senses of it as adopted and advanced by the gospel according to Harold Bloom; not, then, as some kind of intellectual haunting, not as a matter of any great and shadowy anxiety nor in the least as any kind of competition between the past and the present. Nothing of the sort. What I am thinking about is at once more simple and, I would like to think, deeper, though it can be described in a language without the cover and concealment of adroit obfuscation. All of us who try to write poems do so under various influences. In our age, an age (to claim the very least) of the widest kind of literary diversity, of the wildest plurality of forms and voices and tones of voice (and, alas, standards) we are all constantly on the lookout for worthwhile and imitable examples. We seek to learn by and from both good and bad examples. In the absence of widely accepted standards of excellence we are forced not so much to define our own as to find our own from among the apparent practice of our peers and, especially, from the strategies and tactics of the elders, our immediate predecessors who have lived and worked in roughly the same literary world as ourselves. Here John Ciardi's example is particularly important; for he stood as one of the very few among that generation of elders who remained fully active and productive as poets. From many, maybe a majority of the others, the lesson to be learned by their example might well be to quit early, if possible, while ahead, to be dealt out of the game soon enough to rest on laurels, to cut your losses or to take your winnings, adequate or meager, and run.

So that is the first lesson. John Ciardi taught by example: that with a little luck or a lot of hard labor, it may just be possible to continue being a poet, to keep on writing poetry, with, of course, all the risks inherent to that life and calling, a vocation proudly demonstrated by his last book of *new* poems—*The Birds of Pompeii* (1985).

But I am running ahead of myself already. At this stage the only point I wanted to make, a very general one, was that, for the kinds of influence I am thinking of, we of roughly my own generation turn to the elders just behind us, John's generation; for it is from them, their good and bad examples, that we have the most useful things to learn. It is the useful things, what can be begged or borrowed or stolen, even (yes) what can be copied, that we are concerned with. Poets even as near to us in time as Eliot and Pound and Yeats, as Wallace Stevens and William Carlos Williams and Robert Frost, for example, have much less of this to teach us; partly, of course, because they were, each in his own way, so successful in their conventional rebellion from *their* elders that we have already forgotten who most of their prominent predecessors were and what on earth the whole fuss was all about; but partly, also, because the world they lived in and wrote about, though it partakes of a good-size chunk of this selfsame century, is radically different from our own and might as well be (it often seems to me) separated from our times by the dark gulf of many centuries. There are times when it honestly seems to me that we are closer to the lives and times of Wyatt and Chaucer, or Villon, perhaps, and certainly of Virgil, at least the Virgil of the *Eclogues*, than we are to the early Eliot or the later Pound. I am naturally assuming the spontaneous and coterminous equality of all the honored dead, at least in their continual haunting of the present and of the living. And I am not considering the usual contemporary critical distinctions between modernism and post-modernism, distinctions which seem to me about as important, or unimportant as the case may be, as the length of skirts, the height of collars, the width of neckties. Our grandparents witnessed the end of something, itself perhaps an illusion and a brief one, but nonetheless something which might as well be called Civilization. And which may well have been Civilization for all we know. We come along later and deeper in the dark ages of the brutalized twentieth century. We have only the faintest recollection of the almost unimaginable times before. Even our nostalgia is lavished on barbarous times. In John's times and wars, and in mine, which overlap, we have been witness to the murder of hundreds of millions of people. Rivers, maybe oceans of blood have been flowing. Imagine what it would be like for all of us if it were not characteristic of blood to clot and dry quickly. By now half the world would be drowned in human blood, just as the world would be tipped over by the weight of our injustices to each other. Never mind the gothic horror of that image. Instead, consider more simply that John's generation and mine have been witness to many terrible things.

As a matter of course. We share that with each other and have to look to each other for comfort and solace, for some understanding.

Nobody but one among us, a creature of these times, could have written these lines of John's, ripped out of context from "Useless Knowledge," the penultimate poem in *The Birds of Pompeii:*

> . . . These are notes
> for a sermon on the sanctity of survival
> to teach that life is not worth dying for.
>
> But have we a choice? I have flown my hot missions
> in a flammable bottle when I could have been grounded
> on permanent garbage detail. What's wrong with garbage?

Nobody living fully in the second half of this century needs much of a gloss or an explication of those lines.

But maybe equally important, when you cast aside the big cosmic forces and issues, which casting aside is the first gesture of the veteran soldier, throwing away every piece of inessential equipment as he goes into combat; casting aside huge and vague facts for homely truths, we have to admit that the life of the poet, the profession of letters in our time is quite distinctly different for us than it was for that luckier, earlier generation. The social and economic details of this era of ours are at once obvious and tedious to talk about. And I won't trouble you with them except to say that where, with precious few exceptions, they, our literary grandparents, were adequately, if not always well-heeled, there are now precious few ladies and gentlemen of letters left among us. There are, it is true, a few writers, among them poets, who are the fortunate children of considerable inherited wealth, for whom the vocation of literature is, therefore, a matter of free and easy choice, but of next to no risk (except the risk of failing as writer, and there is at least some possible insurance against that if you can afford the extraordinary premiums). But most American poets these days come out of the hard-pressed, overtaxed, American middle class, some quite recently arrived there. Some have arrived there, in a literary paradigm of "the American dream," on their own, from hard and meager beginnings. John Ciardi is one of these latter. Read *Lives of X* (available again, thanks be, in *Selected Poems* (1984)), for the unsentimental story of it. Then maybe read the newer "Audit at Key West" for the other end of the story, the acute awareness of the killing weight of inflation on old and young American dreamers.

> . . . The world is divided
> into those who managed to buy in time, and their children

who can no longer afford to and must wait
for their parents to die.

Enough of belaboring the obvious. I hope I have made the point that since we share a world which is much the same to each other and is distinctly different from the one just before and maybe the one to come after . . .

Well, then, maybe a word about that—the youngsters. I am not sure that our younger poets, some of them our very own students, have very much to teach us except, by merely being there and being young, the immutable veracity, not a cynical syllable in it, of the statement that youth is wasted on the young. It is also possible to learn from them to accept the fact, without undue embarrassment, that we were mostly foolish when we were young. But one does not look to or among them for models on how to live and how to do anything except to be decoratively young. We can, of course, be injured in various ways by the young, but we cannot be seriously influenced by them.

One final, perhaps quirky observation. Though the very young, our children already now young adults, have no choice but to share our world, its same ever-expanding record and inheritance of unbroken and bloody barbarism, the large majority of them, in America at least—finally, it's America I am thinking of and talking about—most of them have only witnessed the bitter truths of these bitter times indirectly and thus vicariously. The overwhelming majority—for the first time in our whole national history—managed adroitly to avoid the national experience of a major war, the war in Vietnam. Except as an abstraction or as something on television. Which, abstraction and / or reduction to cleverly edited two-dimensional representation, begins by being so severely distorted as to be untrue to those of our generations. You will see that I do not consider fleeing to Canada or Sweden or graduate school, no matter how perilous, to be an equivalent experience to military service. Not the same thing, nor even part of it. Those who did not serve were sheltered from it by those who did. All of which means (or *may* mean) that they, the children of the 60's, have yet to learn what others, including ourselves, have by heart; that maybe the influence, like the buck, stops here; that, by and large, they may as yet lack the sad experience to be able fully to understand the work of John Ciardi and, thus, to be influenced by it and by him. Maybe. But though we wish them well, I can't imagine a single manjack among us who believes it is even remotely possible that they will ever manage to get through their lifetimes in this century, and the first of the next one, entirely unscathed, unbruised, and unbloodied.

On the other hand the old masters—if we may so designate the earlier, Eliot-Pound-Yeats generation—were mature and gifted poets of great sensitivity and keen imagination. And yet, tested against the weight of actual experience in

World War I, by which I mean the living work of the brilliant combat poets like Owen and Sassoon, Isaac Rosenberg and Robert Graves and so many others, their work seems somewhat pale. Literary judgments for the moment aside, one has to look to the work of people like John Masefield and Kipling, both honor graduates of the school-of-hard-knocks, to find the gritty impact of experience which can approximate that of the younger poets of that era. And it is interesting to note that those last parts of Eliot's *Four Quartets*, written during and after his direct experience as an air-raid warden during the Blitz, arrive at a kind of poetry more directly experiential than intellectually derivative, something he had not demonstrated before.

To return to the proper subject, then. We, the writers of various kinds of my generation, look especially to the writers of John Ciardi's generation for pertinent and relevant examples; and we are much influenced by them. A good many of us gladly consider ourselves influenced by John Ciardi, as this Festschrift bears solid witness. And I would like to say a few things about the nature of that influence, first in general, then in particular and, finally, personally.

In a general sense John Ciardi has been hugely influential because he placed or found himself in peculiar positions to be so. Nobody sets out to be an influence on others, to be influential, except maybe our natural parents who have a bounden duty to be so, or the varieties of demagogue which the tides of this century have thrown up, demagogues of all kinds and persuasions who seem, in all their guises, to share some common and irresistible itch to be able to manipulate their fellows and to prevail over them, if possible, one and all. But, almost incidentally, there have been various ways, in these our times, by which an individual writer can exercise a considerable influence on others, writers and readers alike. And John Ciardi has been influential in most of the available ways that I know of. I am not speaking here, not yet, of the most important influence of all, the example of his poetry. Which is, of course, the way and means most poets are deeply influential upon each other. I will be speaking to and about that, but as a personal matter (if also, I hope, an exemplary one). Most powerful, that influence is usually most private. Not always. But I think, at least in these times, that the more public the direct influence of a poet the more likely deleterious it will be. A few years ago half the beginning poets in America were writing, as best they could, in the manner of Mark Strand and Charles Simic. There were times when it seemed that most of the younger poets wanted not to be like Strand and Simic, but (by some weird incantation) to *turn into* either one or the other or both indistinguishably. There was a brief period when it seemed possible that every poem being published in America was being written by the same poet. But just when it all seemed too depressing for words, that whole thing vanished like ground fog succumbing to first sunlight. Even Strand and

Simic, separately and equally, slowed down and changed a little and the poetry of young Americans began to assume its appropriate plurality again.

Ciardi has plenty of admirers and disciples, some of them here present and proud of it, but his public influence has been of a different kind. As poetry editor, over years, at *The Saturday Review,* he chose the poems to publish or reject for that magazine. Likewise he determined which books to review or not to review, to praise or to blame. Similarly in his regular columns for the *Review* he had an important opportunity to advance or to challenge ideas. Not merely literary and critical ideas, but others as well. Surely there are readers who still remember well how courageously Ciardi challenged some of the political and social bad habits in postwar America. Editorial positions are, by definition, influential; though it must be said, in honesty, that much of their potential for influence resides in the office and not in the holder. Thus today poets like Howard Moss (*The New Yorker*) or Peter Davison (*Atlantic Monthly*) or even, for example, Reginald Gibbons (*Tri-Quarterly*) or Daniel Halpern (*Antaeus*) have, for a time at least, a kind of automatic power to influence the lives and work of other poets, an influence more weighty and significant than their own achievements might ever allow. And, indeed, the whole matter of editorial integrity and influence, the uses and abuses thereof, merits serious examination as a central part of the literary history of the age. And certainly John Ciardi's time at *The Saturday Review* is an important example of contemporary editorial influence. My recollection of all this is that Ciardi was an exciting, and sometimes controversial, editor and at the same time a highly responsible one. He was an honest editor—a quality more rarely found than the uninitiated might surmise. For a good many years, then, his influence, honest and moderate, was a powerful one and, I think, a healthy one. Which is more than most editors can ever claim.

I say this as one whose every submission to that magazine at that time was summarily rejected and whose books of poems, when reviewed there at all, were (in my opinion then) roughly handled. I can assure you I wasn't happy about it at the time. But there were positive and useful things to learn from the experience, and I like to think that I learned some of them and that they came to serve me well to help me through darker and rougher times (at the hands of villainous amateurs) later on. I have lived to tell the tale. Which may have been a test the tough-minded editor intended; for anyone who couldn't take the heat, who couldn't pass through the modest obstacle course of regular rejection and critical chastisement and still carry on about his proper business, should no doubt look for another kind of life and art. All of us have had to do some judging and editing along the way. Most of those we pause to praise are unimpressed, being convinced they fully deserve a full measure of praise and devotion. And most of those we criticize hate our guts for it. But it is important to learn what to do with and about negative responses to our work. One learns to question one's own habits and assumptions. Sometimes one learns to change habits, to modify assumptions, upon the strength of just and lively criticism. Sometimes one recovers from self-interrogation with a confirmed and strengthened sense of the worth of something which has been criticized by others. And that, too, is a valuable lesson. Ciardi wasn't always right, not by a long shot. But his criticism raised good questions. It was enormously useful.

Without ever discussing or, for that matter, ever even mentioning the editorial experience to John Ciardi, what it did to and for him and how he may have influenced others, I have an idea that it was an experience from which he learned many things. And once it was over, he discovered that he had given up, with that position, some of the amenities of the literary life which went with it. The truth is that some of John Ciardi's finest poems have been written in the years since he served at *The Saturday Review.* It is important to note, however, that while all of Ciardi's books published before he left *The Saturday Review* were widely reviewed, and regularly reviewed in *The New York Times Book Review,* those published since then have been sparsely reviewed, and none has been reviewed in the *Times.* We have all been witness to, recently, the ugly spectacle of a fundamentally boneheaded (and, at least in that sense, dishonorable) review of Ciardi's *Selected Poems* and Karl Shapiro's *Love & War, Art & God* in *Poetry* magazine (a magazine Shapiro once edited and where Ciardi had often published first-rate poems), in which the young reviewer criticized both distinguished poets for their failure to keep up with the latest trends and fashions. As if to be fashionable, and by choice, were the beginning of wisdom.

Ciardi is, and has proved himself to be, too tough and too honorable for any of this kind of thing, at high and low levels, to have made any real difference to him. It certainly has not injured his poetry, either, or stifled his Muse. One of the things he learned, I imagine, from exercising a certain literary authority as an editor and then losing it when he gave up that position was what he already knew well enough—that, by and large, this world is populated by knaves and fools, some of whom can be dangerous to the health and welfare of others. He has, in fact, written about that truth well and often, and never better, in my opinion, than in the poem "Faces." Look it up and read it in *Selected Poems,* the story it tells of an act of gratuitous and stupid cruelty, almost fatal in its consequences, done to the speaker by a perfect stranger whose face he never clearly saw in the dark and for which (that face) he has been looking and finding models ever since:

> . . . But why tell you?
> It's anybody's world for the living in it:
> You know as much about that face as I do.

It may not be redundant here to note that Ciardi, the critic, has indicated an alert awareness of what is going on in poetry, an eager desire to know what the poets are up to. But (see his piece "The Arts in 1975" in *Contemporary Literary Scene II*) he has also pointed out—and I believe he is the first poet and critic to do so—the wild variety of the present scene in poetry, questioning the capacity of anyone to keep up with it. Allowing that contemporary "American poetry lacks a dominant mode," he writes:

> If anything, it is given over to partisan groupings that ignore what is not of the in-group. Imagine that our publishers, in a spasm of madness, commissioned twenty poets, each to assemble a "representative" anthology to be titled *American Poetry Today*. (The fact is, of course, that the cost of permission fees has seriously inhibited the making of anthologies, but imagination is free.) Now list at random twenty poets to edit these anthologies. How many American poets, do you suppose, would appear in all of these anthologies?—I mean poets alive today. How many who are prominently featured in one anthology would not appear in *any* of the others? Would any one of these anthologies offer a reasonable survey of American poetry now? Would it be possible by reading them all to discover some significant common ground on which American poets meet?
>
> Speculation is for its own sake. I suspect that every answer would find factionalism as our only common ground. But division is not necessarily an evil. It tends at least (or does it?) to heed variety. In art, variety is always the soil of hope.

This description of reality seems to me as accurate as it is profound. The fact that our anthologies of the 1980's gather together the same poets *as if* there were a genuine consensus, as if there were some common ground, just as our professional reviewers tend to review the same poets and the same books, does not contradict Ciardi's view. Rather, it is strong evidence of a certain kind of collusion, precisely the "factionalism" he has pointed out, and, to the extent that it pretends to be definitive or even representative, to precisely that extent it is dishonest criticism. It is often easy to disagree with Ciardi the critic, but his integrity was demonstrably beyond all questioning.

Well then. Ciardi exercised much practical (and often useful) influence as an editor and critic, as a creator of anthologies and textbooks. Also as, for years, a teacher and as director of the celebrated summer workshop at Bread Loaf. As teachers we are (perhaps fortunately) seldom aware of how influential we may have been. Some of our students succeed in the very same subjects we professed to be teaching them. And John had his string of successes of this kind at Rutgers and elsewhere. I am impressed by the variety of the work of the poets he

206

has taught. What do Miller Williams and the late Frank O'Hara have in common? Ciardi was their teacher. Though he gave up full-time teaching some years ago, Ciardi was clearly a born teacher and an experienced one. He taught writers beyond numbering. He taught good things and he set a good example for them. But he has taught even more readers that there are good things to read, even in this rusty age, things which are worth a grown-up's time and energy. And who knows how many children have been taught to relish the delight and instruction of poetry from the experience of his many delightful and instructive books of children's poetry? Certainly there are good lessons, good things to learn there for poets in general as well as for those other poets who wish to learn to write poems for children.

Because I have never set foot on the grounds of Bread Loaf and have always been the kid at the knothole at the ballpark, I think I can speak (briefly enough) with some objective authority about it. At Bread Loaf, which Ciardi directed and managed for such a long time, he exerted a major influence on the future (thus the present) of American letters. Consider that, at the outset, it was a bridge, too, between several generations; for in a real sense it was Robert Frost's show. And Frost was the presiding spirit of the place. If Frost was the Old Man, Ciardi was the executive officer, the troop commander. Years of American poets and fiction writers passed through the basic training, the flash and fire of Ciardi's Bread Loaf. It is a debatable point, one that is argued with some vehemence on both sides, but my best judgment is (still viewed from the knothole) that Bread Loaf ain't what it used to be. Not like it was when it was Ciardi's enterprise. There are new names and a new crew, some of them highly celebrated writers. But some essential link with the spirit of Frost, some basic sense of the energy and the original purpose of the place was lost when Ciardi's resignation was accepted. The reports that I receive, the vibrations I also am attuned to, tell me that Gene Lyons' famous article about Bread Loaf in *Harper's* (or was it *Atlantic*? No matter . . .) a few years ago was a devastatingly accurate account of the new and not-improved regime there.

There were some other gatherings and conferences headed by Ciardi after that—like the Ohio Valley Writers Conference at the University of Northern Kentucky in 1985—where something of the old energy and excitement was regained and restored, enough so that it is easy to believe in the validity of the original model, to have an example of what it must have been like.

All these things, then. Editor and teacher and director, and not to overlook Ciardi's influence as the translator of *The Divine Comedy*, taken together with his innumerable lectures, public appearances, readings (that is, John Ciardi as *performer*), his old days on TV, his appearances on National Public Radio, gave Ciardi a visibility and served the art of poetry in America. Much credit has gone to Frost first, and later to Dylan Thomas, for helping the cause of poetry by popularizing the form by which it reaches its largest numerical audience—the poetry reading. Probably Ciardi gave more readings, over a longer period of time, than Frost and Thomas taken together. Certainly he deserves as much credit as they have earned for establishing this kind of marketplace for the works of poets. And he deserves credit from a multitude of poets for creating this additional possibility for poets to earn a living, sometimes an adequate one, for their work.

I have only touched on the surface of things, but I hope it is clear that we all owe a large debt to the public John Ciardi and his good influence.

Finally, however, it is the private influence of the poet and his work to which other poets, often separately (though there are friends who shared most of all their friendship with and admiration of John Ciardi, those for whom he was known as "The Godfather" and "Big John," among other nicknames), are most beholden. Finally, it is the poetry that matters most, both for the pleasure of reading and for learning from it, to other poets. I am sure that we have learned different things from it, each according to our own needs and hopes. All that I can say and celebrate is what I have learned and most admired.

One of these things has been John's concept, both theoretical and practical, of "the unimportant poem." He spelled out this idea in a number of places, no place more clearly and simply than on the jacket of his own book *For Instance* (1979): "I write only unimportant poems," says Ciardi. "The smaller the better. Perhaps small enough to be life-size. That is never much, but all there is, and therefore everything." Simple, but profound. *"Perhaps small enough to be life-size."* We have lived in and through terrible times full of Big Events, what the Chinese used to mean ironically by the "interesting times" it is a curse to live through. Against the enormity of the times and all the noisy clamor of them some poets have linked arms with the hucksters and hype merchants, seeking some kind of marching band authority, if only by size and scope and apparent originality seeking to say large things. Others have turned away and inward, seeking the inversely important, by the cultivation of the deep and shadowy regions of the subconscious. And, as Ciardi was among the first to admit, some good things have come from both directions. But both, using the chaos of the age as a rationale ("How can you write little poems while people are starving in Ethiopia?"), have turned away from the quotidian wonders which are the beginning of wisdom for poets, especially (it seems to me) American poets who have learned to rejoice in the ordinary experience, even as they explore it. Moreover, it is our special strength and characteristic to treat the reader as an honorable equal not by "talking down" to him nor by, to use the southernism, "bigmouthing," but rather by speaking well about persons, places, and things which both poet and reader can be assumed to know and care about. There is a poem in *For Instance* which shows and tells this thing, what "the unimportant poem" is all about exactly:

## Saturday, March 6

One morning you step out, still in pajamas
to get your *Times* from the lawn where it lies folded
to the British pound, which has dropped below $2.00
for the first time since the sun stopped never
setting on it, and you pick it up—
the paper, that is—because it might mean something,
in which case someone ought to know about it
(a free and enlightened citizenry, for instance)
and there, just under it—white, purple, yellow—
are the first three crocuses half open, one
sheared off where the day hit it, and you pick it up,
and put it in water, and when your wife comes down
it's on the table. And that's what day it is.

Lifting up the terrible abstract weight of all the world's news in the actual *Times,* the poet-speaker uncovers the first three crocuses, "one sheared off where the day hit it." An injured, useless, unimportant thing which becomes art (just as an "unimportant poem" can be) when he saves it, puts it in water for another's delight and thus gives the day its true name, meaning, significance. It is a paradigm of the poet about his proper business.

The paradox of the "unimportant poem" as advocated and practiced by Ciardi is that it does, in fact, allow the poet to deal with all kinds of worldly matters, including events large and small, in ways that few other poets have been able to. The Big Band boys are up there on the tower conducting the half-time show. The Deep Image poets are down at the bottom of the well and can only see a little dark circle of starry sky. It is a strange and exciting thing to see stars in the daytime, but wells deep enough are few and far between and you can't stay down there very long. The concept of the "unimportant poem" liberates us to write out of what we imagine happens to us in the real world, to make something out of our own experience. But poetry really isn't about *experience*, it is all about language. And so the "unimportant poem" is wildly liberating to us, inviting us to use a whole range of language—tones, voices, dialects, high and low modes. Ciardi, a master of the American language and its long history, was ideally suited for this kind of freedom. His precision allowed him to make easy leaps and jumps back and forth between the stages of the spoken and the written, between high and low voices within the context of a single poem, often of a single stanza. There can be, therefore, abrupt shifts, "cuts" in the language of film, as radical and graceful as any created by the seventeenth-century metaphysical poets. Riffle through the pages of *Selected Poems* and you'll find a multitude of good examples. If you want to know one of my special favorites, for the sake of many kinds of living language (including the deliberate use of jargon and cliché, thus, in this context renewing both) take a good look at "Trying to Feel Something." The paradox of "the unimportant poem" is that because it is so liberating, it cries out for forms. To contain the energy. A net and some lines to make some rules for the game. Ciardi was, as it happens, a great and subtle master of verse forms. If you idle through *Selected Poems* you will find yourself in a gallery of forms. If you are a poet, you will be challenged to try your own hand at them, to see if you, too, can put living words and living things within the cage of some strict form and then see if you can hide the cage from all but the most alert and curious observers.

We are moving back into a time of forms—everybody knows it. The good poets will be looking to John Ciardi for examples. So will the bad poets if and when forms are truly fashionable again.

All that I have said about the good influence of John Ciardi, public and private, adds up to the truth that he gives hope to the rest of us. Maybe, just maybe, we, too, can keep writing, growing, changing, becoming long after so many others have settled for rigidities (certainties?) and reputation. Maybe, with his example, we can teach ourselves to be tough enough to continue, hitting and missing, suffering and rejoicing, maybe even arriving gratefully and honestly at the earned place of the last line of "For Myra out of the Album"—"I have been here, and some of it was love."

# The Last Photograph of John Ciardi

## Samuel Hazo

It shows you at your best address—
    behind a podium and speaking
    poetry aloud, your own and Dante's.
Whoever heard you heard grandmothers
    praying in Italian, echoes
    of Pacific gunnery, the deft
    excoriation of the small of soul
    and how a word can grow
    through seven centuries, three
    languages and twenty dialects
    into itself.
                        Prolific phonies
    bored you.
                        Right-angled minds
    from Cambridge bored you more.
Chirpers from Manhattan and the Merritt
    Parkway bored you most.
                                        You
    left them to the pet awards
    they gave themselves and spoke
    an audience to birth that was
    too good for them . . .
                        The language
    called American is less because

you left it, John, but more
because of what you left of it
to us.
      I'm thinking of the poems,
prose and conversations that were
really conversations.
            Once
we talked MacLeish—his boyhood
voice, the perfect carpentry of how
he spoke, his utter lack of cant
or spite.
      I told you that his
final words were to his son:
"You go along."
        It made you think
of someone somewhere in the *Purgatorio*—
a warrior who died with half
the name of Mary on his lips . . .
But nowhere were you better
   than you were in repartee.
         Offered
the *Obituary Journal* by a young
obituarian, you winked and said
it should give birth to *Son
of Obituary Journal.*
        That brand
of Ciardi-ness will never die
as long as I'm alive to quote it . . .
After your death I heard your
   browser's voice on NPR.
"Good words to you," was how
   you closed.
        Had you had time
ahead of time to choose last words,
you might have chosen those
to be your jauntiest goodbye.

# "A Man Is What He Does with His Attention":
## A Conversation with John Ciardi

### Vince Clemente

It was in 1953 during an unscheduled company inspection; I was in my final week of basic training, the 716 M.P. Battalion, Fort Dix, New Jersey. I can see the lunatic as clearly as if he had just walked through my study door—the Company Commander, Col. Walter "Moonstruck" Murphy, storming through the barracks, the day's harvest, my well-worn copy of John Ciardi's *Mid-Century American Poets* crooked under his misshapen arm. It was company policy that recruits weren't allowed to keep books—other than government issued—in their footlockers. Of course, I was given company punishment—confined to barracks—but my first free weekend, I was back burrowing through the stacks at the Strand in New York City, finding another copy, which I since have had inscribed by the author. I've been on the Ciardi prowl ever since.

I finally connected with the man in 1978. He wrote from his Metuchen, New Jersey, home, thanking me for a copy of my *Songs from Puccini*. Many more letters followed, with visits to New Jersey, with John and Judith our houseguests the first weekend in June, 1984, while John was poet-in-residence at the Walt Whitman Birthplace, where I also serve as a trustee.

At Walt's Home he read to an overflow crowd and later that day met with about twenty-five invited poets for some good shoptalk. It was a grand day for poetry, for John, for Whitman—but most of all, for me. We talked a bit. I mentioned the possibility of an interview-article. He liked the idea, and a week later I fired off some questions for him to stare at.

"A man is what he does with his attention," he reminded me in a recent letter, and this declaration may serve to sum up the man's credo. His was an "attention" as much at home in Dante's medieval cathedral as in Yankee saltboxes at

213

Vermont's Bread Loaf School; an attention as much riveted to a ruin in Pompey and a "foot / cast in mountain soot" as to "A Knothole in Spent Time," finding again his Medford, Massachusetts, boyhood at the Craddock School on Summer Street. His was an attention comfortable in an aerial gunner's loft, a World War II B-29, as well as in the classrooms of Harvard and Rutgers.

This poet, translator, critic, anthologist, columnist, teacher, television host, writer of award-winning children's books, and etymologist was, then, an "American Man of Letters." Living on the run, as he did, ever since leaving Rutgers University in 1961, he must be viewed as one of those wandering scholars, one of a band of scholar-rascals, who carried in their skulls whole libraries and civilizations, passing through sleepy medieval towns, on warm summer evenings.

The questions posed aimed to cull from a forty-year career those things that engaged John Ciardi's "attention" and were grounded in an exchange of letters, a friendship, and finally in the love I hold for the man. John was "instructed" to answer "all of the questions, some of the questions—or jettison the project as stupid." In his huge-heartedness, he chose to answer *all* the questions.

The questions, I feel, are not random, nor are they indiscriminate. I begin with the poet's genesis, then move on to his public life, his *ars poetica*, finally towards a synthesis: Ciardi summing up a long and rich life. Here he speaks candidly, in typically no-holds-barred, Ciardi fashion. He is a man on record.


# A Conversation with John Ciardi


CLEMENTE: In *John Ciardi* by Edward Krickel, a volume in the Twayne's United States Authors Series, your biographer attaches great importance to your American-Italian boyhood in Medford, Massachusetts. In fact, he writes, "These and related themes are repeated to the point of near obsession in the mature writer's work . . . and supplied him with a rich subject matter and perspective." How sound an assessment is this? Within the body of your full work, just how central are your "tribal" poems?

CIARDI: Krickel says, "These and related themes are repeated to the point of near obsession." I don't think the point is that my boyhood can be categorized as "American-Italian" so much as that it was my boyhood. Is there any point in listing the poets, especially from the forerunners of Romanticism to Dylan Thomas and beyond, who chased their boyhoods for subject matter? If they were haunted by it, I suspect that the haunting sprang in some part from ghost-memory and in equal part from a need to find subject matter.

My real ghost for many years, long laid to rest, was my father. He was an agent of the Metropolitan Life Insurance Company and was killed in an automobile accident on the job in 1919 when I was three years and three weeks old. I was the youngest child, but the only son of an Italian family. My mother, stunned by her loss, made me over into the image of my father. In a real sense, I was all she had left of her sacramental man. For her, he was reborn in me. Her need to double me into the image of her lost husband was a hysteria she lived by, partly a madness, partly a martyrdom. *That* is a ghost to live with. In time I came to see it in about the way an anthropologist might see the howling dance-rituals of a primitive tribe—a stage of development far back in the chain. But if I became detached from it by time and death, how could I forget that it was also contained in a fierce love?

We were, in some sense, a tribe. It is just possible that I am the tribesman who went to Oxford. I no longer fit into the tribal pattern. I remember its rituals and responses from afar, as if they were a stage of things somewhere back in evolution. If I met the boy I was at, say, twelve, I don't think I would like him. I did pick up some of the emotional reponses of the Italian peasant in America, and I hope a few persist, but generally I had lost touch with the details of how we felt, feared, believed. In Italy, once (I forget the occasion) a friend turned to me and said (an Italian friend): "You're not an Italian: you act like an American Army sergeant!" He finally modified his verdict and decided I was "L'Italiano diracinato"—the deracinated Italian. Fair enough: a human being is a deracinated caveman, as a caveman was a deracinated nephew of an ape. Everyone gets to be something by starting as something else—either that or he stays unevolved.

Does anyone really fit into the categories that others invent for him? Kenneth Rexroth once said he thought of me as an older brother who was an Alitalia pilot. I think he meant that I had managed to solve a few practical problems that had had him stumped because he insisted on being charmingly and airily frivolous about them: that made me an older brother. The Alitalia category was sort of a compliment to my nonexistent flying ability, but basically a free-association on the fact that my name is Italian. When I told him it was an ancient corruption of German, Gehrhardt (which in Italian became successively Gherardi, Cerardi, Ciardi over the centuries) he did not offer to transfer me to the Luftwaffe, and I was grateful for that.

Emily Dickinson did not seem to do much but she had a lot of experiences. I mention that to the category makers. I am partly what I was born of, and at least equally the product of what I have read, thought about, imagined.

CLEMENTE: Is this an overstatement: that for the man, John Ciardi, Dante had become the father the boy lost to an auto accident in 1919?

CIARDI: Simple answer: no. I am not at all sure I would have liked stiff-necked Dante as a living presence. He was a pedantic and self-righteous man with an enormous talent. I honor the talent, but spare me the man. I no longer drink, but I could never imagine in my drinking days that it would be any pleasure to drink with Dante.

CLEMENTE: The Mystic River that runs through Medford, Massachusetts, that ran through your boyhood, surfaces in some of your finest poems, poems like "Mystic River" and "The River." Is it too much to say this river is your Passaic?

CIARDI: Only to the extent that the Mystic was part of my first habitat as the Passaic was WCW's. He tried to do something much more ambitious with his river. The Mystic became a symbol of a sort for me because I was brought up right on its banks, starting in 1920 when we moved to Medford (I was four then), when Medford was almost a rural town and the river was *clean*. In the next ten years (it must have been really the next nine—up to the crash of 1929) I watched field after field go under as builders hammered together rows of dormitory housing for people who worked in Boston (six miles away). Most of the town became crowded, ugly. By 1930 the red flags of foreclosure were nailed up on house after house—a squalid time. And the river had gone dirty, not quite an open sewer, but too dirty to use. It even stopped freezing over in the winter; I don't know why. It had been a festive rink through all my first winters in the twenties, and then even the ice stopped forming. It left me with a sense of good things going bad. In that sense, it flowed straight into the stinking 1930's and their blight. I often think that in an earlier age, I might have felt about that river as Thoreau felt about his pond and his canoe ways. It made me feel, among other things, that most of the good things were long ago.

CLEMENTE: You attended Michigan on John Holmes' urging to become a candidate for the Avery Hopwood Award in poetry, an award that carried with it a stipend of $1,200. Of course, you won the $1,200. Was the award instrumental in shaping your destiny—that to "Lucky John" all things were possible?

CIARDI: I went to Michigan loaded with arrogant assumptions. I went so far as to borrow $200 from John Follo, my godfather, and $200 from my sister Ella, promising to pay back in June, when I won the prize. I would, of course, have paid back the money in one way or another, no matter what: not to pay would have been a betrayal of love.

I have since been a judge for the Hopwoods. I am not at all sure that had I been a judge that year I would have voted for the manuscript I submitted. Louise Bogan and David McCord and someone else I have forgotten did—an act of kindness rather than judgment, or the competition was even duller. William Sloane, later my great dear friend, offered to publish the manuscript sight unseen—he was at Henry Holt. It also got me to Bread Loaf (Bill was on the staff) in 1940. I was a Fellow that year (along with Carson McCullers and Eudora Welty). I made good friends at Bread Loaf. . . .

Meanwhile, having paid my debts, given my mother a little money and cheerfully blown the rest, I was broke and lost when Kansas City University in January of 1940 offered me an actual teaching job (for $900 a semester—and believe it or not, it looked like money!) And that, too, came from the Hopwood and that impoverished manuscript of poems. . . .

The answer is clearly yes. Poor as those poems were, they opened the way to important things and important friendships. I have been egregiously lucky. I grew up on a series of miserable jobs for pennies an hour. I have, I may say, an experience aversion to poverty—and to the Army. But once the damned Army was out of the way, having grudgingly consented to let me live, I have managed to make a fair living doing almost exactly as I please. I think that will do as a definition of luck.

As for the Hopwood manuscript,—I think I got far more than I deserved from it, and how can I not be grateful? Those may have been better days for a young writer. I think perhaps they were. Certainly there were more places that would accept a poem and even pay a few dollars for it. But yes, I was lucky and I wish as much to anyone starting out today.

CLEMENTE: In a letter dated April 25, 1983, you write, "I was blessed by good teachers, and at times, even great ones." I'm sure you had in mind John Holmes of Tufts and Roy W. Cowden of Michigan. What special "gifts" did each give you?

CIARDI: John Holmes is a far better poet than he is recognized to be. Making all allowances for the fact that I loved the man, I believe he has left some thrilling, enduring poems. To understand his greatness as a teacher, one needs a historic note.

Tentatively in the late '20's, a few writers began to be attached to our English departments as tolerated nonacademics. These first writers on the faculty rarely had more than a B.A. degree. By the '40's there were more of them, and they tended to have an M.A. (I was one of those.) Nowadays there are many, they have gone through highly organized graduate programs and tend to have a full union-card Ph.D. In the beginning, however, Ph.D. teacher-writers were unheard of, and the curriculum was securely in the hands of academic Ph.D.'s. I transferred from Bates to Tufts in the middle of my sophomore year, and so in early '35 I signed up for John Holmes's writing course. Almost at once I knew what I was going to do with the rest of my life, if I lived that long.

. . . At Bates I attended a reading by Coffin and had found his seriousness to be ludicrous. John was the real thing. My other teachers at Tufts were good men, well-trained Harvard humanists as far as the English department was concerned, sound and outgoing. But they were historians of music, to speak figuratively. John was a piano player: he knew what to do with ten fingers on eighty-eight keys. I knew at once it was the kind of learning I was hungry for. Of many good teachers, he alone talked about the insides of a poem. His sort of technical analysis is common enough today with good writing coaches, but it was rare then; it was not recognized as an area of study by the rest of my teachers (or not much recognized), but to me it was an explosion.

John, moreover, was a loving teacher. Generally, I think, he was indulgent with the hopeless. He did me the honor of being tough with me. I once wrote a poem about watching shark fins circling me in a small boat. I wrote:

A sense of process, a name of the hunting sea
Haunts me.

He wrote in the margin: "Haunts you, hell. When does it haunt me?"

He made his point. I never again tried to be pretty in any mirror. Time after time, John Holmes nailed down what I had done that was false, weak, dull, random. He didn't have to hammer: his last nudge told me. He fired me up. He knew how the piece should be played and which piece wasn't worth playing, and he made me see—by reproof, by example, by being forever available. I lived on his shoulder like a forty-four-pound monkey, and he accepted me, though the addiction was mine rather than his. I read his library, I haunted his house, I sat while he pulled my poems apart.

I even disagreed with him at times. The Spanish Civil War raged on. By the time I graduated in 1938, there was marching in Europe. I was certain we were going to push through the ivy one splendid day and find ourselves at war. I insisted he was too complacent. One of his poems, "Evening Meal in the Twentieth Century," was in answer to my arguments that he was being too complacent in the face of the thunder. He sent me that poem when I was at Michigan in 1939. By then we had become almost colleagues rather than teacher-student.

That difference was never to settle. He was by nature a man to count the blessings of small, daily things. I was more nearly a son of the tempest. But he always knew that keyboard and could always point out the passages I blurred. I wrote once, "Ah, John, you should have been a Wordsworth of unevent!" In a greener world, he could have been a nature poet. In any world, he was the teacher I most needed, and bless his great memory. . . .

CLEMENTE: Although you left Rutgers in 1961—your last full-time teaching position—you have never left teaching. In a sense, the nation has become your classroom.

I recall, now, the poem I selected for broadside publication in honor of your being poet-in-residence at the Walt Whitman Birthplace, "Memoir of a One-Armed Harp Teacher." In a letter dated March 6, 1984, you isolate the lines, "I, who have been the teacher of many failures, / do not blame everything on the student body," then go on to add—"For whatever reason, these lines belong to me." Why are they *your* lines?

CIARDI: I began to teach because I couldn't make a living as a writer. In 1961 I was a part-time editor for *The Saturday Review*—hardly enough to live on—and also doing a fair amount of flying out to lectures between classes.

I liked teaching and tried seriously to be a good teacher within my limits. But teaching is a full-time job and so is writing. I had to decide whether to teach nine months and try to write three months, but my compromise cheated one thing or another. I decided that writing came first. I did an afternoon or two a week for *SR*, spent about three months on the lecture circuit, and had the rest of my time for writing. In 1961–1962 I did a TV show called *Accent*, a weekly for CBS, but it was not demanding nor was I good at it. There was a hectic though pleasant summer of 1962 when we went on the road with a series called *The Summer American*. We traveled from Sea Island, Georgia to Hawaii and got a prime-time slot, Thursday at 7:30. As a final verdict on that interlude, I was taken off the air in September of 1962 and replaced by *Mr. Ed, The Talking Horse*—from one end of the horse to the other, and no regrets.

It was in any case the right decision. In the three years after I quit teaching, I published eleven books. I did not write eleven books: I finished off eleven projects that had been stalled on my desk while I tried to teach.

I do like the classroom. I may fail a student because of ignorance; I have never tried to defraud a class or an audience. Were I independently wealthy, I would like to do a little classroom visiting from time to time. But I do more than that and in simplest terms, I do it for money. I have become a professional lecturer. I do not travel as much as I used to when my energy was nearly limitless. But I need some lecture income to live. It becomes a test of character: when I am offered $3,000 plus expenses to visit a school or attend some convention, do I stay home and read and write, or do I take the money? As a practical answer, I take the money—about fifteen times a year. At lesser rates, I also do a certain amount of talking for good friends, or at return engagements to places that have been good to me in the past. If that makes the nation my classroom, the school system is in trouble (which it is, of course). In any case, the terms of the question are not mine.

You also ask why the lines you cite are somehow mine. All I can say is that they ring right to my feeling. To be a writer is to accept failure as a profession—which of us is Dante or Shakespeare?—and could they return, wouldn't they fall at once to revising, knowing they could make the work better. In our dwarfed way, we are trying for something like perfection, knowing it is unachievable (except of course that trying and failing is a better way of living than not trying). As a teacher, I have coached many students to their own failures. Shall I blame their failures on them? I don't. It is in the human condition. E. E. Cummings once declared, "I am a man, a poet, and a failure"—three equal affirmations.

CLEMENTE: During your tenure (1956–1977) as poetry editor of *The Saturday Review*, what do you feel were your contributions to the vitality of poetry in this Republic?

Have you any regrets? I have in mind your review of Anne Morrow Lindbergh's *The Unicorn* in January 1957, a revew that provoked the harshest reader protest in the magazine's thirty-three-year history.

CIARDI: I doubt that I contributed anything to the "vitality of poetry in this Republic" as poetry editor of *The Saturday Review*. Does pissing into the ocean raise the sea level? *SR* was always relentlessly middlebrow, which is to say, never at the center. Yet it had its moments. Kolodin's music editorship was, I think, the best commentary generally available in the U.S. It also provided advertising that gave him space I could not hope for. If in my limited space I managed a few useful perceptions, that might count toward a good, but I have no claims to make. Poetry is not a vital part of the American culture. Can I claim to have contributed to the vitality of what is today a largely academic corpse? (except—Erato to be praised—for we few loving lunatics who refuse to admit we are obsolete).

My review of Anne Morrow Lindbergh's *The Unicorn* contained a sufficient apology to the social entity who is Mrs. Lindbergh, and enough documentation to support my judgment, my assertion that it was fraudulent stuff in which the publishers (with a first printing of 50,000 copies) and the Book-of-the-Month Club were exploiting Mrs. Lindbergh's social position to exploit bad poetry by Anne Morrow. What has not been recognized is that the furor about that review had little to do with the book, nor with the validity of my judgment of it. The sources of the tempest lie in the American Poetry Society.

When I took over from Amy Loveman as Poetry Editor, *SR* was almost an unofficial house-organ of the A.P.S. When Norman Cousins offered me the job as Poetry Editor, I was a bit surprised. "Why me?" I did not like the poetry *SR* published. I had refused to have anything to do with the magazine because of its tawdry poetry. He said he was concerned about that and hoped I might improve things. I asked for a little time to look at what was in the file of accepted poetry.

220

I found over 100 poems on hand, the bulk of them by members of the APS. I read them through and was forced to conclude that there wasn't one poem in that file that I would have accepted. I reported my conclusions to Norman and said he didn't need a Poetry Editor. At the average of two poems a week, he had enough to hold him for a year, and that I would not let my name go on the masthead while any one of those poems was being published. Since they had been accepted, I supposed they would have to be paid for, but I could not consider the job unless they were returned. *SR*, be it said, had never made money. As editor of a deficit operation, Norman was not about to pay for poems to be returned.

We compromised. I was given permission to return them (without payment) with a letter in which I played the heavy, saying that I had insisted on starting fresh and that N.C. had finally, reluctantly agreed with some reservations, but in fairness to me as the new Poetry Editor.

Within a few days of mailing back those poems, before I had published a word in *SR*, something like 1,000 irate letters poured in lamenting the desecration of the sacred memory of Amy Loveman and generalizing in rather specific ways about my character. (Yes, there were only about a hundred poems, but a hundred accepted-and-then-rejected poems can produce a marvelous ripple effect among friends, associates, relatives, paramours, and unindicted co-conspirators. These ripple out to about ten to one.)

I was in Italy, at the American Academy in Rome when the review was published. (I did my editing by mail.) Instantly, another 1,000 angry letters poured into *SR*. Norman Cousins airmailed me a bundle of them. And at least 80% (probably more) of the signatures were the same as those on my first batch from outraged rejectees. They had nursed their wrath and they poured it out and on. They were so vituperative that their honest estimates of my character touched off a new wave of letter writers. Norman Cousins estimated that there were about 5,000 letters in the second wave and that they were about three-to-two in my favor. The spree went on for at least a month: for two weeks it was a small national sensation. Norman was naturally delighted by the fact that his magazine was drawing such attention. But in all the overblown name-calling, it was never once mentioned that the noise was not about a self-evidently bad book by a great lady with greedy publishers, but the aftermath of rejected pride at the American Poetry Society.

These facts have never been made clear before, largely because the squall was soon over and none of this has mattered to anyone. It has never meant much to me except for a grimace of distaste when some cutesy program chairman decided to introduce me as "the bad boy of American poetry"! I hope I have learned to forgive the stupid while flunking them. The fact that they don't know they are flunking spares their feelings, as it restores mine.

CLEMENTE: Years ago you wrote, "Nothing is really hard but to be real." Is this yet the impetus behind the poems you write?

CIARDI: If you will grant the reality of fantasy, yes.

CLEMENTE: Yours has been described as the quintessential "American voice," that of the wiseguy with a big heart. Is there any truth to this?

CIARDI: Everyone is out to turn a phrase. I have never thought of myself as anything as impressive as a "quintessential American voice"—who could live in such a thought? I hope I shall always be quick to spot a con (if that makes me a wiseguy); I'd like to be quicker in compassion but I sometimes fail through stupidity or preoccupation. None of these terms is mine: I am an old man; insofar as one can say so, I think I have survived ambition; I would like to live my days in some engaged, self-engaging way that includes congenial people without damning those people I am happy to avoid.

CLEMENTE: In *Live Another Day* (1949), in the book's "Foreword to the Reader of (Some) General Culture," you outline your *ars poetica*, thirteen principles out of which you write your poems—"that a poem should be understandable," that "poetry should be read aloud" and be "about the lives of people," that "the subject create its own form," and so forth. Would you care to revise these principles? Are they at work today, thirty-five years later, in the making of a Ciardi poem?

CIARDI: I would never have written such a piece today. I have become less positive and much more ignorant than I was when I wrote it.

CLEMENTE: During your visit, June 3, 1984, to the Walt Whitman Birthplace as its poet-in-residence, you revealed a darker side, warning of Russian missiles, less than thirty miles off Long Island shores, while we load Europe with ours, pointed at the Russians. You insisted that "the human race is playing some kind of joke on itself."

Against such a monition, are you ready to write off the element of hope, carried in lines from "Thoughts on Looking into a Thicket," from *As If* (1955):

> . . . I believe
> if there is an inch or the underside of an inch
> for life to grow on, a life will grow there;
>
> if there are kisses, flies will lay their eggs
> in the spent sleep of lovers: if there is time,
> it will be long enough . . .

Are you saying, we've run out of time?

CIARDI: The distance I gave was not thirty miles but 300. Russian nuclear subs are cruising international waters off our coast, as our submarines are cruising in return off what coast Russia offers. With luck I will die of natural causes blissfully due to my own bad habits. But I do believe beyond a doubt that the bombs will go off, and that the human race has been practicing self-destruction since the first, the present difference being that our ability to destroy is now total—total and, I think, irreversible. Mankind has never been capable of any folly it did not commit.

So far we have just missed. A ten- or twenty-year difference in the technological timetable would have left Hitler with the nuclear bomb and missiles. I cannot doubt that in the end he would have been happy to take everything with him. Nor can I believe that Hitler was the last Hitler. Yes, it will happen. It will happen so certainly that I no longer have time to waste worrying about it, as I have no time to waste in worrying about my own death.

And yes, a life will grow there—everywhere—but some mutant successor species whose sages will preach that the human species was put on earth to prepare the way for their holy froginess or fungoidicity, or whatever the new holiness becomes.

CLEMENTE: "A man is what he does with his attention." Is this the pith of what life has taught you?

CIARDI: If life is subject to aphorisms, this one is as fit as any to rule.

CLEMENTE: In the fall of this year [1984], your *Selected Poems* will be published, the book you took "forty years to write." *Selected* will include, intact, only one of your volumes, *Lives of X*, my favorite Ciardi volume and, I'm sure, an authentic, neglected American classic. In an early letter, one dated November 15, 1978, you write: "My book *Lives of X* was autobiographical and went as deep as I could reach into roots. I gave it everything I had. I will even claim I brought to American poetry a kind of fictional technique that amounted to multiple expansion. No book of mine was more important to me and none was ever more thoroughly ignored."

Would you care to add anything?

Have you gotten over the hurt of this neglect?

CIARDI: I included all of *Lives of X* in the *Selected Poems* because I hope it will be read this time around. I don't know why it went so unnoticed the first time out. I know I have published lesser books that attracted much more attention.

A poet's own estimate of his work is likely to be self-seeking. I am wary of what other poets have told me about their own merit, wary enough to make no great assertions about my own. I think it is a readable book. I tried to make it readable. It pleases me when I reread it, and I am not one to fall in love with every precious word I ever committed to paper. Often enough, I tend to shudder on reading an old poem. What can I say? If it had been read and disliked, that would be a judgment to learn to accept. Instead it has been simply enough ignored. I wish it hadn't been, and I would like it if someone noticed it this time out.

I don't think I feel hurt because of this neglect of the book—I have other things to do. I do feel it deserves better, and ego with us all, I would like someone to read it and like it—a foolish wish, perhaps, but I did not invent it: it comes as an occupational disease.

CLEMENTE: The notion of just what constitutes an authentic "American voice" in American poetry, is this at the root of your anger as you wrote in the November 15, 1978, letter about Lowell commending you for a poem: "I had a longish poem about Italy in the *Atlantic* some years back, and when Robert Lowell wrote to praise its Italo-American voice, I took offense. Did the S.O.B. suppose I had used an American-English inferior to his, one that I had inherited and made mine, less American-English than his?"

CIARDI: American is an anthology of people and accents. I don't think about becoming "an authentic American Voice." Was Whitman authentic to the Creole? Emily Dickinson to the cowboy? Robert Frost to a Texan wheeler-dealer? I try to find the voice in which each poem wants to speak. Let the total theorize itself.

Lowell's card was really an effort to be gracious, and why should I offend a man who says he likes one of my poems. In so doing he assumed that his ancestors had somehow made him more American than I was, and that a poem about my Italian-named ancestors was less American than his life-study blathers about Grandfather Winslow (some of his worst stuff). He didn't mean to be smug about it, he was just bred to it. The S.O.B. label belongs on his assumption rather than on him, but fat heads write good poems, too.

CLEMENTE: Could there be a *Late-Century American Poets* book for you? If so, which poets would you sound out? What are some of the questions you would ask them?

If such a book is not possible—then why not?

CIARDI: I have already suggested to you, and as it would take too long here, I see no way to achieve a consensus on which living poets are doing the best work—not in this fragmented poetic scene. This is a poetic age in which no ten people admire the same thing. As I say, I have suggested to you elsewhere how to run an impartial poll.[1] Perhaps that might lead to a *Late-Century American Poets*. But I doubt it.

CLEMENTE: You always had faith in an audience for poetry, your "reader of (some) general culture," the 600,000 plus readership of the old *Saturday Review*. Does such an audience exist today?

CIARDI: I no longer think about the reader of (some) general culture. A man is what he does with his attention. Poetry—any of the arts—is for those with a willing attention and must not be diluted for those who haven't formed an attention.

CLEMENTE: Looking back over your forty years of writing poems, are you still able to insist you are a "saying" poet rather than a "singing" poet? With which John Ciardi are you most comfortable?

CIARDI: I am always happy when a poem manages to break into song, if only for a line or two. Bless all birds. But I think I am basically a "saying" poet rather than a "singer."

CLEMENTE: "I am an American man of letters . . . with Jefferson, Tom Paine, and even—God save the mark, Emerson—at the roots of my mind and feeling," you write in a letter. What have been the rewards and the responsibilities of such a life in the Republic?

CIARDI: Isaac Asimov once said, "I don't long for the good old days when there was no servant problem. Back in those days, I'd have been a servant."

I suppose I might have found life good had I turned out to be Shiek of an oil-bearing desert. In my lineage of camel-grooms, I like the way it has gone for me in this Republic. The Republic has left me free to my choices. It says in the Constitution that we all have a guaranteed right to make fools of ourselves. I have taken every chance to reap the rewards of that guarantee. If forced to action, I mean to fight to defend that right, which includes the right to be wrong, queer, or just kooky. And how can I defend that unless I defend those kooks and queers who think (wrongly of course) that I am kooky and queer?

CLEMENTE: I'm sure you don't object to being called a "survivor," and I recall the lines in the Willie Crosby poem, "Survival in Missouri"—"Having survived a theology and a war, / I am beginning to understand / the rain." And as a "survivor," you attended last year's reunion of the 73rd Bomb Wing, as one of three living members of an original crew of eleven.

In a recent essay,[2] you included a parable of a cormorant that "turned up in the swimming pool" of your Key West home, and "a pussy cat that tried to stalk it":

> "Like the holy ghost!" my neighbor said.
> "A visitation!" "Shit," I told him, "that
> bird is a bush pilot and knew exactly what

225

it was doing in the most practical terms."
Bush pilots do crash now and then, but first
they line themselves up and fly. And they
don't let themselves be drawn off their flight
plans by imagining that pussy cats may turn
into symbolic lions. Only poet-preachers do that.

Is this, then, our final glimpse of "Lucky John," the "bush pilot," surviving scrape after scrape, outwitting the impractical "poet-preachers"?

CIARDI: Yes, I think of myself as a survivor. I have survived the Catholic Church, the guilt-twisted and poverty-crimped years of my crazy adolescence, the Japanese air force (with some assistance from the USAAF whose clear intent at one time was to incinerate me). I have survived the delusion that I could improve the world by frenzied political stumping for lost causes, and the dream that my vote on anything would be counted as if it counted. In the end I have even survived ambition. Dare I think that I have survived the adolescence of my own children—they are now in their 30s and I begin to hope. Through it all what I have loved has stayed in place. I would like to think I am entitled to veterans' benefits: I have no more wars to go to, but there is still time (perhaps as much as ten or fifteen years by actuarial tables) and I want to concentrate on how to live the days of those years as richly as I can . . . but out of all debt except time and what I love.

About the cormorant—I was talking more about my neighbor than the bird. My neighbor worried about the bird in ways I thought were silly. I saw at once that it knew what it was doing and that it was more than a match for the cat. You are trying to turn it symbolic, but it wasn't. I don't know why or how it stumbled into our swimming pool. The pool happens to be hemmed in by houses and trees, and cormorants need a long runway for takeoff. The bird sized up the one open lane that would serve, waddled off to it, stood backed against the fence, sighted a line under an arching bougainvillea, then climbed steeply for thirty feet to clear the house beyond, and was gone.

Meanwhile the cat kept stalking but (wisely) backing off, and my neighbor kept chortling alarms to which the bird and I were indifferent because it knew what it was doing, and I could see that it knew it. All I find in the story is the difference between silliness (bleeding heart silliness) and knowing how. I have always admired those things in us and in nature that know how.

CLEMENTE: Again and again, you insist you write only "unimportant poems." But in your heart of hearts, aren't you certain you've written some that will last, that will be around long after both of us are gone?

As a poet, mustn't you believe this?

CIARDI: Since your question is pitched to ape-ego, I referred it to my ape and he said, "Yes, of course. Your every poem will live forever." What can you expect from an ape?

As nearly as the rational man can be summoned, the question becomes, "Are you not assuming that only important (big-message) poems will survive?" My thought is that if I can keep the poem small enough, I may yet get it down to human size. I don't see much future for *important declamation*. As above, I don't know how much future there is to foresee for the human race. What does survive—I would at least like to believe—will do so because it is emotionally true to our smallness, not because it is *important* to some Holy Ghost of declared eternal principle. As an international project, I propose that we begin to bury selected chemicals in the Sahara so arranged that when the sands fuse in the last fission-fusion go-round, the buried canisters will solidify into a glassed-in message in as many languages as possible, the message being *Jenny Kissed Me*. If there must be a last message for the species, let it be that.


## Afterword


For John Ciardi's visit to the Walt Whitman Birthplace as its poet-in-residence, I wanted to publish, in broadside for the occasion, a new Ciardi poem. The good man sent me seven or eight from which to choose. I selected "Memoir of a One-Armed Harp Teacher." It was a sound choice, for he soon wrote: "I'm glad you chose 'Memoir.' 'I, who have been the teacher of many failures, / do not blame everything on the student body.' For whatever reason, these lines belong to me. And they go with the anti-Whitman idea of smallness, which is all I can aspire to."

Like John, I've learned to aspire to smallness and would be pleased to hear "Jenny Kissed Me" just before the last light goes out. But were there time—say thirty seconds or so—I'd ask for an encore, a quick bar from John's harp teacher.

### Memoir of a One-Armed Harp Teacher[3]

#### by John Ciardi

Of my three certainly most impassioned students,
one lived over a disco and could not practice,
one split her calluses red and was admonished
by her dermatologist, one married a psychic

and took to listening. There are always available
good, or good enough, reasons for putting by
the incompatible, the painful, the unserviceable.
One decides what is important by what one does.

But the most demanding instrument forgives least.
I, who have been the teacher of many failures,
do not blame everything on the student body.
I could have done better with both hands. Perhaps
with an unamputated mind, and heart for it.
Passion is a crippling hobby, a killing trade.


# Notes


1. In a conversation on June 3, 1984, Ciardi suggested I poll all the poets listed in *A Directory of American Poets and Fiction Writers* and ask each to list ten living American poets certain to endure, to survive this century. I liked the idea but need a sabbatical year for the study.

2. Written for the Walt Whitman Birthplace, to be published in the first issue of the new *Whitman Birthplace Bulletin.*

3. Copyright © John Ciardi, 1984, first published in broadside by the Walt Whitman Birthplace Association, West Hills, Long Island, New York.

# *Notes on Contributors*

TERRI ARRIGON, English teacher and arts-program coordinator at Rocky Point Jr.-Sr. High School, lives in Suffolk County, Long Island, with her husband, six cats, and two dogs.

ISAAC ASIMOV, in 1950, having managed to publish one book in the thirty years of his life, met John Ciardi and, suffused with inspiration, wrote 338 additional books in the next thirty-six years of his life.

PHILIP BOOTH's seventh book, *Relations: Selected Poems 1950–1985*, has just been published by Viking Penguin.

STANLEY BURNSHAW's fourteen books include *The Poem Itself, The Seamless Web, In the Terrified Radiance,* and the forthcoming *Robert Frost Himself.*

VINCE CLEMENTE is a poet-editor whose books include *Snow Owl above Stony Brook Harbor, Broadbill of Conscience Bay, Songs from Puccini, From This Book of Praise,* and *Paumanok Rising.* His work has appeared in *The New York Times, Newsday,* and in many literary journals and anthologies. Founding editor of *Long Pond Review* and *West Hills Review: A Walt Whitman Journal,* he is Professor of English at Suffolk Community College as well as a trustee of the Walt Whitman Birthplace.

NORMAN COUSINS, former editor of *The Saturday Review,* is a faculty member of UCLA School of Medicine, and author of *Present Tense: An American Editor's Odyssey, Anatomy of an Illness,* and *The Healing Heart.*

ROY W. COWDEN for many years directed the Hopwood Awards at the University of Michigan and was one of the nation's great teachers of writing. His books include *Current Glossary,* an etymological study of the military language of World War I.

W. S. DI PIERO's recent book of poems is *Early Light;* he has also translated Leopardi's *Pensieri.*

RICHARD EBERHART's new edition of *Collected Poems: 1930–1976* will be published by Oxford University Press; *Negative Capability* will publish an issue on his work, and two documentary movies are scheduled to appear in 1986.

RICHARD ELMAN is a novelist, poet, and journalist; his latest books include *Little Lives* (published under the name of John Howland Spyker), *Homage to Fats Navarro* and *Cocktails at Somozas.*

GEORGE GARRETT, poet and novelist, is Henry Hoyns Professor of Creative Writing at The University of Virginia.

CHARLES GUENTHER is the author or translator of eight books of poetry and translations including *Modern Italian Poets, Phrase / Paraphrase, Paul Valery in English, Voices in the Dark*, and *The Hippopotamus: Selected Translations.*

DONALD HALL's ninth book of poems is *The Happy Man.*

SAMUEL HAZO is a widely published author of poetry, fiction, and criticism. His most recent book is *Thank a Bored Angel: Selected Poems.*

WILLIAM HEYEN, Poet in Residence at SUNY Brockport, is the author of *Long Island Light: Poems and a Memoir, Erika: Poems of the Holocaust*, and other volumes of poetry including *The Chestnut Rain*, a book-length poem.

JOHN HOLMES was for many years at Tufts University a teacher of poets, and himself a poet of stature. His books include *The Poet's Work, Address to the Living, Map of My Country, The Double Root*, and *The Fortune Teller.*

DAN JAFFE is editor of BkMk Press (University of Missouri-Kansas City) and author of *Dan Freeman* and the forthcoming *Seasons of the River.*

JUDSON JEROME is the author of a dozen books of poetry, fiction, social criticism and books about poetry. He is a frequent contributor to dozens of magazines and has been poetry columnist for *Writer's Digest* for a quarter of a century. He freelances from his home in Yellow Springs, Ohio.

X. J. KENNEDY, formerly an English professor at Tufts University, now writes poetry, textbooks, and children's books in Bedford, Massachusetts.

NORMAN KRAPF, a professor of English at Long Island University, C. W. Post Campus, is editor of *Under Open Skies: Poets on William Cullen Bryant* and the author of seven poetry collections, the most recent being *A Dream of Plum Blossoms.*

EDWARD KRICKEL teaches English at the University of Georgia and is author of *John Ciardi*, a volume in the Twayne's United States Authors Series.

JOANN P. KRIEG teaches American Literature at Hofstra University and is editor of *Walt Whitman Here and Now: A Collection of Scholarly Essays.*

MAXINE KUMIN's newest collection of poems is entitled *The Long Approach*.

JEFF LOVILL lives in Denver with his wife, Debbie, and their three children and is an editor for McDonnell Douglas as well as adjunct professor of English at Metropolitan State College.

JOHN FREDERICK NIMS was Cockefair Visiting Professor at the University of Missouri-Kansas City in March 1986 and gave as his public address, "John Ciardi: The Many Lives of Poetry." His poems have appeared in *The Georgia Review*, *The Sewanee Review*, *The Atlantic*, and *The Yale Review*, in addition to his *Selected Poems*.

KARL SHAPIRO is Professor of English (Emeritus) of the University of California, Davis, and author of countless books of poetry and prose.

WILLIAM JAY SMITH, former Consultant in Poetry to the Library of Congress, has translated poetry from several languages, written books for children, and published a number of poetry collections, including *The Traveler's Tree: New and Selected Poems*.

JOHN STONE is a physician and poet who teaches and practices at Emory University School of Medicine in Atlanta; his books of poetry include *The Smell of Matches*, *In All This Rain* and *Renaming the Streets*.

LUCIEN STRYK's latest books include *Collected Poems: 1953–1983* and *Triumph of the Sparrow: Translations of the Zen Poems of Shinkichi Takahashi*.

JOHN TAGLIABUE, who came to this country from Italy when he was very young, and now teaches at Bates College in Maine, has published five books of poetry, the most recent being *The Great Day*.

LEWIS TURCO's most recent books are *The Complete Melancholick*, a collection of poems, *Visions and Revisions of American Poetry*, and *The New Book of Forms: A Handbook of Poetics*.

DIANE WAKOSKI is Writer in Residence at Michigan State University, and has published a new collection of poems, *The Rings of Saturn*.

ELLY WELT, novelist, author of *Joanna Reddinghood* and *Berlin Wild*, lives in Key West and the Canary Islands with her husband, Peter.

WILLIAM WHITE, author of *John Ciardi: A Bibliography*, taught at Wayne State University and Oakland University; has been a visiting professor at numerous universities in this country, Korea, and Israel; and has edited or written forty books and over 2,400 articles and book reviews, including two best-sellers on Hemingway, *By-Line: Ernest Hemingway* and *Dateline: Toronto*, in addition to six volumes in *The Collected Writings of Walt Whitman*.

RICHARD WILBUR retires this year from Smith College, where he has been Writer in Residence. He recently published a new translation of Racine's *Phaedra*, and in collaboration with William Schuman, composed a cantata for the centennial of the Statue of Liberty, which had its premiere at the New York Philharmonic in October 1986.

JOHN WILLIAMS, editor of *English Renaissance Poetry*, has edited two volumes of his own poems, and written several novels, including *Stoner* and *Augustus*, winner of a National Book Award. Formerly Professor of English at Denver University, he lives with his wife, Nancy, in Fayetteville, Arkansas.

MILLER WILLIAMS' books include *Patterns of Poetry: An Encyclopedia of Forms* and a new volume of poetry, *Imperfect Love*.

# Selected Bibliography

## Works by John Ciardi

### Poetry

*An Alphabestiary.* Philadelphia: Lippincott, 1966.

*As If: Poems New and Selected.* New Brunswick, N.J.: Rutgers University Press, 1955.

*The Birds of Pompeii.* Fayetteville: The University of Arkansas Press, 1985.

*For Instance.* New York: Norton, 1979.

*From Time to Time.* New York: Twayne, 1951.

*A Genesis.* New York: Touchstone Publishers, 1967.

*A Grossery of Limericks,* with Isaac Asimov. New York: Norton, 1981.

*Homeward to America.* New York: Henry Holt, 1940.

*I Marry You: A Sheaf of Love Poems.* New Brunswick, N.J.: Rutgers University Press, 1958; London: Paterson, 1958.

*In Fact.* New Brunswick, N.J.: Rutgers University Press, 1962.

*In the Stoneworks.* New Brunswick, N.J.: Rutgers University Press, 1961.

*Limericks: Too Gross,* with Isaac Asimov. New York: Norton, 1978.

*The Little That Is All.* New Brunswick, N.J.: Rutgers University Press, 1974.

*Live Another Day: Poems.* New York: Twayne, 1949.

*Lives of X.* New Brunswick, N.J.: Rutgers University Press, 1971.

*Other Skies.* Boston: Little, Brown, 1947.

*Person to Person.* New Brunswick, N.J.: Rutgers University Press, 1964.

*Phonethics: Twenty-Two Limericks for the Telephone.* North Carolina: Palaemon Press Limited, 1985.

*Selected Poems.* Fayetteville: The University of Arkansas Press, 1984.

*39 Poems.* New Brunswick, N.J.: Rutgers University Press, 1959; London: Paterson, 1959.

*This Strangest Everything.* New Brunswick, N.J.: Rutgers University Press, 1966.

## Poetry for Children

*Doodle Soup.* Boston: Houghton Mifflin, 1985.

*Fast and Slow: Poems for Advanced Children and Beginning Parents.* Boston: Houghton Mifflin, 1975.

*I Met a Man.* Boston: Houghton Mifflin, 1961.

*John J. Plenty and Fiddler Dan: A New Fable of the Grasshopper and the Ant.* Philadelphia: Lippincott, 1963.

*The King Who Saved Himself from Being Saved.* Philadelphia: Lippincott, 1965.

*The Man Who Sang the Sillies.* Philadelphia: Lippincott, 1961.

*The Monster Den or Look What Happened at My House—and to It.* Philadelphia: Lippincott, 1966.

*The Reason for the Pelican.* Philadelphia: Lippincott, 1959.

*Scrappy the Pup.* Philadelphia: Lippincott, 1960.

*Someone Could Win a Polar Bear.* Philadelphia: Lippincott, 1970.

*The Wish-Tree.* New York: Crowell-Collier, 1962.

*You Know Who.* Philadelphia: Lippincott, 1964.

*You Read to Me, I'll Read to You.* Philadelphia: Lippincott, 1962.

## Nonfiction

*A Browser's Dictionary and Native's Guide to the Unknown American Language.* New York: Harper & Row, 1980.

*Dialogue with an Audience.* Philadelphia: Lippincott, 1963.

*Manner of Speaking.* New Brunswick, N.J.: Rutgers University Press, 1972.

*On Poetry and the Poetic Process*, with Joseph B. Roberts. Troy, Ala.: Troy State University Press, 1971.

*A Second Browser's Dictionary and Native's Guide to the Unknown American Language.* New York: Harper & Row, 1983.

## Translations

*The Divine Comedy* (includes *The Inferno, The Purgatorio*, and *The Paradiso*), by Dante Alighieri. New York: Norton, 1977.

*The Inferno*, by Dante Alighieri. New Brunswick, N.J.: Rutgers University Press, 1954. Reprinted in paperback by the New American Library, 1954.

*The Paradiso*, by Dante Alighieri. New York: New American Library, 1970.

*The Purgatorio*, by Dante Alighieri. New York: New American Library, 1961.

## Works Edited

*How Does a Poem Mean?* Boston: Houghton Mifflin, 1959, rev. ed. with Miller Williams, 1975.

*Mid-Century American Poets.* New York: Twayne, 1950.

*Poetry: A Closer Look*, with James M. Reid and Laurence Perrine. New York: Harcourt, Brace, 1963.

# Works about John Ciardi

## Bibliography

White, William. *John Ciardi: A Bibliography*. With a note by John Ciardi. Detroit: Wayne State University Press, 1959. Limited to Ciardi's early years, but still the only fully realized Ciardi Bibliography.

## Books

Krickel, Edward. *John Ciardi*. Boston: Twayne, 1980. The only book-length study of Ciardi to date. A lucid and readable biography, especially evenhanded in discussing the poems.

Williams, Miller, ed. *The Achievement of John Ciardi*. Glenview, Ill.: Scott, Foresman, 1969. The poems are selected from *Other Skies* through *This Strangest Everything*. Williams' introduction, "John Ciardi—'Nothing Is Really Hard But to Be Real,'" is the most perceptive essay on Ciardi to date as Ciardi considered Williams to be his "best reader."

## Extracts and Articles

Acocella, Joan Ross. "The Cult of Language: A Study of Two Modern Translations of Dante." *Modern Language Quarterly*, 35 (June 1974), 140–56. Comparison of Dorothy Sayers and Ciardi translations.

Bergin, Thomas G. "Dante Translations (Ciardi's *Paradiso*; Singleton's *Divine Comedy*)." *The Yale Review*, 60 (1971), 614–17.

Bogan, Louise. "Verse: Ciardi's *Homeward to America*." *New Yorker*, 15 (January 27, 1940), 52–54.

Carruth, Hayden. "Further Unanswered Questions about Translating: Dante's *Purgatorio* and *In the Stoneworks*." *Poetry*, 100 (June 1962), 198–200.

Cifelli, Edward. "The Size of John Ciardi's Song." *CEA Critic*, 36 (November 1973), 21–27. A close reading of "The Size of Song," a poem that illustrates Ciardi's "poetic principles in action."

Cousins, Norman. *Present Tense: An American Editor's Odyssey*. New York: McGraw-Hill, 1967. An insider's view of Ciardi at *The Saturday Review*.

Crane, Milton. "Elegies, Rich and Strange." *New York Times Book Review*, 57 (May 25, 1952), 27. *From Time to Time.*

Dick, Bernard F. Rev. of Dante's *Inferno*, trans. by Mark Musa. *Saturday Review*, 54 (May 22, 1971), 37–38. Comparison of Musa (former Ciardi student) and Ciardi translations.

Gaskin, J. R. "New Words: Ciardi's *A Browser's Dictionary*." *Sewanee Review*, 90 (Winter 1982), 147–48.

Hall, Donald. "The New Poetry: Notes on the Past Fifteen Years in America," *New World Writing: Seventh Mentor Selection*. New York: New American Library, 1955. Calls

Ciardi one of the "Wurlitzer Wits" because of the richness of his treatment of the commonplace.

Humphries, Rolfe. "Verse Chronicle." *Nation*, 171 (August 12, 1950), 152–53. *Mid-Century American Poets*.

Hughes, John W. "Humanism and the Orphic Voice." *Saturday Review*, 54 (May 22, 1971), 31–33. A review of *Lives of X* but has much wider implications.

Jacobsen, Josephine. "Ciardi's *39 Poems*." *Poetry*, 96 (July 1960), 235–37.

Jerome, Judson. "Among the Nightingales." *Antioch Review*, 16 (Spring 1956), 115–25. The poems in *As If* and an examination of Ciardi's distinctive poetic techniques.

——. "Ciardi's Art." *Writer's Digest*, 65 (October 1985), 16–20. *Selected Poems* as an eminently "readable book" that examines "what it means to be a poet in our times."

Kenner, Hugh. "Problems in Faithfulness and Fashions." *Poetry*, 85 (January 1955), 225–31. Compares Binyon and Ciardi translations of the *Inferno*.

Laing, Dilys. "Some Marrying and Some Burning." *Nation*, 187 (September 13, 1958), 137–39. A review of *I Marry You* that touches upon Ciardi's craft in general.

Langland, Joseph. "Ciardi's *Person to Person*." *New York Times Book Review* 69 (October 4, 1964), 22.

Lattimore, Richmond. "The *Inferno* as an English Poem." *Nation*, 179 (August 28, 1954), 175. Brief but insightful appraisal.

MacAllister, Archibald T. "The Literature of Italy." *The Yale Review*, n.s. 44 (September 1954), 155–59.

Meredith, William. "The Problem of the Second Volume." *Poetry*, 72 (May 1948), 99–102. *Other Skies*, relationship to *Homeward to America*.

Mickelberry, William. "An Interview with John Ciardi." *Florida Quarterly*, 5 (1973), 69–84.

Nemerov, Howard. *Poetry and Fiction: Essays*. New Brunswick, N.J.: Rutgers University Press, 1963. "A Few Bricks from Babel" includes a review of Ciardi's translation of the *Inferno*; it appeared originally in the *Sewanee Review* in 1954.

Parisi, Joseph. "Personae, Personalities, Ciardi's *The Little That Is All*." *Poetry*, 126 (July 1975), 220–22.

Peragallo, Olga. *Italian-American Authors and Their Contribution to American Literature*. Ed. by Anita Peragallo. New York: S. F. Vanni, 1949.

Perrine, Laurence. "Ciardi's 'Tenzone.'" *Explicator*, 28 (May 1970), Item 82.

Ponsot, Marie. "Poems for Children." *Poetry*, 101 (December 1962), 208–209. *The Man Who Sang the Sillies* is "so good that . . . adults can read aloud without pain."

Rexroth, Kenneth. "Animals, Stars and People." *New York Times Book Review*, 63 (August 3, 1958), 6. The poems in *I Marry You* are "'simple, sensuous, passionate'—what goot poetry must always be."

Scott, Winfield Townley. "Three Books by John Ciardi." *University of Kansas City Review*, 16 (1949), 119–25. The books are Ciardi's first three volumes.

Southworth, James G. "The Poetry of John Ciardi." *English Journal*, 50 (1961), 583–89. All volumes through *39 Poems*.

Spender, Stephen. "Poetry vs. Language Engineering." *New Republic*, 143 (August 15, 1960), 17–18. Challenges the working premise of *How Does a Poem Mean?*

Stuttaford, Genevieve. "Review of *Selected Poems*." *Publishers Weekly*, 226 (July 6, 1984), 59. Brief review but underscores the range and achievement of a book in which the poet "leaves virtually no aspect of modern life untouched."

Walsh, Jeffrey. *American War Literature: 1914 to Vietnam*. New York: St. Martin's Press, 1982. Includes a trenchant reading of Ciardi's World War II poems found in *Other Skies*, *As If*, and *39 Poems*.

White, Gertrude M. "Six Poems by John Ciardi." *Odyssey: A Journal of the Humanities*, 4 (1979), 12–19. A close and lively reading of six poems from *For Instance*.

White, Lawrence Grant. "Dante for Americans." *Saturday Review*, 37 (September 18, 1954), 13, 27. Limited to the *Inferno* and focuses on Ciardi's adaptation of Dante's terza rima.

Wright, James. "Four New Volumes." *Poetry*, 93 (October 1958), 46–50. A poet responding to some of the poems in *I Marry You*.

### Dissertations

Lovill, Jeffry. "The Poetry of John Ciardi: How Does It Mean?" Arizona State University, 1985, 382 pages. The title of the dissertation doubles as its thesis: to analyze the "how" of John Ciardi's poetry in terms of Ciardi's own criticism.

MacBride, Doris. "John Ciardi: Poet, Literary Critic, Oral Interpreter. His Literary Concepts and Their Significance for the Field of Oral Interpretation." University of California, Los Angeles, 1970, 183 pages.

# Index

Albert, Sam, 28
Allen, Donald, 68
American Poetry Society, 221
*The American Scholar*, 45
American Youth for Democracy, 52
Anderson, Maxwell, 42
Antioch College: Ciardi visit in 1957, 137
*The Antioch Review*, 135
Aquinas, Thomas: Ciardi's pen name for
    Hopwood Award manuscript, 10
Arizona State University, 61
Arrigon, Terri: on writing "Ciardi's Dia-
    logue with Children," 156
"Ars Poetica" (MacLeish), 88
Asimov, Isaac: 225
  at Bread Loaf, 142
*Atlantic Monthly*, 14
Auden, W. H., 52
Barone, M. Robin, 33
Bates College: 26
  Ciardi's transfer from, 40
Baudelaire, Charles, 91
Baum, L. Frank, 150
*The Beautiful Changes* (Wilbur), 52
Bechet, Sidney: 21
  Ciardi's ghostwriting *Treat It Gentle*,
    79–81
Benét, William Rose: contrasted with
    Ciardi at *The Saturday Review*,
    114
Berryman, John, 52
*Best Science Fiction of the Year:* 1950 an-
    thology that included Ciardi's
    story "Hypnoglyph," 183

Bishop, Elizabeth, 69, 70
Bogan, Louise: judging the Hopwood
    Award in 1939, 10
Boston Center for Adult Education: po-
    etry workshop conducted by John
    Holmes that included Ann Sex-
    ton, Maxine Kumin, Sam Albert,
    George Starbuck, Theodore Weiss,
    28
*The Bourgeois Poet* (Shapiro), 86
Bread Loaf Writers' Conference: 31, 44,
    57
  workshops as opposed to clinics, 133
  Ciardi misunderstood at, 134
  touched by the political events of
    1968, 138
  galaxy of writers, 142
Brooke, Rupert, 105
Burnshaw, Stanley: 21
  *The Seamless Web*, 119
  Ciardi and *The Poem Itself*, 120
*Cantos* (Pound), 31
Carroll, Lewis, 89
Caudwell, Christopher, 52
Ciardi, Carminantonio:
  significance of death, 8, 29
  boyhood in Italy, 6
  political tradition of Sacco & Vanzetti,
    8–9
  in Ciardi's poems, 163–64, 214–15
Ciardi, Concetta De Benedictis:
  death of husband, 29
  life in Italy, 4
  death of, 5

239

Ciardi, John:
  Anne Morrow Lindbergh controversy,
    114–16
  as a children's poet, 145, 150–52,
    157–61
  as an etymologist, 143, 146, 209
  as a narrative poet, 34, 35–38, 189
  as protagonist in his poetry, 162–77
  as a science fiction writer, 180–84
  as a social critic, 171–73
  at Bates College, 9, 42
  at Bread Loaf, 11, 31, 44, 126–30,
    131–34, 141–42, 207, 216
  at the Ohio Valley Writers Conference
    at the University of Northern Ken-
    tucky, 1985, 207
  at Tufts, 32–40, 42–43
  "Audubon of Poets," 92
  career as a poet, 91–113
  childhood of, 3–8, 24–25, 35, 42,
    214–15
  credo as a writer, 143–44
  death of, 22, 86
  distinctive voice of, 123–25, 143
  exhibition of manuscripts and books at
    Wayne State University, 1959, 123
  ghost-writing *Treat It Gentle*, 82–83
  *John Ciardi: A Bibliography*, 123
  homes in Key West, 21–22
  in Metuchen, 62, 155
  host for CBS *Accent*, 65
  like Donne, 196
  like Frost, 107, 121
  like Horace, 111
  MacLeish friendship, 62
  method of self-editing, 92–94
  Mystic River in poetry of, 24–26, 42,
    216
  new fictional techniques in *Lives of X*,
    223
  on the "unimportant poem," 194–95,
    208–10, 226–27
  on translating Dante, 45–46, 65,
    74–77
  pen name of "John Anthony," 182
  popularizing poetry as a spoken art,
    207–208
  prizes from *Poetry*, 44

  productivity in old age, 199–200
  proposed festschrift, 21
  reviewed in *The New York Times Book
    Review*, 205
  teacher at Harvard, 16–17, 40, 43–
    44, 52–53
  at Rutgers, 55–56
  at University of Kansas City at Mis-
    souri, 11–12, 43, 217
  war experiences (WW II), 12–15, 20,
    44, 141
  war poems suggest Wilfred Owen, 105
  and Walt Whitman, 21, 113, 125, 133
  with Henry Wallace's Progressive Party,
    17, 53
  with John Holmes, 9–10, 217–18
  with Roy W. Cowden at Michigan, 41,
    49–50
  with *The Saturday Review*, 85, 114–
    16, 117, 204, 219
  works:
    ARTICLES
    "The Arts in 1975," 206
    "On the Importance of the Unimpor-
      tant Poem," 195
    BOOKS, CHILDREN'S
    *Doodle Soup*, 155
    *I Met a Man*, 118
    *The Man Who Sang the Sillies*, 150,
      154, 155
    *The Reason for the Pelican*, 155
    *Scrappy the Pup*, 155
    *You Read to Me, I'll Read to You*,
      150, 155
    BOOKS, POETRY
    *As If*, 46–47, 93, 95, 106, 135
    *The Birds of Pompeii*, 22, 109, 122,
      144, 150, 200, 201
    *For Instance*, 110, 124, 192, 195,
      198
    *From Time to Time*, 45, 106–107
    *Homeward to America*, 41, 42, 92,
      192
    *I Marry You*, 84–85, 98
    *In the Stoneworks*, 154
    *The Little That Is All*, 95, 102, 124,
      144, 147
    *Live Another Day*, 45, 92, 222

240

*Lives of X*, 24–31, 34, 85, 92, 97, 102, 104, 106, 119, 141, 201, 223

*Other Skies*, 17, 41, 42, 44, 92, 93

*Selected Poems*, 21, 30–31, 41, 92–94, 98–99, 102–103, 106–107, 118, 122, 190, 192, 210, 223

BOOKS, OTHER

*A Browser's Dictionary*, 113

*Dialogue with an Audience*, 143

*The Divine Comedy* (translation), 71–73, 74–78, 119, 153

*How Does a Poem Mean?*, 36, 87–90, 119, 137, 158

*Manner of Speaking*, 190

*Mid-Century American Poets*, 32, 45, 68–70, 85, 135, 137, 140, 158, 193, 213

*A Second Browser's Dictionary*, 196

POEMS, CHILDREN'S

"As I Was Picking a Bobble-Bud," 153

"How To Tell the Top of the Hill," 158, 159

"Last Word about Bears," 160

"The Lesson for Tonight," 160

"A Loud Proud Someone," 159

"The Man Who Sang the Sillies," 160

"Mummy Slept Late and Daddy Fixed Breakfast," 157

"My Cat, Mrs. Lick-a-Chin," 62

"Poor Little Fish," 64–65

"Rain Sizes," 157, 158

"Someone," 159

"Sometimes I Feel This Way," 161

"Speed Adjustments," 157–59 *passim*

"The Stranger in the Pumpkin," 160

"There Once Was an Owl," 150

"There Was a Hunter from Littletown," 153–54

POEMS, OTHER

"An Apology for Not Invoking the Muse," 113, 124

"An Inscription to Richard Eberhart," 33

"Audit at Key West," 201–202

"Aunt Mary," 95

"Autobiography of a Comedian," 165–67

"Back Home in Pompeii," 109

"Ballad of the Icondic," 111

"The Benefits of an Education," 26, 30

"Bird Watching," 108–109

"Birthday," 105, 198

"A Box Comes Home," 172

"Boy," 100–101, 174

"Bridal Photo, 1906," 97, 163–64

"The Cartographer of Meadows," 107

"Censorship," 194

"Christmas Eve," 163, 172–73

"Coming Home on the 5:22," 103, 176

"Coq au Vin," 169

"Death of a Bomber," 44

"Dialogue of Outer Space," 93

"Donne ch'avete intellètto d'amore," 112–13

"Driving Across the American Desert and Thinking of the Sahara," 189

"Elegy," 43, 47–48, 131

"Elegy Just in Case," 44, 93–94, 111, 170, 193

"Epilogue: The Burial of the Last Elder," 102

"Epithalamium at St. Michael's Cemetery," 97

"The Evil Eye," 170

"Exit Line," 102, 146–47

"Faces," 205

"Fast as you Can Count to Ten," 174–75

"Feasts," 29

"Firsts," 198

"A Five-Year Step," 29–30

"For Myra out of the album," 31, 210

"Fragments from Italy," 163, 169

"The Gift," 20, 144

"The Glory," 105

"Goodmorning with Light," 170

"The Graph," 106
"The Health of Captains," 171
"The Highest Place in Town," 26–28
"Image of Man as a Gardener After Two Wars," 106
"I Meet the Motion of Summer Thinking Guns," 174
"In Some Doubt but Willingly," 109–10
"Interstellar," 150–52
"In the Hole," 93, 122, 197
"The Invasion of the Sleep Walkers," 93
"It Is for the Walking Man to Tell His Dreams," 1
"Jackstraws," 198
"Joshua on Eighth Avenue," 176
"Kiss Me, Hardy," 179
"A Knothole in Spent Time," 34–38
"Knowing Bitches," 196
"Landscapes of My Name," 169
"Letter to Mother," 95–96
"Machine," 110–11
"Memo: Preliminary Draft of a Prayer to God the Father," 110, 122
"Memoir of a One-Armed Harp Teacher," 227–28
"Men Marry What They Need, I Marry You," 85, 100, 131, 135
"Mutterings," 122
"My Father Died Imperfect as a Man," 97–98, 102, 164
"Mystic River," 25–26
"My Tribe," 172
"Nona Domenica Garnaro," 190
"Nothing Is Really Hard but to Be Real," 163
"No White Bird Sings," 198
"Obsolescence," 111
"October 18, Boston," 118
"On a Photo of Sgt. Ciardi a Year Later," 94, 102–103, 175
"On Leaving the Party After Having Been Possibly Brilliant for Certainly Too Long," 65

"On Sending Home My Civilian Clothes," 44
"On the Orthodoxy and Creed of My Power Mower," 110
"On the Patio," 106–107
"Oration," 172
"Philosophical Poem," 176
"A Poem for Benn's Graduation from High School," 102
"Poem for My Thirty-Ninth Birthday," 164
"Poem for My Twenty-Ninth Birthday," 93, 171
"Praise," 105
"Reflections While Oiling a Machine Gun," 44
"Saturday, March 6th," 190, 209
"The Shaft," 189
"Small Elegy," 109
"Snowy Heron," 108, 168
"S.P.Q.R.," 93
"Stations," 196
"Suburban," 196
"Survival in Missouri," 225
"Tenzone," 103–105
"Thoughts on Looking into a Thicket," 108, 135–36, 168, 191, 222
"Three Views of a Mother," 122, 131
"To Judith Asleep," 100, 168
"To Lucasta, About That War," 171–72
"Tree Trimming," 98, 167, 196
"True or False," 144
"Trying to Feel Something," 210
"Tuesday: Four Hundred Miles," 198
"Two Egrets," 108
"Useless Knowledge," 201
"V-J Day," 44
"Washing Your Feet," 197
STORIES
"The Hypnoglyph," 181–83
Ciardi, Judith Hostetter: 16, 32, 34, 185–87 *passim*
marriage to Ciardi, 43
Clemente, Ann, 22

242

Clemente, Vince:
Walt Whitman Birthplace conversation with Ciardi, 29, 40–41, 81, 159
letters from Ciardi, 157
*Songs from Puccini,* 213
Coleridge, Samuel Taylor, 88
Columbia University, 68
"The Congo" (Lindsay), 88
Corman, Cid, 12
Cousins, Norman: 21
describes Ciardi, 61
role in Ciardi-Lindbergh dispute, 114–16, 220–21
Cowden, Row W.: writing seminar at Michigan, 10, 41, 42
Ciardi's Hopwood Award, 49–50
Crane, Stephen, 88
Crews, Harry, 142
Da Capo Press: publishing *Treat It Gentle,* 79
Dante, 5, 105, 112, 117
Ciardi's translation of, 71–73, 74–78
Decker, Clarence R.:
President of University of Kansas City at Missouri, 11
hires Ciardi to teach, 16, 217
De la Mare, Walter, 88
"The Descent" (Williams), 71
De Voto, Bernard, 11
Dewey, Thomas, 53
Dickinson, Emily, 215
Dies Committee, 12, 19
"Directive" (Frost), 120
*A Directory of American Poets and Fiction Writers,* 140, 228
"Don du Poéme" (Mallarmé), 120
Donne, John, 88, 142
*The Double Root* (Holmes), 28
Dryden, John, 91
Eberhart, Richard:
Festschrift in *New England Review,* 33
in *Mid-Century American Poets,* 69
on Ciardi, 32–33
*Ecologues* (Virgil), 200
Eisenhower, President Dwight D., 136
Eliot, T. S.:
eminence of, 52, 70

on Dante, 77
"Prufrock," 88
World War II and *Four Quartets,* 200, 203
Emerson, Ralph Waldo: and Ciardi, 17, 38, 90, 225
"Étude Réaliste" (Swinburne), 100
"The Eve of St. Agnes" (Keats), 142
Feinberg, Charles E., 123–25 *passim*
Fitts, Dudley:
on Ciardi's *Dante,* 45–46
on the Ciardi voice, 47, 119–20
Florida, University of, 32
Frost, Robert:
John Holmes correspondence, 29
at Bread Loaf, 11, 120–21
at Rutgers, 56
"Stopping by Woods," "Departmental," 88
"The Hill Wife," 107
Ciardi compared to, 107–108
Ciardi's *Saturday Review* memorial essay on, 121–22
Mark Van Doren's tribute to, 188–89
Fuller, Edmond: on Ciardi's *Dante,* 45
*The Generation of 2,000* (Heyen), 68
Gilder, Gary, 79
Ginsberg, Allen, 135, 137
Giotto, 71
Gorey, Edward St. John, 53–54
Half Hollow Hills (Long Island, New York) School District, 156, 157
Hall, Donald:
with Ciardi at Harvard, 52–54
editing *The Harvard Advocate Anthology,* 53–54, 70
Hannah, Barry, 142
Hardy, Thomas, 41
Ciardi compared to, 198
*The Harvard Advocate,* 53
*The Harvard Advocate Anthology:* Ciardi's role in creation of, 53–54
Harvard University: 27
Briggs-Copeland appointments, 43
Ciardi's Phi Beta Kappa poem, 44
Ciardi teaching English C in 1947 at, 52–54

243

Heaney, Seamus, 71
"He Makes a House Call" (Stone), 146
Heyen, William, 68
Hill & Wang: publishing *Treat It Gentle*, 80, 83
"The Hill Wife"" (Frost), 107
Holmes, John:
　as a teacher, 9, 27–28
　assessment as a poet, 9, 28, 69, 217
　death of, 28
　Ciardi's role in publication of his *Selected Poems*, 28
　Holmes-Frost correspondence, 29
　teaching Ciardi at Tufts, 9, 32, 40–41, 217–18
　role in *Homeward to America*, 11
　in *Mid-Century American Poets*, 69
　mentor to Maxine Kumin, 131
Hopkins, Gerard Manley, 100
Hopwood Award:
　to Ciardi for *Homeward to America*, 10–11, 42, 49–50, 216–17
　Ciardi as Award speaker in 1958, 57
Horace, 111
House Un-American Activities Committee, 53
"Howl" (Ginsberg), 135
Humphries, Rolf, 88
"The Hypnoglyph" (Ciardi): published under the name of "John Anthony" in *Fantasy and Science Fiction*, 181–83

"I Saw a Man" (Crane), 88

"Jabberwocky" (Carroll), 88
Jarrell, Randall, 52, 69, 70, 135
Jeffers, Robinson, 70
Jefferson, President Thomas, 225
Jerome, Judson, 136
John Reed Society, 53
Juvenal, 111

Kansas City at Missouri, University of, 11, 16, 43, 217
*Kansas City Review, University of*, 43
Keats, John, 99, 142
Kees, Weldon, 52
Kehl, D. G., 61
Krickel, Edward, 214

Kumin, Maxine, 28–29 *passim*
　at Bread Loaf, 142
Larkin, Philip, 31
Lattimore, Richmond: on Ciardi's *Dante*, 45
*Laughing Time* (Smith), 153
Lea, Sydney, 33
LeMay, Gen. Curtis, 12
Lindbergh, Anne Morrow: Ciardi's *Saturday Review* condemnation of, 114–16, 137
Lindsay, Vachel, 88
"The Listeners" (De la Mare), 88
Longboat Key Writers Conference, 58
*Lord Weary's Castle* (Lowell), 52
Loveman, Amy, 114
"Love Poem" (Nims), 52
"Love, The First Decade" (Jerome), 137
Lowell, Robert: 52, 69, 135, 137, 170
　on Ciardi's "Italo-American voice" in poetry, 224
MacAllister, Archibald T., 46
MacArthur, Gen. Douglas, 15
MacLeish, Archibald, 47, 62, 88, 183
McCord, David, 10
Mallarmé, Stéphane, 120
"The March into Virginia" (Melville), 106
Matthiessen, F. O., 53
*Maximus Poems* (Olson), 31
Mayo, E. L., 69
Melville, Herman, 106
Meredith, William, 142
"Money" (Larkin), 31
Montaigne, 92
Moore, Marianne, 52
Morrison, Theodore, 11, 16, 44
Moss, Howard, 52
"Mr. Flood's Party" (Robinson), 88
*The Nation*, 45
National Council of Teachers of English, 155, 157
*The New American Poetry* (Allen), 68
New Directions, 52
*New England Review*, 33
*The New Yorker*, 16–17, 53, 92
*The New York Times Book Review*, 45

Nims, John Frederick, 52, 69, 120, 138, 142, 147
Northern Kentucky, University of, 207
Oakland University, 124
O'Donnell, Gen. Rosie, 15, 19
O'Hara, Frank, 53–54, 207
Owen, Wilfred, 105
Pack, Robert, 138, 142
Paine, Thomas, 225
Parini, Jay, 33
"The Parlement of Foules" (Chaucer), 108
*Paterson* (Williams), 31
Perse, St. John, 76
*Poesis: A Journal of Criticism*, 22
*Poetry*, 11, 30–31, 44, 52, 205
"The Polo Grounds" (Humphries), 88
Pound, Ezra, 52, 68, 104, 137, 197, 200, 202
Pratt, Fletcher, 11, 180, 181
Princeton University, 46
The Progressive Party: 17, 53. *See* Wallace, Henry
"Prufrock" (Eliot), 88
Quasimodo, Salvatore, 77
Ransom, John Crowe, 46, 52
Rexroth, Kenneth, 198, 215
"The Rime of the Ancient Mariner" (Coleridge), 88
Robinson, E. A., 88
Rocky Point School District (Long Island, New York), 156, 157
Roethke, Theodore: 27, 29, 69, 70
   Ciardi compared to, 170–71
Rukeyser, Muriel, 18, 69
Rutgers University, 43, 56
Rutgers University Press, 45
Sacco & Vanzetti, 8–9
"Sasquatch" (Turco), 38–39
*The Saturday Review*, 114–16 *passim*, 133, 136–37
Schwartz, Delmore, 69
Scott, Winfield Townley, 69
Sexton, Anne, 28–29 *passim*, 70
Shapiro, Karl, 22, 52, 69, 86, 205
Singleton, Charles, 71
Sloane, William, 11, 126, 127, 142, 216

Smith, William Jay, 153
*Songs from Puccini* (Clemente), 213
"Sonnet CXXX" (Shakespeare), 56
Starbuck, George, 28
*Starting from Paumanok* (Walt Whitman Birthplace), 22, 125, 225–26
Stevens, Wallace, 26, 52, 80, 83, 200
Stone, John, 141
Summers, Hollis, 85, 138
Swinburne, Algernon Charles, 100
Tate, Allen, 52
Tennyson, Alfred, 34
Thomas, Dylan, 70, 170
Thoreau, Henry David, 17, 216
Three Village School District (Long Island, New York), 156, 157
*Treat It Gentle* (autobiography of Sidney Bechet):
   Ciardi meeting Bechet, 79–81
   Ciardi's ghostwriting of, 80
   compared to Faulkner, 80
   Bechet as a "back-country Wallace Stevens," 80
Truman, President Harry S., 18, 52–53
*The Tuftonian*, 41, 42, 49
Tufts University, 22, 24, 25, 26, 32, 42, 46, 49
Turco, Lewis, 38–39
Twayne Publishers, 44, 53, 61, 83
Uberti, degli Farinata (The *Inferno*), 5
*The Unicorn* (Lindbergh), 114–15
Untermeyer, Louis, 11, 68
"A Valediction Forbidding Mourning" (Donne), 142
Van Doren, Mark, 188
Vendler, Helen, 156
Viereck, Peter, 52, 69
Virgil, 5, 200
*Virginia Quarterly Review*, 192
*V-Letter* (Shapiro), 52
Wakefield, Dan, 127
Wakoski, Diane, 133, 142
Wallace, Henry:
   Ciardi's role in his 1948 Progressive Party presidential campaign, 17, 53
   Ciardi's assessment of, 53

Walt Whitman Birthplace, 21, 125, 213, 222
*Walt Whitman Newsletter*, 125
Weiss, Theodore, 28
White, Gertrude M., 124
Whitehead, James, 142
Whitman, Walt: 22, 76, 113, 190
  Ciardi's assessment of, 68, 125
Wilbur, Richard, 52, 69, 70
Williams, John, 22
Williams, Miller, 128, 138, 142, 145–46, 207

Williams, Oscar, 68
Williams, William Carlos, 52, 68, 70, 71, 198, 200, 216
"Winterset" (Anderson), 42
*The Wonderful Wizard of Oz* (Baum), 150
Wordsworth, William, 35, 218
*Writer's Digest*, 135, 138
Yeats, William Butler, 99, 202
*Yes, Giorgio* (film), 63–64